Evolution and Syncretism of Religion

An Integral and Evolutionary World View
Volume 2

Craig R. Vander Maas

Integral Growth Publishing
Grand Rapids, MI

Integral Growth Publishing
Grand Rapids, MI
www.integralgrowthpublishing.com

Copyright © 2017 by Craig R. Vander Maas.

All rights reserved. No part of this book may be reproduced or transmitted in any form or by any means whatsoever without express written permission from the author, except in the case of brief quotations embodied in critical articles and reviews.

For information regarding bulk purchases of 10 or more copies, please email: info@integralgrowthpublishing.com

For more information about the author please visit: www.craigvandermaas.com

Unless otherwise noted, Scripture quotations are from the New Revised Standard Version Bible, copyright © 1989, by the Division of Christian Education of the National Council of the Churches of Christ in the United States of America.

Scripture quotations marked KJV are from the King James Version.

First Edition
ISBN 9780997238815 pbk

Acknowledgments

I want to express my thanks to Mark Lodenstein, Dr. Richard Rotman, Jon Propper, and Dr. Robert Cross for feedback on this book and their support for this project.

That which is called the Christian religion existed among the ancients, and never did not exist, from the planting of the human race until Christ came in the flesh, at which time the true religion, which already existed, came to be called Christianity.

Augustine, ca 410 AD, *Sermo 10, De Sanctis*

Contents

Forward   1

Chapter 1   Prehistoric religion   17

- Prehistory   18
- Archeology   20
- Archeological Dating Methods   22
- Evolution   25
- Taxonomic Hierarchy   27
- Earliest Hominids   28
- Stone Age   32
- First Human Migration   34
- The Second Great Migration   35
- DNA   38
- Race   39
- Population Genetics   40
- Adam, Eve and Eden (Y chromosome and Mitochondrial DNA)   42
- Paleolithic Religion   44
- Bear Cults   46
- Upper Paleolithic   47
- Venus Figurines   50
- Neolithic Religion   52
- Anthropology, Ethnography, and Recent "Primitive" Cultures and Religions   56
- Sociology   57
- Animism   58
- Ancestor Cults   59
- Cult of the Dead   59
- Fetishism   60
- Totenism   61
- Polytheism   61
- Shamanism   62
- Sacrifice   62
- Cannibalism   63
- Myth and Ritual   65

| Chapter 2 | Mesopotamia | 70 |

- Mesopotamia — 72
- Chalcolithic Period (or Copper Age) — 74
- City-States — 75
- Sumerian King List — 77
- The Sumerians — 78
- Semites — 79
- Invention of Writing — 80
- The Akkadians — 81
- Third Dynasty of Ur — 83
- Hammurabi — 84
- Hittites and Kassites — 84
- Religion — 85
- Death — 86
- Mesopotamian Pantheon — 86
- Worship and Sacrifice — 88
- The Epic of Gilgamesh — 90
- Code of Hammurabi — 94
- Atrahasis — 99
- Enuma Elish — 99
- Enki and Ninhursag — 101
- The Sumerian Job — 101
- Sumerian Proverbs — 102
- Lamentations — 102
- Syncretism — 103
- Abraham — 106

Chapter 3   Egypt   111

- Jacob — 112
- History of Egypt: 5000 to 3000 BCE — 113
- Manetho — 116
- Early Dynastic Period (3000-2686 BCE) — 117
- Old Kingdom (Dynasties 3-6) (2686-2160) — 117
- First Intermediate Period
  (Dynasties 9-11) (2160-2055) — 121
- Middle Kingdom
  (Dynasties 11-14) (2055-1650) — 121
- Second Intermediate Period
  (Dynasties 15-17) (1650-1550) — 123
- New Kingdom
  (Dynasties 18-20) (1550-1069) — 124
- Moses — 134
- Egyptian Religion — 141
- Creation — 143
- Divinity of Kings — 145
- Magic — 145
- Afterlife — 146
- Mummification — 148
- Maat — 149
- Egyptian Pantheon — 149
- Creator Sun-gods — 150
- Other Egyptian gods — 151

Chapter 4   Syria-Palestine   156

- The Sinai   157
- The Transjordan   160
- Crossing the Jordan   165
- Archaeology   167
- History of Syria-Palestine   170
- Ugarit   172
- Religion of Syria-Palestine   173
- Sacrifice   177
- Human Sacrifice   180
- Gods of Syria-Palestine   189
- Yahweh   193
- Syncretism in the Religion of the Israelites   197

Chapter 5   Ancient Empires   202

- Judges   203
- Assyrian Empire   206
- Babylonian Empire   212
- Cosmic Religion, Solar Deities and Astrology   216
- Persian Empire   223
- Zoroastrianism   226
- The Axial Age   229

Chapter 6	Hellenistic-Roman	236

- Greek Empire — 237
- Philosophy as Religion — 242
- Middle Platonism, Neoplatonism and the Trinity — 246
- Mystery Religions — 249
- The Eucharist — 255
- Baptism — 256
- Roman Empire — 257
- Judaism during the Roman Period — 260
- Jesus of Nazareth — 263
- Miracle Workers of the Day — 264
- Early Christianity — 268
- Apotheosis — 272
- Mithraism — 273
- Gnosticism — 275
- Manicheism — 277
- Proto-Orthodox Christianity — 278
- Common Religious Themes — 278
- Church Fathers Explain — 283

Conclusions — 286

Group Discussion Questions — 300

Appendix A — 308

Bibliography — 314

Index — 328

Author's Notes

In researching this book I found many varying opinions about dates for events, particularly in prehistory. For many events there appears to be no clear consensus on specific dates. Although I tried to be as accurate as I could in citing dates, my purpose in writing this book is not historical fastidiousness, but rather the presentation of more general information that affects one's historical perspective and world view.

Also, there has been custom of using a capital letter "G" when writing about the one true god of Judaism and Christianity and then using a small "g" when writing about false gods. In writing about the evolution of the concept of god I find it impossible to try to stick to this convention. Therefore I will always use a lowercase "g" when writing about god.

Evolution and Syncretism of Religion

An Integral and Evolutionary World View
Volume 2

Forward

My early belief about religion was that it began with revelation by God. God revealed himself to the earliest humans. For some reason individuals strayed from God and they started creating false religions. At some point God chose one particular group of people, the Jews, to be his favored people. Although Jews often strayed from the worship of the one true God, God stuck by them.

Many fundamentalist Christians and some evangelical Christians have the belief that the world and religion are 6,000 years old. This is often called "Young Earth Creationism", and it is based solely on a literal interpretation of verses in the book of Genesis. Others known as "Old Earth Creationists" interpret the seven days mentioned in the first two chapters of Genesis metaphorically, i.e. that the world was not created in six literal 24-hour periods. These individuals believe that God was the creator of the world but that this happened in a time period that was much longer, as has been revealed by science.

Although growing up I would never have called myself a "young earth creationist", my world view really was one of approximately 6,000 years. I was taught that the world began with two individuals, Adam and Eve, and that "religion" began with them as well. If religion were to be thought of as a belief in the divine, then according to Genesis Adam and Eve certainly had this. They reportedly had an intimate relationship with God; they strolled and chatted in the Garden of Eden together.

Although early Christian church fathers such as Augustine and Origen did not believe in the Genesis creation myth as being literally true, the view of the earth as being under 10,000 years old was the dominant belief until the 18th century with the dawning of the "Age of Enlightenment" and the "Scientific Revolution". It was learned that the world was in fact approximately 4.5 billion years old! That would be 750,000 times older than previously thought!

$$6,000 \times 750,000 = 4.5 \text{ Billion}$$

With this scientific knowledge in mind, I wondered how religion actually did begin and how it evolved. This book is about what I've learned through research in the disciplines of archeology, anthropology, sociology and history. I particularly researched the influence of other cultures and religions on Judaism and Christianity. The word "syncretism" applies here; in regards to religion the word refers to the merging and assimilation of religious beliefs and practices. My goal in this book is to show how Judaism and Christianity evolved from its earliest beginnings.

As I grew up as a child I viewed the world through the lens of the culture that I grew up into. This included broadly my American culture, but also specifically for me a Calvinist, evangelical culture. Everyone is affected by the culture that they grow up in. I am sure if I had grown up in a pre-historic, head hunting culture, I would have grown up accepting their views. If I had grown up in a fundamentalist Islamic madras, I would have grown up accepting their views. And if I am not confronted with conflicting evidence later on in life that I am willing to consider, I likely will continue to accept and not question the views I grew up with for the rest of my life. Up until adolescence we are indoctrinated by our culture. It is only in adolescence that we begin to develop the ability to think critically. Unfortunately, many adults never learn to critically think.

Education is the key to growth and spiritual evolution. Ongoing, lifelong adult education has been very important to me personally in my spiritual journey, and I think it is also important for us as a society and as a species. That is the reason I am writing this series of books; to share what I've learned in what I hope is an easily understandable format that will be accessible to the average adult reader.

In chapter 6 of this book I mention Plato's "Myth of the Cave" from the *Republic*. Plato's point in this story is the importance of contemplation and seeing the "light" and then sharing/teaching these insights to others. That is what I'm trying to do.

Many readers may be surprised and taken aback by my conclusions, particularly those from an evangelical background. My goal is not to shock or upset. My goal is not to denigrate religion (Judaism and Christianity in particular). Religion is important to me. I believe in God. I consider myself a Christian. Although the research I present in this book might contradict some common religious beliefs that have come to be considered "orthodox", I believe that data and evidence from various academic disciplines give us new information and insights about god that is very exciting, if we are able to be open-minded to new discoveries, insights, and paradigms. As the slogan of the United Church of Christ says, "God is still speaking."

It is arguable whether religion has been more a source of good or ill in the world overall. Religion does not have to be doctrinaire, rigid, close-minded, and antithetical to reason. I believe that religion can, and sometimes has been, a force for good and progress. I personally believe that *all* of the problems of this world are spiritual problems; it will take spiritual growth by humanity to solve them. Remaining stuck in old religious paradigms will keep us in our problems and misery.

I no longer believe in direct revelation or special revelation. I do not believe that God spoke directly to Moses to give the Ten Commandments or the Torah. I do not believe that God spoke directly to Paul the Apostle to influence his writings and letters. I do not believe God spoke directly to Mohamed to give us the Quaran. I do not believe God spoke directly to Joseph Smith to give us the Book of Mormon. I believe that religious beliefs evolved and that various cultures and beliefs had influence on other cultures and beliefs. That is what I hope to demonstrate in this book.

My Current World View
and a summary of what I've learned through research about the history of religion

The earliest evidence suggesting the possibility of religion or belief in a divinity comes from the Middle Paleolithic Age (300,000 to 35,000 years ago). During this period there was evidence for burials of deceased humans. The first primates first evolved around 65 million years ago, and the earliest apes evolved around 39 million years ago. The beginnings of the human lineage was believed to have been about 7 million years ago. Hominids began walking upright (on two legs) between 3 and 4 million years ago. Up until 1,800,000 years ago no fossils of hominids were found outside of Africa. Our own species, Homo sapiens, began to look like modern man about 100,000 years ago.

Starting around 225,000 years ago remains of various hominid species were found that suggested a primitive form of burial. The earliest "true" burials occurred around 100,000 years ago. This is an important development. Animals do not bury their deceased; they simply leave the remains. Because early hominids were nomadic, there was no reason to bury the deceased for reasons of sanitation. Some of these buried individuals had food or "grave goods" such as tools buried with them. This might suggest a belief in an afterlife as a spirit. Grave goods may have been included to serve the dead in an afterlife.

The Neolithic Age began about 10,000 years ago. During this period were the beginnings of agriculture and the domestication of animals. Humans began settlements, rather than the previous nomadic existence. One characteristic of prehistoric, neolithic religion was believed to be animism, i.e. the belief that animals and non-living things had a spirit. From this belief in spirits developed a belief in gods; that some spirits had control over various aspects of nature. Over time a hierarchy of gods developed. Humans wanted to influence these gods, for example to persuade the gods to make it rain. *Ritual* was the method by which humans attempted to influence the gods. The most common ritual was *sacrifice*. There is evidence of sacrifice of humans as well as of animals to the gods. It is believed that later *myth* developed to explain the reasons for the rituals.

Mesopotamia is often called the "cradle of civilization". The first cities and written language first developed there. Written language is first credited to the Sumerians around 3200 BCE. Sumerian writings were carved into stone, and many of these writings are still in existence and are able to be translated. Many of these writings deal with religious beliefs. From these early Sumerian writings we know the Sumerian pantheon, early myths, and early law codes. Sacrifice continued to be the main way of worshiping the gods.

It is from Mesopotamia that the patriarch, Abraham, was said to have been from. Abraham (earlier known as Abram) has been traditionally placed at 2000 BCE, although others place him as late as 1400 BCE. Some scholars doubt the historicity of Abraham altogether. The book of Genesis tells us that Abram's father, Terah, intended to move to the land of Canaan. He ended up settling with his offspring, including Abram, in Haran, however. At the age of 75 Abram was told by god to proceed on the journey to Canaan. Who was this god? Presumably it was a Mesopotamian god, as this was where Abram and his ancestors lived. Abram and his wife and nephew made it to Canaan and built alters to their god. For some reason they continued moving southward to the Negeb desert, and then because of famine continued down to Egypt. He later returned to Canaan.

When Abram was 99 years old god appeared to him and told him that he would be "the ancestor of a multitude of nations". Abram's name was changed at that time to Abraham. In return for getting offspring, god required a ritual: the circumcision of all male offspring now and in the future. Interestingly, circumcision was a practice of the Egyptians where Abraham had purportedly recently lived for a time.

Abraham's offspring would continue to have some contact with their homeland, Mesopotamia. Abraham sent servants to Mesopotamia to obtain a wife for his son, Isaac. Isaac's son, Jacob, also traveled to Mesopotamia to obtain a wife. He actually got two wives there who were sisters and his first cousins. Jacob remained in Mesopotamia for twenty years before returning to Canaan with his offspring and servants.

Jacob and his entourage secretly fled his home in Mesopotamia from his father-in-law, Laban, when Laban was away. Laban pursued when he found they had left and caught up to them several days later. One of the issues was that Rachel, one of Jacob's wives, had stolen some of her father's "household gods". These were idols to various gods. It was common in Mesopotamia to worship not only the gods of the pantheon that were well known, but also to have personal gods or gods of one's household; they would be akin to "guardian angels" perhaps. Laban and Jacob made peace together and invoked the names of each of their gods in the agreement; "May the God of Abraham and the God of Nahor...."

Once Jacob and his family were in Canaan, Jacob told everyone to get rid of their idols. He made an altar to "the God who answered me in the day of my distress and has been with me wherever I have gone." Who was this god? Many have assumed it was YHWH, but this god would only be mentioned for the first time (to Moses) many hundreds of years later. Most likely Jacob made an altar to his personal Mesopotamian god, who was also the god of his father and grandfather, Abraham and Isaac.

Jacob and his family settled in Canaan. From there we have the story of Jacob's son, Joseph, being sold by his brothers into slavery. Joseph was taken to Egypt. Eventually, because of his ability to interpret dreams, he became the pharaoh's right-hand man. At this point he was 30 years old. There was a famine throughout the middle east, and the only place where there was food was Egypt. Without going into all the details of the story, Jacob and his family ended up moving to Egypt because of this food shortage. The descendants of Jacob remained in Egypt for 430 years.

Over the years the Israelites became a people disliked by the pharaoh, who oppressed them with forced labor. We are told in Genesis that the pharaoh even sought to kill male Israelite infants in order to decrease their numbers. One of these infants, Moses, was saved and raised by the daughter of the pharaoh. Moses prospered until he came upon an Egyptian beating a Hebrew; he killed the Egyptian and then fled. He went to the land of Midian. There he married the daughter of a Midianite priest. Just who was this god that the Midianite priest served?

While Moses was watching the flock of his father-in-law, Jethro, the Midianite priest, god appeared to him in the form of a burning bush and said "I am the God of your father, the God of Abraham, the God of Isaac, and the God of Jacob." This god later identifies himself as "I Am Who I Am" and later gives his name YHWH. This is the first time that this god is identified. This god tells Moses to lead the Israelite people out of bondage in Egypt and to tell the Israelite people who he is, i.e. the god of their distant ancestors.

What would have been the religious beliefs of the Israelite people at this time? Likely having lived and been part of the Egyptian culture for 430 years, they would have adopted the Egyptian religious beliefs. The Bible tells us that Jacob and Joseph were embalmed after their deaths in the Egyptian fashion. It is unlikely that they would have retained any of the religious beliefs of Mesopotamia where the family was said to have originated from.

YHWH sent numerous plagues against the Egyptians, and finally due to the power of YHWH the Israelites escaped the Egyptians and went on their journey to a land promised to them by YHWH, Canaan, the land where the Israelite ancestors had briefly lived hundreds of years earlier. Just who was this god that Moses was serving?

Many scholars believe YHWH originated in the land of Midian. Likely this was the god that the priest Jethro, Moses' father-in-law, was a priest for. YHWH likely originated as a typical warrior god. Sigmund Freud and other scholars believe that the god Moses served actually originated in Egypt. A pharaoh by the name of Amenhotep IV initiated a period of relative monotheism in Egypt. He advocated the worship of one god, Aten, a sun god. He changed his name to Akhenaten to reflect his devotion to Aten. Freud notes that Akhenaten "worshiped the sun not as a material object, but as a symbol of a divine being whose energy was manifested in his rays." In one of Akhenaten's hymns to Aten he states "O Thou only God, there is no other God than Thou."

Freud believed that the religion of the Israelites was a conflation of the religion Moses brought from Egypt (the worship of Aten which rejected anthropomorphisms, magic, and focus on an afterlife) with the religion that Moses learned from the Midianites (the worship of YHWH, a god probably not unlike the other gods of the middle east). Freud believed Moses retained the ancient Egyptian custom of circumcision to set the Israelites apart from other cultures in the Levant. Another characteristic that set the Israelites apart from these other cultures was henotheism, i.e. the worship of only one god, even though there may be belief in other gods.

When the Israelites, led by Joshua, eventually crossed over the Jordan River to enter Canaan, we are led to believe in the book of Joshua, that the Israelites with the help of YHWH destroyed the native Canaanite peoples. However, archaeological evidence does not bear this out. There is no archaeological evidence for a *mass* exodus of peoples out of Egypt, and there is no Egyptian writings attesting to such an event. However, we do know that there was forced labor by the Egyptians, and there may have been a more limited exodus. However, the huge scale exodus suggested by the book of Exodus should have left archaeological evidence. Archaeology also tells us there was no widespread destruction in Canaan during the time period described in the book of Joshua. Archaeologists now predominantly agree that the Israelites developed from within Canaanite society and that there was not a widespread foreign invasion in which the indigenous peoples were destroyed.

The Israelites consisted of a number of tribes that coexisted with other Canaanite tribes. The religion of Canaan was polytheistic. Sacrifice continued to be the primary way of honoring the gods and soliciting their help and favor. This included instances of human sacrifice, and there is some evidence that this was done in the name of YHWH as well as other gods of Canaan. The chief god of Canaan was known as "El". A majority of scholars believe there were several writers of the Torah (Genesis, Exodus, Leviticus, Numbers and Deuteronomy), and that Moses did not write these books as has been commonly believed. The "Documentary Hypothesis" is subscribed to by many Biblical scholars; this theory hypothesizes four principal sources. They are known as the Yahwist source (J), Elohist source (E), the Deuteronomist (D), and the Priestly source (P).

The earliest source is believed to be the Yahwist source who refers to god as "YHWH". This god is described extremely anthropomorphically; he walks, talks, enjoys pleasing odors, and has a bad temper. The Elohist source calls god "Elohim"; this god is more benevolent and transcendent. This god resembles the Canaanite "El" who is depicted as an aged man with a gray beard and is described as "the father of mankind" and the "head of the divine council". Many scholars believe that El was the original god of the Israelites as suggested by the name Isra*el*, and that YHWH and El over time became combined into a single entity. YHWH originated in the south, and El originated in the north.

The early Israelites did not dispute that there were various gods, but they did insist on the worship of only the god

YHWH. It was not until the writings of Deutero-Isaiah (chapters 40-55 in the book of Isaiah) that we have an unambiguous statement of the belief that there is no other gods other than YHWH. This was written during the Babylonian Period (600 to 540 BCE).

Judaism changed and evolved tremendously since its beginnings. Initially the religion of the patriarchs (Abraham, Isaac and Jacob) was the same as the other peoples of the near east. It was polytheistic, and the worship of the gods consisted of rituals, primarily sacrifice. As societies got larger, there was a need for rules and laws. The earliest seem to have come from Mesopotamia (e.g. Code of Hammurabi), but this developed with the Israelites as well many centuries later (Ten Commandments, Deuteronomistic laws).

A tremendous evolution in religion occurred between 800 BCE and 200 BCE; this period has been termed the *Axial Age*. Many great spiritual sages lived during this time period including Buddha, Confucius, various Greek philosophers, and the great Jewish prophets. It was during this time period that ritual decreased in importance, and justice, helping the downtrodden, and spiritual growth became important. Morality became important in religion.

The nations of Israel and Judah were conquered by a number of empires. The first were the Assyrians; they totally dispersed the peoples of the northern kingdom of Israel. These Israelites were to become known as the "lost 10 tribes" never to be heard from again. But in Judah there was a religious renaissance under the rule of King Josiah. Josiah due to the purported discovery of deuteronomistic laws in the temple, initiated numerous reforms in his kingdom. There was a new focus on following YHWH's laws, although the reforms did not last after Josiah's death.

Then the Babylonians conquered the Assyrian empire, including Judah. Eventually most of the Judean citizens were exiled to other places, including Babylon. Certainly when people are living in another country with a foreign culture, they are influenced by that culture. One of the ways that the Judeans were influenced by the Babylonians (and the Assyrians) was with astrology. Astrological ideas permeated the Mediterranean world, and although the prophets Isaiah and Jeremiah preached against it, it continued to have influence. In the Gospel of Matthew magi use astrological signs to find the infant Jesus.

Then the Persians conquered the Babylonians. The Judean exiles were able to return to Judah, and they were allowed to rebuild the Jewish temple which had been destroyed by the Babylonians. The main religion of the Persians was Zoroastrianism, and this had great influence on Judaism (the Essenes) and particularly later Christianity. Zoroaster taught that the great creator god, Mazda, created the world in seven stages. He created and ruled other beneficent deities but was in conflict with the evil god, Ahriman, who was the leader of other evil gods. There is a duality between good and evil, and each person needs to choose which path to take. Upon death there will be a judgment of each soul. The good would go to paradise, and the evil would be eternally punished. Before the final judgment, there will be a cosmic savior that arrives. This was a novel theology for the time. The Israelite religion, and all of the other religions in the near east for that matter, had no teachings about a final judgment, or a belief in a heaven or a hell.

Then the Greeks conquered the Persians. It was a goal of the Greeks to *Hellenize*, i.e. to spread Greek culture throughout the world. There was increased emphasis on logic and rational thinking to replace myths. It was the beginning of science. Greek philosophy, particularly Plato, had great influence on Judaism and later Christianity. Greek became the *lingua franca,* i.e. the common language for the whole empire. The New Testament writings were written in Greek.

Then the Romans conquered the Greeks. During this time there were four major sects of Judaism: Sadducees who focused on sacrifices, Pharisees who focused on laws, Essenes who focused on the battle between good and evil and the final judgment, and the Zealots who wanted to restore Jewish rule over their homeland and to defeat their oppressors, the Romans. During the Greco-Roman age, "mystery religions" became very popular. They emphasized having a personal relationship with the divine, promised a blessed afterlife, offered fellowship between congregants, and offered forgiveness of sins. Baptisms and sacred meals were common elements. These mystery religions had much influence on Christianity.

I grew up believing that religion was the revelation from god about who god is, who we are, and what the ultimate purpose of life is. Actually, religious beliefs evolved over millennia. And interestingly, it appears that various religious themes evolved independently and simultaneously throughout the world. In my childhood I believed there was the right religion (coincidentally the one I was raised in), and then there were the false religions. Many people still believe this. My conception of religion now is that from the earliest history of mankind there has been belief in a divinity, and that beliefs about ultimate truth have been evolving over the ages.

It is my belief as a religious person that I should not "cling" to my old religious beliefs and have antipathy toward people who are not like me (to paraphrase Barak Obama's 2008 quote), but to continue to evolve spiritually and to be open to new beliefs. President Obama got a lot of flak for using the term "cling", but if the term means to hold onto beliefs simply because that it what one grew up believing, despite evidence to the contrary, then I think that is an apt term.

I strongly believe we need to be open to other cultures, other viewpoints, and other ideas. Then it is necessary to critically examine these new ideas and to re-examine old conceptions. The "kingdom of god" is a process- a process that I (and all) should be actively involved in creating. Many believe the kingdom of God is a place, but Jesus said "The kingdom of God is not coming with things that can be observed; nor will they say, 'Look, here it is!' or 'There it is!' For, in fact, the kingdom of God is among you" (Luke 17:20-21). Jesus also said "'You shall love the Lord your God with all your heart, and with all your soul, and with all your mind.' This is the greatest and first commandment. And a second is like it: 'You shall love your neighbor as yourself.' On these two commandments hang all the law and the prophets" (Matthew 22: 37-40).

This was the essence of religion for Jesus as well as for the other great religious prophets and leaders since the Axial Age. Very many people have not gotten to this place in their personal spiritual development. Instead their focus is on the power of sacrifice and ritual or the importance of following rules. If we are to solve the problems of this world such as starvation, oppression, and war, we need to further develop as a world spiritually, for it is spiritual retardation that is the source of *all* of mankind's problems

Chapter 1

Prehistoric Religion

Prehistory

The term "prehistoric" refers to <u>before</u> "history", or <u>before</u> language. History is the study of past events, primarily by studying writings of the time period. But how do we study events that happened prior to the development of language? If there is no written record, how do we know what happened? That is the purview of Anthropology and Archaeology. Anthropology is the broader scientific discipline; it is the study of humanity from both biological and cultural perspectives. Anthropology's four sub-fields are:

- Cultural and social anthropology
    - This is the study of current, living cultures including "primitive" peoples as well as modern, industrialized cultures. Ethnography is employed; this is direct observation of groups of people by living near or among them.
- Biological or physical anthropology
    - This is the study of how humans evolved over millions of years. It also includes the exciting new work using DNA to trace human migrations and evolution.
- Linguistic anthropology
    - This is the study of how languages evolved.

- Archaeology
  - This is the study of humans in the past by examining the material evidence they left behind, rather than studying writings, which in some cases were nonexistent.

The focus of Anthropology and Archaeology is the study of <u>humanity</u>. Paleoanthropology is the branch of anthropology that deals with prehistoric hominids. Paleoarcheology focuses on hominid fossils ranging from 15 million to 10 thousand years ago, and the majority of paleoarcheology sites are found in Southern and Eastern Africa. Hominids is a term that refers not only to modern human beings (homo sapiens) but also to extinct species of erect, bipedal primates. There are other scientific disciplines that deal with the past. These include:

- Geology
  - This is the study of earth and its materials, e.g. rocks and soil. It focuses on non-organic, non-living materials.
- Paleontology
  - This is the study of dinosaurs and other fossils from other earlier life forms. It should be noted that dinosaurs and humans <u>never</u> lived during the same time period. The dinosaurs died out millions of years before the appearance of the first humans, contrary to what one might see on the Flintstones and other popular televisions shows and films.

- Population Geneticists
  - Using DNA the migrations of human populations have been tracked from earliest times.
- Historical Linguists
  - This discipline has traced back the developments of language from earliest times.
- Primatologists
  - This discipline has studied chimpanzee and bonobo societies through ethnography.
- Evolutionary Psychologists
  - This discipline investigates how psychological traits have evolved due to natural selection.
- Evolutionary Biology
  - This is a sub-field of biology that studies evolutionary processes.

Archaeology

The discipline of archaeology started during the Renaissance, but it became much more scientific in the 19th century and particularly after World War II when more modern scientific techniques were developed. A key concept of archaeology is stratigraphy; that sedimentation takes place according to uniform principles, and that upper layers of soil are newer than lower layers. Many cultures over the centuries existed in the same geographical areas as earlier cultures. As we excavate various sites, the deeper we dig, the farther we go back in time to even earlier cultures.

The purpose of archaeology is to learn about past cultures and to learn about the evolutionary development of humanity. Most hominids lived in prehistoric times. Written language has only been around about 5,000 years, and hominids have been around perhaps 3.5 million years. So well over 99% of the time that hominids have existed has been prehistoric.

Sophisticated equipment is used to find potential archaeological sites. Although humans likely walked over much of the earth, there were relatively few areas that were home to settlements. Remote sensing equipment for finding such settlements includes:

- Infrared aerial photography that can show patterns invisible with normal photography.
- Radar systems that can also show patterns invisible with normal photography.
- Proton magnetometers which detect minute deviations in the earth's magnetic field which are caused particularly by metal objects.
- Satellite imagery that is multispectral; again, this can see patterns that our eyes cannot perceive.

Once a site is identified, an archaeological dig might occur. Heavy equipment such as a backhoes might be employed initially to remove topsoil, but as one gets closer to the stratum one is interested in, the area is hand-cleaned carefully with trowels so as not to destroy artifacts (which are any objects made by humans). Ecofacts is a term used by archaeologists to refer to objects used by humans without modification, e.g. animal bones left from a dinner. However, once an item is modified by a human (such as carving a bone into a spearhead, it becomes an artifact. Features refer to anything made by humans that are too large to be transported back to a laboratory, e.g. graves, building foundations, etc.

When artifacts are found, how do we know how old they are?

Archaeological Dating Methods

When artifacts, ecofacts and features are discovered it is very important to ascertain the culture and time period they are from. There are a number of dating methods that archaeologists employ to determine the date of their origin. Some methods are "direct", meaning the artifact itself is dated. Other methods are "indirect", meaning we assume the date of an artifact based on something else it is associated with that we can date. Some methods give us "relative dates" rather than absolute dates, i.e. something's relative age in relation to something else. Relative dating includes:

> 1. The Law of Superposition
> As already mentioned, artifacts found deeper in the ground are generally speaking older than artifacts found nearer to the surface.

2. Fluorine absorption dating
This method is used to determine how long items such as bones have been buried. Bones will absorb fluoride ions which are in ground water over time. Based on the amount of fluoride that is absorbed, the amount of time the bone has been in the ground can be estimated. However, in order to estimate a date for a bone, another bone needs to be present for which you do have a known date in order to compare the two bones.

There also are "absolute" methods for dating items:

- Radiocarbon dating
  All living things take in carbon (primarily through food) and contain an equal proportion of the carbon-12 isotope to carbon-14 (14C). When an organism dies, 14C begins radioactive decay. This happens at a known rate. It can only be used on organic specimens, i.e. things that were once alive. It also only can be used on organisms within 50,000 years (so specimens older than this cannot be dated by this method. Accelerator Mass Spectrometry (AMS) is a refinement of radiocarbon dating that requires far less material in order to date.

- Dendrochronology
  This is a method for dating trees and wood products. It is also important for calibrating radiocarbon dates.

- Potassium-argon dating
  This is the primary way of dating fossilized hominid remains. It measures the decay of a rare radioactive

isotope of potassium that results in its becoming argon gas. With this method fossils can be dated that are millions of years old.

- Archaeomagnetic dating
  This is a method for dating features within the last 10,000 years. When soil is heated (e.g. clay hearths for cooking) the iron particles in the soil align themselves with the earth's poles. The direction and strength of the magnetic field varies with time and leave a signature on the soil allowing one to date when the heating of the soil happened.

- Thermoluminescence dating
  This method is used on ceramics and often with stones that had been heated by fire. By measuring accumulated radiation dose, one can determine the amount of time that has elapsed since being exposed to sunlight or being heated.

- Rehydroxylation dating
  This is a method again used on ceramics that measures the extent of rehydroxylation.

- Amino acid dating
  This dating method is used on deceased organisms. All biological tissues contain amino acids, and the ratio of some of these amino acids to each other starts to change upon death. The process is called racemization.

- Optical dating
  This is a method for determining how long ago minerals were last exposed to daylight for items between 100 and 200,000 years old.

- Tephrochronology
  Each volcanic eruption has a distinctive signature. This is a technique that allows for the dating of materials within an ash layer.

Evolution

Evolution is considered a "theory", a term with a scientific meaning that is different from what the general population thinks of when they hear this term. Theories are more than hypotheses. A hypothesis is an educated guess that is based on observations. You may hear a friend say in response to an explanation about something that "that is just a theory". It might be more accurate for him to say "that is just a hypothesis". Theories are explanations that are generally accepted to be true. If evidence accumulates to support a hypothesis, it becomes a theory. It is not considered a scientific "law" because it cannot be expressed in a mathematical equation, which is the requirement to be a "law". "Laws" are not better than "theories". Unfortunately, theories and laws cannot be proven true; they can only be disproven. I may have hundreds or thousands of examples to support a particular theory that I have, but that still doesn't prove that it is always true. There may be some instance out there that I haven't run across that doesn't support my theory. The difference between facts and theories is that facts are observations and theories are the explanations for the facts.

Biological evolution refers to the change that happens to living organisms over time. The concept was introduced by Charles Darwin in his 1859 book "On the Origin of the Species". Biological evolution occurs as the result of natural selection as opposed to "artificial selection". Examples of artificial selection include farmers breeding cows that give more milk and dog breeders who select certain animals to breed that have certain traits they want. Dogs' ancestors were wolves; it is amazing that with artificial selection over the years we have such diversity in dog breeds as Saint Bernards, Poodles and Shitzus.

Natural selection occurs when it is environmental factors that "choose" which animals or plants are likely to survive. It is "survival of the fittest", i.e. the organisms that have the traits that most enable them to flourish and reproduce are most likely to survive to pass on their genes. There is much evidence supporting the theory of evolution including from biochemistry, comparative anatomy, molecular biology, and the fossil record. Because there is very much evidence to support it and no evidence to prove it false, it is a theory accepted as true by science. Those who reject the theory of evolution in the United States seem to base their rejection entirely on their interpretation of the Bible, a very literal one. Most fundamentalist Christians and many evangelical Christians have a six-thousand year old world view in which every species was created by God simultaneously. They really reject the scientific disciplines of geology, anthropology and archaeology. Their only argument against evolution is their literalist interpretation of Genesis. In "War of the Worldviews", a book available at the Creation Museum in Kentucky, the worry about evolution is explained:

"The more that generations are trained to disbelieve the Bible's account of origins, the more they will doubt the rest of the Bible, as all biblical doctrines (including marriage) are founded (directly or indirectly) in the history in Genesis 1-11. We see the direct result of this doubt and compromise reflected in the increasing number of moral battles concerning gay marriage, abortion and so on. Again, the more people believe evolution and reject Genesis 1-11 as history, the more they will reject the rest of the Bible- including the morality that is based in that history."

Taxonomic Hierarchy

Biologists have developed a system for organizing and classifying organisms by their evolutionary relationships: it is called the taxonomic hierarchy. All living organisms fall into one of three domains: bacteria, archaea, and eukarya (which include animals, plants, mushrooms and seaweed). Life then can be organized into smaller and smaller groups:

- Kingdom
- Phylum
- Class
- Order
- Family
- Genus
- Species

Our species, Homo sapiens would be classified thus:

- Kingdom: Animalia
- Phylum: Chordata
- Class: Mammalia
- Order: Primates
- Family: Hominidae
- Genus: Homo
- Species: H. sapiens

Organisms that are not in the same species are for the most part unable to reproduce with each other. Ancestors of Homo sapiens not only were in different species but also were from different genuses.

Earliest Hominids

Our earliest hominid ancestors first evolved in a geological epoch known as the Pliocene (5.332 million years ago to 2.588 MYA)*, although most of the evolution of hominids occurred in the succeeding epoch, the Pleistocene, which was our last ice age, covering the period from 2.588 MYA to 11,700 years ago. Primates diverged from other mammals over 65 MYA, and the earliest apes evolved around 39 MYA. It is believed that the human lineage split off from that of chimpanzees approximately 7 MYA. It once was believed that the human lineage was a straight line going from apes to homo sapiens (modern man). Now it is believed that our lineage is much more complicated than that with the overlapping and coexistence of several hominid species at one time.

Chapter 1: Prehistoric Religion

Fossils have been uncovered that shed light on the origins of our species. The following is a chronology of some of these fossils with their scientific names:

- Proconsul (27-17 MYA)
  This species had the size and build of a monkey, but a larger brain and no tail like an ape. This is believed to be an ancestor of both humans and apes.

- Pierolapithecus (13 MYA)
  This species had many features in common with modern apes.

- Sahelanthropus Tchadensis (7-6 MYA)
  This species lived around the time of the split in lineages between apes and humans. It is unknown whether the species lived before or after the split and whether it is an ancestor of apes, humans, or both.

- Orrorin Tugenensis (6.1-5.8 MYA)
  This may be the oldest known biped, however there is disagreement about which side of the ape/human divergence it belongs.

One of the most important distinguishing features between humans and apes is bipedalism, i.e. walking upright on two legs. All of the species below were believed to have been bipedal.

- Australopithecus Anamensis (4.2-3.9 MYA)

- Australopithecus Afarensis (4.1-2.8 MYA)
  This species is thought to be the ancestor of the genus Homo. The famous fossil "Lucy" belongs to this species

- Australopithecus Bahrelghazali (3.6-3 MYA)

- Australopithecus Africanus (3.3-2.8 MYA)

- Australopithecus Garhi (3-2 MYA)
-
- Paranthropus Aethiopicus (2.7-2.3 MYA)

- Paranthropus Boisei (2.5-1.2 MYA)

- Paranthropus Robustus (1.8-1.4 MYA)

- Homo Habilis (2.2-1.5 MYA)
  This is the first member of the genus Homo (the same genus as modern humans). This species had a larger brain than the genus Australopithecus, and there is evidence that this species used stone tools.

- Homo Rudolfensis (1.9 MYA)

- Homo Ergaster (1.8-600,000 YA)
  This species was as tall as modern humans and with a similar build (arms of human length rather than ape length). This may have been the first in the human line to shed fur in favor of skin, allowing it to sweat in the warmer climate. It extensively used stone tools. It is probably the ancestor of all subsequent species of Homo.

Up to this point, all of the fossils had been found in Africa. It was not until around 1,800,000 years ago with the genus Homo that migrations might have started out of Africa.

- Homo Antecessor (1.2 MYA-800,000 YA)
  Only a few fossils of this species were found- in Spain.

- Homo Erectus (1 MYA-50,000 YA)
  Many fossils of this species were found in Asia, but fossils of the species also have been found throughout Africa.

- Homo Heidelbergensis (600,000-250,000 YA)
  This species was probably the common ancestor of both Homo Neanderthalensis and Homo Sapiens. Fossils have been found across Africa and Europe.

- Homo Neanderthalensis (350,000-30,000 YA)
  This species lived throughout Europe. They coexisted during much of the same period as Homo Sapiens, and there is much speculation about how much they interacted with each other. They thrived for 300,000 years. They were accomplished toolmakers. There will be much more about this species which went extinct later in this chapter.

- Homo Sapiens (150,000-present)
  This is our own species. The species started to look like modern humans about 100,000 years ago. 150,000 years ago sounds like a long time, but if we were to put it on a geological timescale of one calendar year in which the origin of the earth 4.5 billion years ago occurs at midnight on January 1st, the

appearance of Homo sapiens would not occur until December 31st at about 11:49 pm!

The first word in these scientific names is the name of the Genus, and the second word is the name of the Species. As one can see, there is overlap between the different geneses and species in the various time spans.

Stone Age

This is the term for the prehistoric period in which stone tools were widely and predominantly used. Archeology divides human technological prehistory into three periods: the Stone Age, the Bronze Age, and the Iron Age. Certainly technology is not the only measure to demonstrate evolution, but from an archaeological standpoint it is one of the easiest ones since we can find relics that demonstrate a culture's technology. It also should be kept in mind that various cultures went through these technological ages at different times. For example, in southeastern Europe the Iron Age began around 2,500 years ago, but it took centuries more to reach northern Europe.

The Stone Age is divided into three stages: The Paleolithic Era or Early Stone Age (which is further divided into the Lower, Middle and Upper Paleolithic Eras), the Mesolithic or Middle Stone Age, and the Neolithic or New Stone Age.

- Paleolithic
  Lower Paleolithic (2.5 MYA). This period begins with the earliest known use of primitive stone tools.

The earliest species of hominids to use stone tools were probably the australopithecines.

Middle Paleolithic (300,000 YA). It is during this time period that the Neanderthals (Homo neanderthalensis) predominated in Europe, and our ancestors (Homo sapiens) were leaving Africa. Religious practices appear to have begun during this period, and this will be discussed in some detail later in this chapter. Language also likely first developed first during this period.

Upper Paleolithic (35,000 YA). Although Homo sapiens of 100,000 YA appeared like modern humans, they did not behave like them. This changed during the Upper Paleolithic period. Tools became more sophisticated and differentiated. We start finding art works from this period, including the famous paintings in the Lascaux caves in France. Religious ritual developed.

- Mesolithic.
The Mesolithic stage begins with the end of the Pleistocene epoch and the earth's climate warming from the last ice age. It is a transitional period from hunter-gatherer to agricultural societies. There was a shift from dependence on big game (such as the wooly mammoth) to hunting smaller animals and fishing.

- Neolithic (10,000 YA).

    This period is marked by the beginning of agriculture and the domestication of animals. It truly was a revolution as people began to settle down in various places rather than the previous nomadic existences, and the Levant (present day Israel, Lebanon, Syria and Jordan) was where the Neolithic culture was believed to have begun.

First Human Migration

About 1.8 MYA early humans started leaving Africa. Most of the earliest fossils suggest variants of the species Homo ergaster. Once separated from the African population from which they came, these other populations evolved on their own. Over time they developed into Homo neanderthalensis and Homo erectus. Fossils of Homo neanderthalensis are found throughout Europe with none found in Africa. Fossils of Homo erectus are found in East Asia as well as in Africa. It is believed that Homo neanderthalensis evolved from a species known as Homo heidelbergensis, a likely descendent of Homo ergaster. Homo heidelbergensis likely lived from 600,000 to 250,000 YA and probably migrated from Africa at a later date than the first migration of Homo ergaster.

Homo neanderthalensis and Homo erectus are not species that are the ancestors of Homo sapiens, our own species, which has been determined in part by DNA evidence. It is believed that Homo erectus became extinct around 50,000 YA , and Homo neanderthalensis became extinct around 30,000 YA. So around 50,000 YA it is believed that there were four distinct species of hominids that lived concurrently!

- Neanderthals who lived in Europe
- Homo erectus in East Asia and Africa
- Homo floresiensis, a dwarf species that lived on the island of Flores in Indonesia. Fossils have been dated to less than 38,000 YA. The species is believed to be descended from Homo erectus and evolved independently and in isolation on this island.
- The ancestors of Homo sapiens who were in Africa

Many hominid species appeared to have died out. These include:

- Homo neanderthalensis
- Homo erectus
- Homo antecessor
- All species of the genus Paranthropus

Our species, Homo sapiens, likely evolved from

- Homo heidelbergensis
- which evolved from Homo ergaster
- which evolved from Homo habilis
- which evolved from the genus Australopithecus

The Second Great Migration

It is believed by geneticists that our ancestors, Homo sapiens, shrank to a population size of as few as 5,000 people between 60,000 and 40,000 YA due to a dry climate that shrank the forests and dried the savannas. It is believed that our ancestors originated in what is now Ethiopia, or at least somewhere in East Africa. It is believed that our ancestors left Africa about 50,000 YA, and that language had developed shortly before this. Some believe the group left Africa as early as 65,000 YA. Geneticists believe there was a single immigration of our ancestors out of Africa, and the number of people leaving may have been as small at 150 individuals.

Our ancestors were hunter-gatherers and did not settle down, and so they continued to cover significant distances. They initially went from Africa to the Arabian Peninsula. They likely often followed coastlines. While some people continued to push on into new territories, others remained in various geographical locations, and so the population of the world from this small group of people appeared to be quite orderly. From the Arabian Peninsula the migration moved to India. From there some migrated on to Asia and some continued on to the Australian land mass, China and Japan. Others went northwest into present day Iran and Turkey and probably eventually met and maybe combated the Neanderthals. By about 30,000 YA the Neanderthals went extinct. It is surprising that the earliest fossils of Homo sapiens outside of Africa have been found (thus far) in Australia, and so the migration which likely followed shoreline went fast. Homo sapiens did not appear to get to North and South Americas until 14-15,000 YA, although again once they were able to cross the Bering Land Bridge the migration all the way to the tip of South America appeared to go quite quickly.

Although Neanderthals and Homo sapiens were of different species, there is DNA evidence of some interbreeding. Interbreeding between species is not unheard of. For example, female horses can breed with male donkeys, which results in a *mule*. Mules are unable to reproduce. Male lions have reproduced with female tigers; offspring are known as a *ligers*.

DNA evidence has suggested that 1% to 3% of DNA in present-day people of European and Asian descent comes from Neanderthals. This is not found in present-day people of African descent. So it is believed that Homo sapiens after leaving Africa were involved with very limited interbreeding with the Neanderthals. There also has been a relatively new discovery of a possible new species known as the *Denisovans*. They interestingly have significant genetic similarities to present-day Melanesians. So there appears to be evidence that Homo sapiens also bred with this other species, the Denisovans.

Our knowledge about the story of early hominids continues to unfold, and undoubtedly new knowledge will continue to be discovered, particularly due to research with DNA. The Genographic Project of the National Geographic Society is involved with collecting DNA from around the world to understand genetic origins. Their website describes it as "a multiyear research initiative led by National Geographic Explorer-in-Residence Dr. Spencer Wells. Dr. Wells and a team of renowned international scientists are using cutting-edge genetic and computational technologies to analyze historical patterns in DNA from participants around the world to better understand our human genetic roots."

DNA

DNA (deoxyribonucleic acid) is our genetic blueprint; it carries instructions for all of our personal traits. James Watson and Francis Crick figured out it was a double helix. The Human Genome Project had the incredibly ambitious task of mapping the entire DNA sequence of 24 human chromosomes, 20-25,000 genes, and 2.85 billion units of DNA: this was completed in 2003. This allowed us to have a map of just where each individual gene was situated on a particular chromosome. Since then scientists have been involved with genetically modifying organisms, such as crops. This has been controversial.

We each have our own genetic "fingerprint". Although human beings are extremely similar (99.9% of our DNA is the same as in every other human being), we each also have our differences which make us unique and like no one else. You may be aware of DNA's practical implications in solving crimes and determining paternity. DNA evidence has enabled many individuals who were wrongly convicted of crimes to be released from prisons.

DNA also allows us to investigate evolutionary relationships of life on earth. The more differences there are in DNA, the more evolutionarily dissimilar are two organisms. The genomes of chimps and humans are 99% identical. By looking at DNA we know that gorillas are more dissimilar to us than chimps, and orangutans are even more dissimilar and distant on the family tree. When we look at different races and ethnic groups we find humans who have shared genetic similarities. People can currently go on internet sites such as dna.ancestry.com, get kits to collect saliva, and then get results that "uncover your ethnic mix, discover distant relatives, and find new details about your unique family history with a simple DNA test."

Race

In the United States from the 17th to 19th centuries and even later many people understood the races as being primordial (existing since the beginning of time), enduring and distinct. The various races were actually seen by many as subspecies of Homo sapiens. That perception was explained by the judge in the case against Richard Loving and Mildred Jeter who were charged by the State of Virginia in 1958 for violating the state's ban on interracial marriage. Judge Leon Bazile said:

"Almighty God created the races white, black, yellow, malay and red, and he placed them on separate continents. And but for the interference with his arrangement there would be no cause for such marriages. The fact that he separated the races shows that he did not intend for the races to mix."

In actuality, we all had the same ancestors in Africa. After our ancestors left Africa and migrated to the rest of the world, they settled on the various continents and then evolved independently from each other genetically and culturally. Most anthropologists see "race" as a social and cultural construction that really has no validity. We now have a world culture in which people readily travel and intermingle with each other. "Interracial" marriages are more and more commonplace, and it is my belief that in a relatively short period of time (i.e. a century or two) the general public will no longer think in terms of "race".

Population Genetics

Population geneticists have analyzed DNA of living individuals and then have worked backwards to investigate the human genetic history. The two parts of the human genome that are very important for this work are the Y chromosome and mitochondrial DNA. Every human being has 23 pairs of chromosomes that carry our entire genetic makeup. Mitosis is a process in which cells replicate and make more cells that are identical. Meiosis, on the other hand, is a very different process for sexual reproduction. When we reproduce we do not want our sperm and egg cells to be identical in terms of DNA; if they were, we would create clones of ourselves. We want our offspring to be unique individuals; meiosis is the process that makes this happen.

Every human has a total of 46 chromosomes: 23 of our chromosomes come from our mother, and 23 chromosomes come from our father. Each of these 23 chromosomes is part of a pair. In the figure below you will see that chromosome 1 from the father matches up with chromosome 1 of the mother, chromosome 2 of the mother with chromosome 2 of the father, etc.

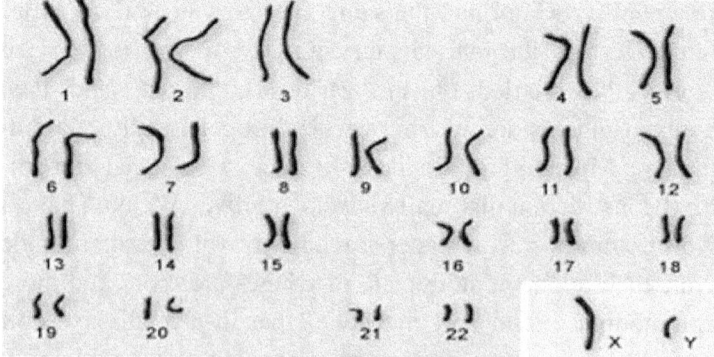

Courtesy of U.S. National Library of Medicine

Chromosome 18 is important for a genetic disorder known as Edwards Syndrome (or Trisomy 18), and chromosome 21 is important for Downs Syndrome (also known as Trisomy 21). Every cell of our bodies contains these 23 <u>pairs</u> of chromosomes.

Before sperm and eggs are generated, there is the process of meiosis in which DNA is shuffled between chromosomes. Men create sperm cells which have 23 chromosomes, and women create egg cells which also have 23 chromosomes. Because of the process of meiosis, there are 8.4 million possible gene combinations for each sperm cell and 8.4 million possible gene combinations for each egg cell. When the sperm and egg cells join together, the resulting zygote has 26 chromosomes; half from the mother and half from the father. This makes the genetic possibilities for this resulting zygote almost unlimited (i.e. 8.4 million times 8.4 million possibilities).

This process of meiosis happens for all the sets of chromosomes with the exception of chromosome pair #23, our sex chromosomes. Men have both an X and a Y chromosome; it is this combination that makes them genetically a male. Women have two X chromosomes; this is what makes them genetically a female. During the process of meiosis these two chromosomes do not swap genes as the other 22 chromosomes do with the exception of at their very tips. Therefore, as a man, my Y-chromosome is passed down exactly from my father unchanged (with the exception of the genes at the very tip). The Y-chromosome for the most part is passed down unchanged from generation to generation.

In women, it is mitochondrial DNA that is passed down unchanged from generation to generation. Mitochondria are components in cells which generate energy. Both sperm cells and egg cells contain mitochondria, but upon fusing of the two the mitochondria from the sperm dies and only the female mitochondria remain. The female mitochondria (which has DNA) is passed from mother to each offspring. If the offspring is female, that is passed down then to the next generation and so on. And so all men living in the world today carry the same Y-chromosome, and all people living in the world today have the same mitochondrial DNA.

Adam, Eve and Eden (Y chromosome and Mitochondrial DNA)

Remarkably, it is believed by geneticists that all of the people living in the world today descended from a single male individual, whom we might call "Adam". It is believed also that all people in the world descended from a single female individual, whom we might call "Eve". How in the world could this be? It happened due to a process called "genetic drift". I refer the reader to Nicholas Wade's fascinating book "Before the Dawn" for a much more detailed discussion of population genetics. Wade said:

"It's a curious fact of genetics that one version of a gene, especially in small populations, can displace all the other existing versions of the same gene in just a few generations, through a purely random process called genetic drift. Consider how this might work among surnames, which are passed on from father to son just like Y chromosomes. Suppose a hundred families are living on an island, each with a different surname. In the first generation, many of those

families will have only daughters or no children at all. So in just one generation, all those families' surnames (and accompanying Y chromosomes) will go extinct. Assuming no new male settlers arrive on the island, the same unavoidable winnowing will happen each generation until only one surname (and Y chromosome) is left" (Wade, 2006).

Wade said that the Y chromosomes of "all the other Adams" died out, and now all human males are descended from one male, the father of all mankind. Wade reports that "Adam" probably lived between 40,000 and 140,000 years ago with perhaps the most probable date being 59,000 years ago. Like the men's lineage, women's mitochondrial DNA seems to have come from a single woman, "Eve" if you will, who likely lived considerably earlier than "Adam", perhaps 150,000 years ago. So although evidence suggests that homo sapiens are descendants of one man and one woman, they were not a couple. Homo sapiens most likely descended from east Africa, likely specifically what is now Ethiopia. So Ethiopia might be considered the "Garden of Eden" if we want to use a Biblical metaphor.

Over the years mutations occurred on the Y chromosome and with the mitochondrial DNA. When mutations occur, they are passed on to offspring. This allows geneticists to trace when one lineage breaks off from another. The earliest mutation of the Y chromosome appears to be M168. All human beings outside of Africa have this mutation and a few who live in Africa also have it. So the Homo sapiens who migrated out of Africa would have left after this mutation occurred. The first Homo sapiens to enter Europe are thought to have another mutation called M173: these are the humans who brought the Aurignacian culture. This culture was succeeded by another European culture, the Gravettian culture who were bearers of the M170 mutation. There will be more about these two cultures later in this chapter. The M242 mutation is seen in individuals in the Americas and was believed to have occurred shortly before the migration over the Bering land bridge from Siberia to the Americas 15,000 YA.

According to Wade, "The mitochondrial genealogy of humankind has three main branches, known as L1, L2 and L3. L1 and L2 are confined to Africans who live south of the Sahara. The L3 branch gave rise to a lineage known as M, and it was the descendants of M who left Africa." All of the women who live outside of Africa belong to the M or N mutations (descendants of L3).

Paleolithic religion

The earliest evidence for some type of religion appears to be in the Middle Paleolithic Age (300,000 YA to 35,000 YA). It is in this period that there is the first evidence for burials. Burying of the dead is a behavior that is unique to humans. Most animals simply ignore the dead and leave the bodies for scavengers and bacteria. Why during the Middle Paleolithic Age did humans start to bury their dead? After all, they were hunter-gatherers who did not live in settlements, and so there was no need for disposing of bodies for sanitary reasons. Although we cannot know the reasons for sure, it is assumed that religious beliefs played a role in the burials (possibly a belief in an afterlife or a belief in a "living corpse"). The earliest examples of hominid remains were found in caves rather than true burials, but they are suggestive of deliberate disposal of bodies. Examples include:

- 225,000 YA 5-15 Neanderthal remains were found in Pontnewydd Cave in Wales
- 200,000 YA 32 individuals of Homo heidelbergensis were found at the bottom of a deep shaft at Atapuerca in Spain
- 100,000 YA fragmentary cranial remains of at least 22 Neanderthals were found in Charente, France.
- 100,000 YA 70 Neanderthals were found at Krapina Cave in Croatia.

There have been many more examples of remains being found in caves. The earliest true burials that have been discovered were of more anatomically modern humans beginning around 100,000 YA. Findings have been found in Israel and in the Nile Valley. Some of these individuals had simple grave goods buried with them.

Neanderthals also began having true burials of their dead beginning about 70,000 YA. Findings have been found in southern France, the northern Balkans, Israel/Syria, and possibly from Central Asia. The Neanderthal remains were sometimes accompanied by food and implements, and stone slabs or animal horns might be used to demarcate graves. The latest burial found of Neanderthals was around 35,000 YA in St. Cezaire in France.

Bear Cults

During the Middle Paleolithic period "bear cults" seem to have arisen. In caves in Germany and Austria skeletons of bears were found, especially skulls. The evidence suggests that bears were at the center of ritualistic cults. Scholars believe that supernatural beliefs of some sort did exist among the Neanderthals. Offerings of stone tools and food would suggest a belief that the deceased in some way benefited from these offerings, i.e. that there continued to be the existence of a soul or spirit.

Bears today are certainly an impressive animal, but during the Palaeolithic period they were truly imposing and extraordinary. I took a photograph of a model of one of these animals at the Field Museum of Natural History in Chicago:

Upper Paleolithic

During this period modern humans were displacing the Neanderthals. There were a number of cultures that appeared in Europe during this period, sometimes referred to as "Advanced Hunting Cultures". One of the earliest of these cultures was populated by Cromagnon man, a very early Homo sapien. Remains of them were first discovered in a cave in France. The earliest known remains we now know go back to 43-45,000 YA in Italy and Britain. Their successors were a culture known as the Aurignacians (38-29,000 YA). They appear in Afghanistan, Iran, and the Levant and spread west into Europe. They were believed to have been the first artists. They produced figurines and also some cave art.

This figure is dated at 32,000 years old and is associated with the Aurignacian culture. It was found in a cave in Germany. This anthropomorphic animal figurine might have religious significance.

The Aurignacian culture was followed by the Gravettians (29-22,000 YA) who made further advances in the arts. They were strongly established in Greece, Italy, southern France, Spain and Portugal. This culture was succeeded by the Magdalenians (17-12,000 YA), the culture that produced the great cave paintings in Altamira, Spain, the Chauvet Cave in France, and the Lascaux Caves in France.

Lascaux cave painting

Venus Figurines

During the Aurignacian, Gravettian, and Magdalenian cultures Venus figurines were often produced. They are made from bone, ivory, soft stones or ceramics and include some of the earliest examples of prehistoric art. What are characteristic of these figurines are exaggerated abdomens, hips, breasts, thighs or vulvas. Although they are termed "Venus" figurines, they predate the Roman goddess Venus. There is some speculation that the figurines might be representations of a mother goddess or fertility icons and so might be considered religious symbols or idols.

With the Upper Paleolithic burials there were increased use of grave goods to accompany the deceased including the bones of large herbivores such as aurochs, mammoth, bison or reindeer (animals often depicted in cave art during this period). Burials also incorporated the heavy use of red ochre to color the skeletons, perhaps to symbolize blood or life. Annemarie de Waal Malefijt (1958) sums up the characteristics of Upper Paleolithic burials:

"Burial was careful; attempts were made to protect the bodies by partially covering them with stone slabs; the skeletons were stained with red ochre; animal bones were placed near the bodies, as were tools and ornaments (the latter usually of shell), and small stone discs to which no utilitarian function can be assigned. The skeletons are either in extended or flexed positions, some with the knees almost touching the chin, others with the legs drawn up in a more natural position.

The presence of animal bones, tools, ornaments, and discs indicates something more than mere respect for the dead. Burial with ornaments, tools, and food is frequent in contemporary non-literate societies, as it was also in the literate civilizations of Egypt, Sumer, and Greece. In these instances the burial objects have most often the stated purpose of serving the dead in the afterlife. It is possible to conclude that such beliefs might have existed in Paleolithic times, and most interpreters agree that this was the case."

Neolithic Religion

The Neolithic Age (also called the New Stone Age) begins with the domestication of plants and animals in the Near East. A culture known as Natufian existed in the Levant that had a way of life that was intermediate between hunter-gatherer and farmer. This culture existed between 12,000 and 8500 BCE and succeeded a previous society of hunter-gatherers, the Kebarans (18,000 to 12,000 BCE). The Natufians settled in an area where the ancestors of wheat and barley grew wild. It is also possible they herded gazelles. Their population grew, and there has been evidence of villages as large as 50 huts. However, this culture had no domesticated plants and animals and relied on hunting small game for much of their diet.

Large cemeteries have been found for the Natufians. With the burials there is some evidence of social ranking; only some burials have elaborate grave furniture such as stone bowls while the majority have no grave goods. One particular Natufian burial particularly stands out; it is of a 45 year old woman who was in a single (rather than mass) grave. Ten large stones were placed on her body at the time of burial, and she was accompanied by a number of remarkable grave goods including a complete human foot of a much larger person placed upon her left leg, 50 complete tortoise shells, a basalt bowl, wing tip bones from a golden eagle which may have borne colorful feathers, a male gazelle horn, and parts of other animals. Excavators believed she was a shaman for she was buried with animal objects that have had powerful supernatural associations in many societies.

Two of the earliest areas believed to have had cultivation of wheat and barley and then domestication of sheep are the Levant and Mesopotamia.

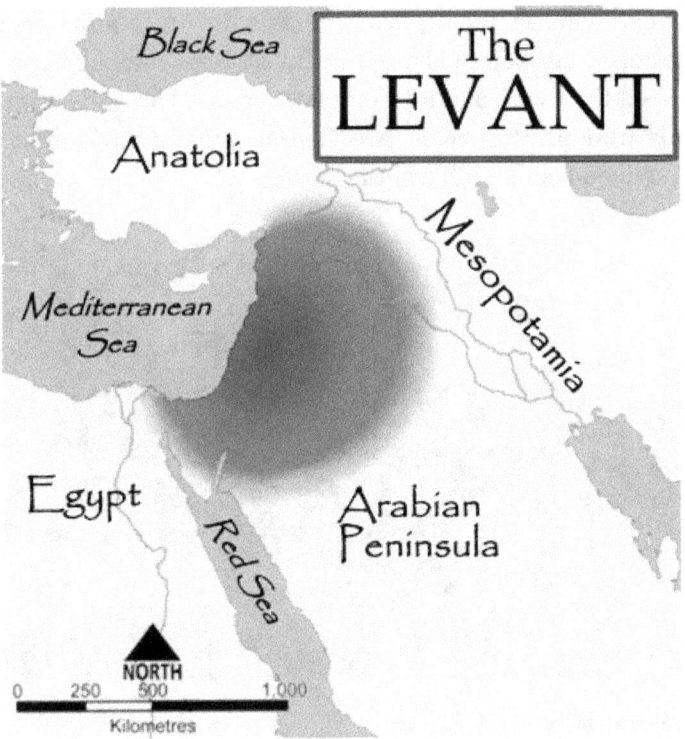

Perhaps the two oldest towns in the world to ever have existed were Catal Huyuk which would have been in today's Turkey, and Jericho which would have been in today's Israel. Jericho dates back to 9-10,000 BCE. By 8,000 BCE Jericho had some 2,000 residents (of Natufian descent). The inhabitants of Jericho buried their dead underneath or among their houses. Toward the end of the millennium Jericho was deserted for a while and then repopulated around 6,800 BCE. The dead were still buried under houses (far better houses than in the previous settlement) but many of them were decapitated. Also found were nine skulls that were covered in plaster to reproduce the flesh of the deceased individual. Shells were inserted for eyes. Many archaeologists believe this represents an ancestor cult, i.e. that the heads of revered ancestors were kept and were believed to be intermediaries between the living and the spiritual worlds. These plastered skulls were also found in Ain Ghazal (present day Jordan) and some other Neolithic sites.

From the British Museum

Around the same time that the above civilization existed in Jericho, the town of Catal Huyuk flourished in modern-day Turkey. Scattered among the houses of Catal Huyuk were ornately decorated shrine rooms which contained idols. Many of the idols were of goddesses. The principal divinity in this culture was a goddess, who was portrayed in three aspects: as a young woman, as a mother giving birth to a child (or a bull or ram), and as an old crone (sometimes accompanied by a bird of prey). Below is a photo of one of

Chapter 1: Prehistoric Religion

the more famous Catal Huyuk goddess figurines; the very rotund woman is sitting between two large cats. The masculine divinity often appears as a youth or as a bearded adult, often mounted on a bull. The masculine divinity is also often symbolized by a bull, ram, stag or boar. Many bulls' heads were found in the shrines at Catal Huyuk.

From the Anatolian Civilization Museum in Ankara, Turkey.

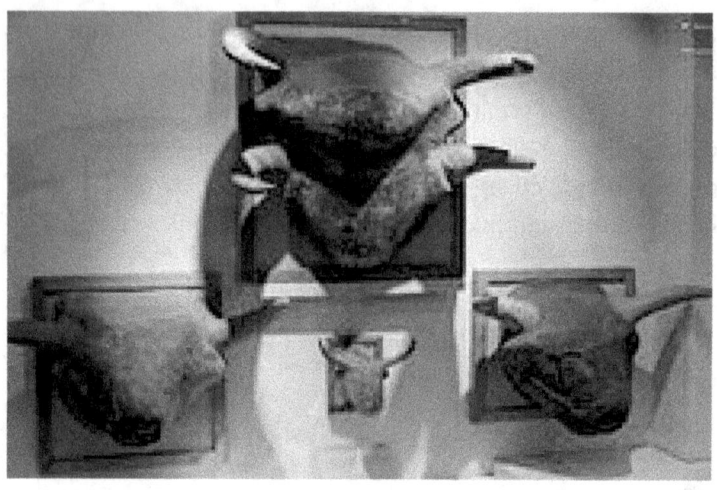

From the Anatolian Civilization Museum in Ankara, Turkey

Anthropology, Ethnography, and Recent "Primitive" Cultures and Religions

Although archaeology has uncovered artifacts from many thousands of years ago that suggest religious practices, we really can only hypothesize about their meanings. Because they are from prehistoric times, there was no written language and no writings to inform us about their meaning. One method of gaining understanding about non-literate societies is to study contemporary cultures that are similar. Anthropology is a scientific discipline that studies not only cultures of the distant past but also contemporary cultures. Ethnography is the systematic study of cultures through observation.

We do, however, have to be very careful with our generalizations from modern non-literate societies to ancient non-literate societies. Although their ways of living, technologies, and practices may have been very similar, the reasons for their behaviors might not have been necessarily the same. An interesting book which describes and categorizes hunter-gatherer societies is the Cambridge Encyclopedia of Hunters and Gatherers (Lee and Daly, 1999). It describes the ethnographies of 67 hunter-gatherer societies from around the world.

Sociology

Another field of study that has examined religion is sociology. Sociology is a social science involving the study of the social lives of people, groups, and societies. Three names known for the sociology of religion are Karl Marx, Max Weber, and Emile Durkheim. All three explored the functions of religion. Karl Marx (1818-1883) had the famous line that "religion is the opiate of the masses". He believed that religion served a social purpose; to provide reasons and excuses to keep a society functioning and to keep the status quo. It is an illusion that keeps people happy. Emile Durkheim (1858-1917) on the other hand did not see religion as imaginary but as an expression of a society. He noted that every society has had religion. He saw religion as an expression of a collective consciousness. As societies become more complex, their religions become more complex. Durkheim (1912) defines religion as "a unified system of beliefs and practices relative to sacred things, that is to say, things set apart and forbidden- beliefs and practices which unite into one single moral community called a Church, all of those who adhere to them." He sees religion's function as being to unite people. Max Weber (1864-1920) believed that religion was a core force in society. He proposed a socioevolutionary model of religious change, i.e. that societies evolved from believing in magic, to polytheism, to pantheism, to monotheism, to an ethical monotheism.

Animism

A prominent characteristic of prehistoric religion likely was animism, the view that plants, non-living things and especially animals possessed a spiritual essence. Humans were considered a part of nature. Sir Edward Burnett Tylor (1832-1917), sometimes considered the founder of social anthropology, believed this was one of the earliest religious conceptions. Tyler defined religion then as "the belief in Spiritual Beings". Animism has some similarities and also some differences with Pantheism, which is the belief that the physical universe and God are one. With animism, belief is of *separate* spirits.

Tyler saw two principal dogmas in animism: the belief in souls continuing to exist after death, and also a belief in other spirits including deities. Tyler believed that early man thought souls would wander during one's sleep and appear to others in dreams. Other people's souls would appear to us in our dreams. After one's death, the soul would depart the body permanently but would continue to exist; after all, the dead appear in dreams as well. Tyler believed that the belief in the soul of humans generalized to other living things and inanimate objects as well; they too appear in dreams. These types of beliefs are supported by more contemporary hunter-gatherer societies that have been studied. Tyler said these beliefs become a religion once they are institutionalized through communal rituals.

From this one can see how polytheism might have developed, e.g. trees being governed by a god of the forest, waves governed by water deities, lightning governed by sky deities, etc.

Ancestor Cults

The belief in the continuation of souls leads, in Tyler's opinion, to the veneration of ancestors, which appears to have been common. This could lead to an actual worship of ancestors. Tyler (1874) states:

"The dead ancestor, now passed into a deity, simply goes on protecting his own family and receiving suit and service from them as of old; the dead chief still watches over his own tribe, still holds the authority by helping friends and harming enemies, still rewards the right and sharply punishes the wrong."

Graves often contained food offerings, tools, weapons and ornaments. Red ochre often was used to color the deceased (to represent life? blood?). Perhaps there was a fear of vengeance of the dead or of revivification. Skulls or jaw bones of the dead may have been kept in homes. The above examples of the plastered skulls found in Jericho and Ain Ghazal are good examples of this.

Cult of the Dead

This term refers to a different belief about the deceased. Instead of venerating the dead and wanting to keep their souls around, some feared the dead. Sometimes survivors of the deceased would give grave goods and offerings to try to keep the dead happy and contented so that they did not return to earth. Ritual offerings were thought to be quite frequent at first and then diminished over time; there seemed to have been a belief that the <u>recently</u> deceased were more dangerous than the long departed. Again, evidence for these beliefs has been supported by more contemporary non-literate cultures.

Tyler believed that other "doctrines" developed from animism:

- Doctrine of Continuance: the idea that departed souls must reside somewhere gave rise to the idea of an afterlife.
- Doctrine of Embodiment: this is the idea that released souls and spirits can enter other bodies and objects when they want.
- Doctrine of Possession: this is the idea that evil souls can enter other people and make them ill, i.e. demon possession.

Fetishism

The belief in possessions may have led to a "doctrine of fetishism", which is the belief that objects may be possessed by a spirit and have power. These objects may be carried around in the belief that they possess power to ward off illness or catastrophe. This can lead to idolatry, the worship of a fetish object.

Totenism

Animism may have been a precursor to totenism, which is a perceived relationship between individuals or groups of individuals with a particular animal or other natural object. For example, members of my clan might perceive us as being descended from a common ancestor of the bear. We feel an affinity with the bear; it is our totem. People may view their totem as a relative or as a protector (like a guardian angel). Generally it was prohibited to eat one's totem except for special times during a ritual ceremony in which the meal was considered an assimilation of the gods. It is believed that individual totenism predated group totenism, which likely had a more social function. There have been several relatively modern "primitive" societies that have subscribed to totenism such as native peoples of Australia, New Guinea, Malaysia, India and Africa as well as native peoples of North America. Most people are familiar with the "totem pole", a carved wood pole with totemic symbols that is particular to American indigenous peoples. Neolithic artwork where animal drawings predominate (including drawings of half-human, half-animal beings) and the inclusion of animal parts in graves may be suggestive of totenism. In this period there may have been beginnings of animal worship.

Polytheism

From the belief in spirits or souls being loose in the world and capable of possessing living and inanimate beings, comes the viewpoint, according to Tylor, that all of nature is possessed or animated by these spirits. Some are good, and some are evil. From this comes the idea that spirits become gods and rule various aspects of nature, e.g. gods of the water, gods of the earth, etc. Over time a hierarchy of the gods developed; some gods more important and more powerful than others. From this developed monotheism, a belief in a supreme deity. This developed many millennium later.

Shamanism

A shaman is a person who is regarded as having special access to the spiritual world. Shamans would typically enter a trance during a ritual in order to have contact with the spirit worlds. The goal would be to elicit help for the human world from guardian spirits, who often would take animal form. Some scholars see the origins of mysticism in Neolithic shamanism. The presence of shamans is thought to be a crucial step in the development of organized religion in that there is now a "professional" to take charge of spiritual matters. Hunter-gatherer societies were very egalitarian; all individuals were of equal status. Shamans achieved an elevated status, and this is seen in burials. Occasionally archaeologists have uncovered Neolithic graves that have been filled with extraordinary grave goods; these are believed by researchers to have been the graves of shamans.

Sacrifice

Some anthropologists believe the idea of sacrifice arose from totemic ritual meals (i.e. where one's totemic animal is eaten in a special feast in order to subsume the power of the god). William Robertson Smith (1846-1894) was a proponent of this view. He saw sacrifice as being both a communion between members of a group (in sharing of a sacrificial meal) and also communion between the group members and their god by their eating of the sacred animal.

Edward Burnett Tyler saw sacrifice as originating as a gift to gods in order to obtain favor, i.e. to gain favor or protection or to atone for past offenses. The goal was very utilitarian: I give in order than I receive. It was an effort to coerce the gods. Tyler believed that the idea of sacrifice evolved into homage, i.e. sacrifices are made to gods in order to express gratitude and respect, not to get something tangible in return. Max Weber agreed with Tyler that the main reason for sacrifice was to gain something from the gods, but he also agreed with Smith that sacrifice had social importance; it provided communion between the participants.

There is evidence for human sacrifice as well as animal sacrifice. At Jericho there is evidence of possible child sacrifice; surrounding the skeleton of an infant were skulls of small children who were decapitated. Stonehenge in England, believed to have been constructed in the Neolithic period between 3,000 and 2,000 BCE, was believed to have been a place of ritual and worship. There is some evidence that human sacrifice was a possibility here as well (Atkinson, 1960).

Cannibalism

Fragments of 40 hominids were discovered and recovered from a cave near Chou Kou Tien, about 40 miles from Beijing in the 1920s. They have become known as "Peking Man". They are of the species Homo erectus and are dated to around 700,000 YA. It is believed that individuals of this culture were cannibals. Skulls in the cave were broken at the bottom of the skulls at the foramen magnum, suggesting that the brains were extracted there and perhaps then consumed. Long bones also were split open, perhaps to get at the marrow. Another skull of Homo erectus known as "Java Man" which was found in Java is dated to between 1 and 1.7 million years ago seems to have been treated in the same way as the skulls from Chou Kou Tien.

In a cave near Monte Circeo in Italy a Neanderthal skull was discovered in 1939. This would have been from the Middle Paleolithic period. The skull was surrounded by a circle of stones and by bones of animals. Like the skulls found near Chou Kou Tien, the skull was broken at the base, again suggesting that the brain was extracted and possibly consumed. Another skeleton from this period was found in a cave near the village of La Chapelle-aux-Saints in France. The body was buried in a fetal position. Although the foramen magnum was not enlarged, the nose bones were missing; brain might have been extracted from here. Game was not believed to have been scarce for the Neanderthals, and so many scholars believe that the eating of their own kind was primarily for ritual purposes rather than for nourishment.

Cannibalism and head hunting are found in a number of contemporary cultures, particularly South Pacific cultures and parts of tropical Africa. The reasons for these practices are to prevent souls from reoccupying the bodies (due to fear of the spirits of the deceased) and also to acquire the powers of the deceased. It is believed that by consuming the brains of the deceased, one can take in their positive qualities. Similarly, the Sambia tribe in New Guinea has an initiation ritual to transform the boys of the tribe into men. Their belief is that the boys must ingest semen from the men of the tribe in order to become strong warriors. The Jivaro of South America take the heads of their enemies in order to acquire their souls.

Myth and Ritual

Both myth and ritual are integral aspects of early religion, and there has been argument about which came first. Making a sacrifice is an example of a ritual. A ritual is done because of a belief, for example sacrificing an animal in the belief that it will make it rain. Robertson Smith 2002) believed that ritual proceeded myth and was at the core of religion. Myth is a story, a narrative with a plot, created to express a *truth*. In that way it is different from folktales or legends, although myths over time may become folktales or legends. Myths deal with the supernatural, and although fairy tales may also deal with the supernatural, they are *not* believed to be true. Robertson Smith explains myths as the verbal explanation of rituals.

Psychologist Merlin Donald (1991) explains the evolution of humans from episodic to mimetic and then to a mythic culture. Episodic culture is the culture of apes and our hominid ancestors. Our distant hominid ancestors lived entirely in the present; these individuals had no abstract symbolic memory representations. Things changed with Homo erectus. "Erectus developed a variety of sophisticated manufactured tools and spread over the entire Eurasian landmass, adapting to a wide variety of climates and living in a society where cooperation and social coordination of action were central to the species' survival strategy." Although erectus was not believed to have had spoken language, it is believed they could communicate with mime, imitation, and gestures. Whereas in episodic culture individuals could react to situations based on memories of their pasts, with mimetic culture individual's learning could be passed on to other individuals. For example, if I learned that a particular berry made one sick, I could gesture to others to stay away from it.

A transition was made from mimetic culture to mythic culture with the advent of spoken language. Spoken language was believed to have developed in Homo sapiens shortly before the migration out of Africa around 50,000 years ago. Individuals now passed on knowledge to each other in the forms of oral lore, totemic art, mimetic song, dance, and ritual. Narrative stories, myths, were passed on orally from generation to generation. Donald writes "Their mythical thought, in our terms, might be regarded as a unified, collectively held system of explanatory and regulatory metaphors."

Another transition happened with the development of *written* language; we moved from mythic culture to having external symbolic storage and theoretic culture. It is only within the last 8,000 years or so that written language has existed. This has enabled new learning to be passed down to subsequent generations. What a tremendous difference this has made! Homo sapiens have lived for 150,000 years, and during that time there has been little change in their hunter-gatherer, nomadic culture. Since the advent of written language, in 5% of that time period, we have gone from the first small cities, to cars, radios, television, airplanes, the internet, and space exploration. No longer did new knowledge die with individuals; progress was able to be passed on!

David Christian explained the timescale of the universe by converting a billion years to one year. With this timescale the 13.5 billion year old universe becomes 13.5 years old.

- The sun and solar system began 4.5 years ago
- The first single celled organisms on earth arrived between 4 and 3.5 years ago
- The first multi-cellular organisms arrived 7 months ago
- Homo sapiens arrived 50 minutes ago
- Agricultural communities arrived 5 minutes ago
- The science and technology revolution occurred in just the last second

Chapter 2

Mesopotamia

Mesopotamia Timeline

5000	BCE	Ubaidian culture dominant throughout Mesopotamia
4000		Bronze Age
3500		Sumerians enter southern Mesopotamia
3500		Uruk, first city in the world
3300		Development of cuneiform writing in Sumeria
2900		Amorites settle to the north of Sumer
2500		City of Ur is major center of trade and manufacture
2400		foundation of Akkadian dynasty in southern Mesopotamia
2334-2279		Sargon the Great of Akkad
2111		Ur-Nammu establishes Third Dynasty of Ur
2100		Epic of Gilgamesh
2100		Construction of Ziggurat at Ur in Sumer
2000		Abraham?
1792-1750		Hammurabi, first great king of Babylon
1750		Code of Hammurabi
1700		Atrahasis
1595-1157		Kassites rule Mesopotamia
1150		Enuma Elish

Hebrew Timeline

900 BCE	Yahwist (J) source for the Pentateuch
800	Elohist (E) source for the Pentateuch
700	Combination of "J" and "E"
700	Deuteronomist
600	Priestly source
550	Formation of the Pentateuch

One can see that the Hebrew timeline was much later than the Mesopotamian timeline. I will discuss in this chapter many Mesopotamian writings that predated and likely significantly influenced the Hebrew scriptures.

Mesopotamia

The land we call "Mesopotamia" is the area of the Tigris and Euphrates river systems. The word "mesopotamia" means in Greek "the land between the rivers". It covers areas in what are now Syria, Kuwait and Iraq. It is a fertile area because of these rivers, and it is part of what is referred to as the "fertile crescent" which includes not only Mesopotamia but also the Levant (Lebanon and Israel) and the Nile valley in Egypt. This fertile land is surrounded by desert and sea. Chapter 3 of this book will be dealing with Egypt, chapter 4 with the Levant, and in chapter 5 we will again return to Mesopotamia.

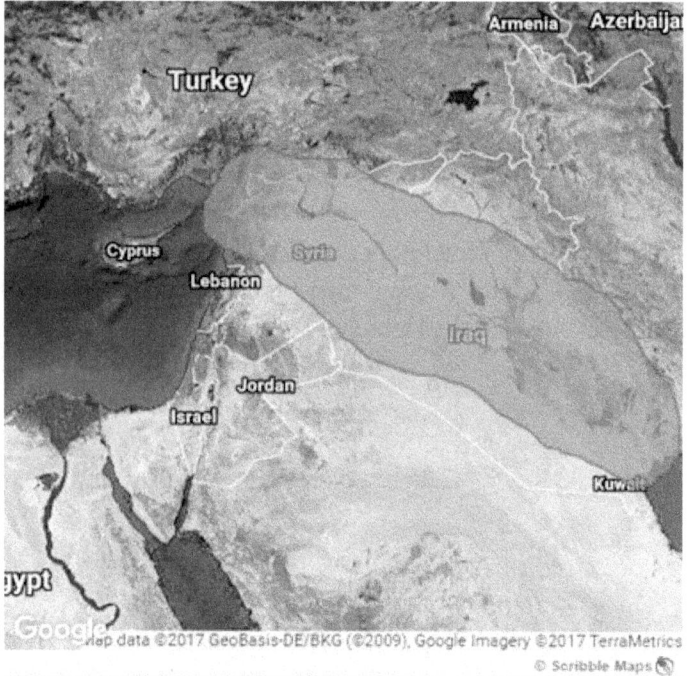

Mesopotamia

Chapter 2: Mesopotamia

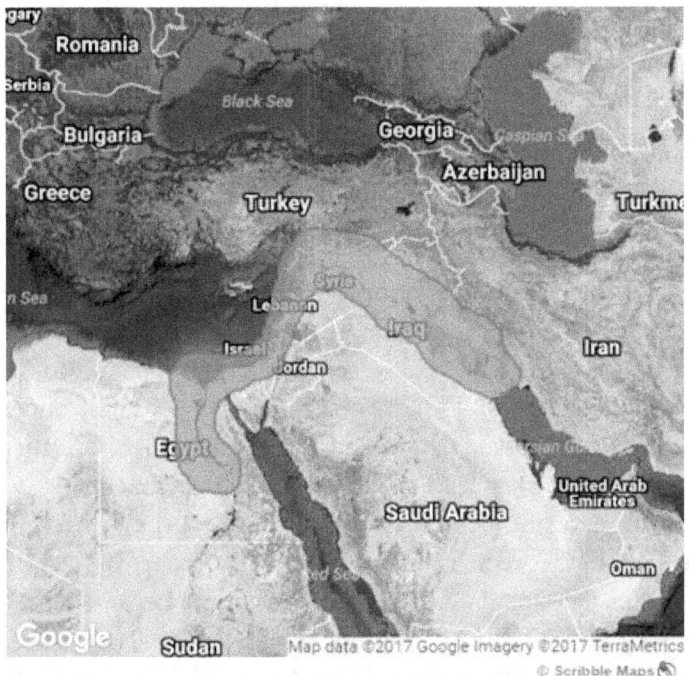

Fertile Crescent

Mesopotamia truly was the cradle of civilization. It was where cities began and where writing was invented. By at least 7000 BCE farmers occupied the Assyrian plains. Farmers known as the Samarrans occupied land south of the land that was occupied by another culture known as the Hassunans, which was replaced by the Halafians. The Halafians and the Samarrans maintained regular contact. This was around 6000 BCE, and it is believed that chiefdoms developed around this time. This is an important cultural development. Hunter-gatherer societies are made up of "bands", groups of families made up of no more than 25 to 100 people. A "tribe" is a group of people that are linked by common ancestral ties. They contain bands, and they may be as large as a few thousand people. "Chiefdoms" are societies between 5,000 and over 20,000 people. Because they are so large, they require hierarchical leadership, a chief. They continue to be kin-based. Whereas hunter-gatherer societies were very egalitarian, chiefdoms are quite hierarchical.

Chalcolithic Period (or Copper Age)

We move from the Stone Age to the Copper Age in Mesopotamia around the 5th or 6th millennium BCE. Copper was used for ornamentation and eventually for tools, especially when it was learned how to combine it with tin to make bronze (the beginning of the Bronze Age). Around 4500 BCE the region was settled by a group of people known as the Ubaidans. The Ubaidan culture became dominant around the whole of Mesopotamia. Perhaps the earliest city of all was the Ubaidan city of Eridu. By 4500 BCE its population may have been as high as 5,000 people. A great temple (ziggurat) was built there, perhaps to honor the god Enki who according to Sumerian legend founded the city. This temple, dated to 4500 BCE was, according to archaeological evidence, built upon ten earlier shrines. Ziggurats were huge stepped pyramids that had a temple or shrine at the top. It would appear they represented mountains where at the top gods resided and where worshipers could encounter them.

Ziggurat

City-States

By 2800 BCE Mesopotamia had several city-states and each one had a ruler. Earlier on the rulers were the temple priests, but later the rulers became more secular. The various city-states rose and declined in power through various periods of history. There was competition and strife between them, and there also were threats from nomadic peoples who migrated from the desert and mountains. Each city-state had its own god who was the center of worship.

Uruk was one of the great early cities of Mesopotamia. It dates to before 4600 BCE, and by 2800 BCE it covered 617 acres. It probably had 50 to 80,000 residents at this time and was the largest city in the world. In the 27th century it was reportedly ruled by the legendary king, Gilgamesh (according to the Sumerian king list). Like other Mesopotamian cities, the ziggurat complex was the center of life in the city. Uruk is believed to be the city named as "Erech" in Genesis 10:10 of the Bible. The gods worshiped were Inanna (the goddess of love, fertility and warfare) and Anu (the great sky god).

Kish was another prominent Mesopotamian city-state. This city's patron deities were Zababa and his wife, Inanna. This is the area that the founder of the Akkadian Empire, Sargon the Great, came from. He will be discussed later in this chapter.

Ur dates back to around 3800 BCE, within the Ubaid period, although there is archaeological evidence suggesting occupation as early as 6500 BCE. It is located south of Uruk. Around 2030 to 1980 BCE it may have been the largest city in the world with a population of approximately 65,000. The city's patron deity was Nanna, the moon god. The ziggurat of Ur which contained the shrine of Nanna was built around 2200 BCE. It was excavated in the 1930s and has been partially restored.

The ruins of Sumerian Ur with the ziggurat in the background.

The city of Ur also has significance for the Jewish, Christian and Islamic religions as it is known to many as the birthplace of the Hebrew patriarch, Abram (Abraham, Ibrahim). In the Torah the birthplace of Abram is called "Ur of the Chaldees". Although many believe the great city of Ur is what is referred to, other scholars believe the birthplace of Abram to be further north, the city of Urfa which is in modern day southern Turkey. Also, traditionally the lifetime of Abram is attributed to around 2000 BCE (this date being arrived at by working backwards from the Jewish Exodus using the lengthy life spans stated in Genesis). Because these lengthy life spans are unlikely, many scholars dispute the traditional dating of Abram and place him at around 1400 BCE.

Sir Leonard Woolley led excavations of the city of Ur in the 1930s. A tremendous find was the Royal Cemetery of Ur. These tombs date to the third millennium. A total of 1,850 burials were uncovered, several of which appeared to have been royal tombs which contained many valuable artifacts. The many goods and artifacts found in these tombs indicate extensive trade links with other cultures. The tombs of the wealthy individuals also contained the remains of servants. One particular tomb contained the remains of 59 people (courtiers and soldiers) who were dressed in their official uniforms and apparently took poison in order to die with their master.

Sumerian King List

Many clay tablets from ancient Mesopotamia have been unearthed in modern times which describe a list of Sumerians kings. The oldest tablet has been dated to 2000 BCE.

The manuscript lists both prehistoric (mythical) kings as well as historical figures from the ancient city-states, including Ur, Kish and Uruk. The Sumerians had a story about a great flood that destroyed all of mankind, with the exception of one sage and his wife who became immortal. There is a list of rulers that were "antediluvian" or before the flood, and these mythical rulers lived extraordinarily long lives, i.e. anywhere from hundreds of years to several thousand years. Scholar Gary Rendsburg reports that people of the Near East were very fastidious in memorizing their genealogies but were not reliable in reporting ages of their ancestors or even of themselves, which Rendsburg said is still true of people in the Near East to this day.

The Bible also lists antediluvian people, and true to the custom of other peoples in the Near East, they also are described as living extraordinarily long lives:

- Adam   930 years
- Seth   912 years
- Enosh   905 years
- Kenan   910 years
- Mahalalel   895 years
- Jared   962 years
- Enoch   365 years
- Methuselah 969 years

The Sumerians

Around 3000 BCE a Sumerian culture developed in southern Mesopotamia. It is not really known whether the Sumerians were an immigrant people coming from the north or from

Iran, or were a combination of indigenous peoples, i.e. an outgrowth of the Ubaidans combined with some Semites who were drifting into the area from western deserts. However, there is a myth of "seven sages" in Sumerian culture which explains that the southern Mesopotamian population was wild and rough-hewn, and that the population was "initiated into all that constituted civilized life" by strange beings who came from the sea. The myth might have developed out of some past actual history. Many do consider Sumerian culture as being the first civilization, particularly due to the invention of writing.

Semites

William Robertson Smith (2002) said the Semites are "the Arabs, the Hebrews and Phoenicians, the Aramaens, the Babylonians and Assyrians, which in ancient times occupied the great Arabian Peninsula, with the more fertile lands of Syria, Mesopotamia, and Irac, from the Mediterranean coast to the base of the mountains of Iran and Armenia." The Semites also included the Canaanites and the Akkadians. We do not know the most ancient history of the Semites. They may have originated on the Arabian Peninsula prior to desertification where they raised sheep and were semi nomadic. At the end of the third millennium bands of them began moving into more fertile lands where they could enjoy a more sedentary existence.

Invention of Writing

One of the greatest inventions by far of mankind has been writing, and it was invented by the Sumerians around 3200 BCE. This written language was believed to have started with simple pictograms used for accounting purposes. Eventually phonetic writing had developed (i.e. that signs could stand for sounds). Their system of writing is called "cuneiform"; scribes would use sharpened reeds to make wedge shapes onto clay tablets which would then be baked until they were hard. They were so hard that they have survived to this day. The language is called "Sumerian". Sumerian is a "lost language" like Latin; people stopped speaking it around 2000 BCE, although like Latin it continued to be taught in schools as a classical language until the first century BCE when it completely disappeared. Because the Akkadians knew Sumerian, and because scholars are able to translate the Akkadian language (which is related to other Semitic languages such as Arabic and Hebrew), we are now able to translate Sumerian writings.

A couple centuries after the Sumerians the Egyptians developed their hieroglyphic writing, and about this same time the Elamites developed a geometric script, probably inspired by their foes, the Sumerians. Elam was a civilization along the Persian Gulf in present day Iran. Its capital was Susa. Like Sumerian writings, Egyptian hieroglyphics were not able to be translated until the discovery of a stone slab by Napoleon's soldiers in Egypt near the city of Rosetta; the stone slab is now referred to as the Rosetta Stone. The stone contains a passage of writings in three different languages: Egyptian hieroglyphic, Demotic script (an ancient Egyptian script), and ancient Greek. This enabled scholars to decipher the Egyptian hieroglyphics since the Greek was a known language.

The Akkadians

Farther north in Mesopotamia lived a Semitic population known as the Akkadians. Their language was very different from the Sumerians and was related to other Semitic languages such as Eblaite, Canaanite, Aramaic and Arabic. They likely came to Mesopotamia from the desert, but it is not known when these peoples first arrived. It's believed the earliest settlers likely predated the Sumerians, and more and more of them came in successive waves. And so in the third millennium BCE there were two civilizations in Mesopotamia: the Sumerians in the south, and the Akkadians in the north. They had completely different languages and ancestries. The two cultures had great influence on each other and lived side by side, although it was the Sumerians who were the more culturally advanced. Although they had different languages, all documents were written only in Sumerian, which makes it difficult for scholars to separate Sumerian from Akkadian culture.

The first time that many Mesopotamian city-states were united under a central government was by the Akkadian king Sargon the Great (2334-2279). Sargon destroyed the walls of the cities he conquered and then installed governors of his choosing to oversee the cities. He was the first king to have a standing army. He founded a new capital, Akkad, although that city's location has been lost to history. Sargon's empire lasted until around 2100 BCE. Sargon's beginnings are related on an ancient Sumerian tablet. Sargon was said to be the illegitimate son of a temple priestess of the goddess

Inanna. Sargon's mother bore him in secret and placed him in a basket of reeds, sealed the basket's lid with pitch, and cast the basket adrift on the Euphrates River. He was found by a man named Akki, who was a gardener for Ur-Zababa, the king of the Sumerian city of Kish. Akki raised Sargon. Legend has it that he rose to power by winning the favor of the goddess, Ishtar. Compare this to the story of Moses (written over a thousand years later) whose mother bore him, hid him for three months, and then got a papyrus basket for him which was lined with pitch. She placed Moses in it and placed the basket among the reeds on the bank of the river. Moses was discovered by the pharaoh's daughter who raised him. Later Yahweh chose him to lead the Israelites out of bondage in Egypt.

Sargon	Moses
Mother bore him in secret.	Mother bore him in secret.
Placed in a basket of reeds sealed with pitch.	Placed in a papyrus basket sealed with pitch.
Set adrift on Euphrates River	Set in reeds of the river.
Discovered and raised by the gardener of the king.	Discovered and raised by the daughter of the pharaoh.
Rose to power by winning the favor of the goddess, Ishtar.	Chosen to lead the Israelites by the god Yahweh.

Third Dynasty of Ur

A Sumerian dynasty from Ur reunited much of Sargon's territory. The ruler was Ur-Nammu (2112-2095), who like Sargon appointed governors to oversee the cities. Ur-Nammu was known for building ziggurats, including the ziggurat dedicated to the god Nanna in Ur. This shifted power in Mesopotamia from the north to the south. By around 2000 this dynasty gradually disintegrated, partly due to attacks by the Amorites and the Elamites. The Elamites devastated the city of Ur in 2004. Power once again returned to the individual city-states. During this time period groups of nomadic Semitic peoples migrated into Mesopotamia; they were given the name "Amorites". Their language, related to Akkadian, was Canaanite (which later developed into Ugaritic and Hebrew).

Hammurabi

By the beginning of the second millennium BCE power centered in Asshur in the north and Babylon (or Babylonia) in the south. The Babylonians were Amorites who took over Sumerian culture and religion (although the gods' names were Akkadian). The dominant language at this time became Akkadian. King Hammurabi (1792-1750) brought Babylon to prominence at this time. Hammurabi is known for his law code which will be discussed later in this chapter. Hammurabi was known as "King of the Amorites", and he made Babylon his capital. He controlled southern Mesopotamia but did not gain control over the northern areas. The Amorite Period (also known as the Old Babylonian Period) lasted about 150 years.

Hittites and Kassites

In 1595 Babylon was sacked by a group of people known as the Hittites, who came from the north-west. The Kassites, who came down from the Zagros Mountains, spoke an unknown language that was neither Semitic nor Indo-European. They ruled Mesopotamia for longer than any other Mesopotamian dynasty: 300-400 years. They called their kingdom "Babylonia". They adopted the Akkadian customs and language, including the Babylonian religious culture. It was during this time that Aramaic, a Semitic language, began to replace Akkadian as the dominant language in the region.

Religion

In Mesopotamia gods are the beings who live in heaven, whereas earth is where human beings live. To be a god is to be superior, although the Mesopotamian gods were very human-like in terms of their emotions. They were ambitious, jealous, violent, flawed, and sexual. They ate and drank, and sometimes drank too much. Unlike humans, they were immortal. They also had a mysterious power called *me*, an essence that made them superior to humans. Some humans had superhuman powers or were great sages, and so were considered god-like, but not fully god or immortal.

While most gods reside in heaven (the Igigi), there are other gods who reside in the underworld (the Anunnaki). There is a hierarchy of gods, with the lowest gods being relegated to manual labor. Because these lower gods rebelled against doing this type of work, human beings were created to do the worst tasks. It is the job of humans to serve the gods. The gods made the plans, and it was up to humans to follow the divine orders.

The gods also could be found in their temples in the ziggurats. The belief was that the gods had divided up the city-states and their surrounding territories between them. Each city-state had a principal or patron god. The largest complex in each city-state was the ziggurat, which was located in the center of town. The ziggurats were palaces for the gods. Bedrooms were included for the gods/goddesses and their spouses and sometimes rooms for offspring as well. The gods received ritual offerings of meat and incense, and there were worship rituals of prayer and song. Priests were employed to serve the temples.

It was also customary in ancient Mesopotamia for individuals to have a "personal god" and/or "personal goddess" who would care for them and to whom individuals could turn in times of trouble. A similar concept in today's world would be "guardian angel". While the major gods controlled the major elements of the world such as the sun and weather, personal gods cared for individuals.

In regards to suffering, the Sumerian belief was that all human suffering was deserved. If bad things happened, it was because of something the individual did or did not do. The gods were never to blame.

Death

When people die, they descend to a netherworld where life is a dim and dismal reflection of earthly life. With the exception of the Egyptians who believed in an enjoyable physical afterlife, the rest of the ancient near east believed the afterlife was a gloomy, dreamlike existence where individuals would lead a semi-conscious existence for eternity. It did not matter what kind of life one led; all people, good and bad, would ultimately end up there. The Hebrew term for this was Sheol, and the Greeks called it Hades. Other peoples of Mesopotamia and the Levant also held this view.

Mesopotamian Pantheon

The earliest surviving list of Mesopotamian gods is dated to 2600 and lists 560 gods by Sumerian names. The following is a list and description of the more important gods (with both their Sumerian and Akkadian names). It should be noted that there are some contradictions in the stories about the various gods, for example whom is the offspring of whom. As power shifted from one city-state to another, the importance of gods shifted accordingly.

- An (Anu in Akkadian) was the god of the sky. He lived the highest in the heavens and was superior to the other gods. His consort was the earth goddess (originally Urash and then Ki). Their sexual intercourse did not produce offspring but rather vegetation on the earth. This is a metaphor for the rain from heaven combining with the earth to produce crops.
- Enlil (Ellil in Akkadian) was the chief god of Sumer and the god who ruled over human affairs. His consort was the goddess Ninlil, and their children included the gods Ishkur, Nergal, Ninurta, Urash, Nanna, and the goddess Inanna.
- Inanna (Ishtar in Akkadian) was originally a fertility goddess who eventually evolved into the "Queen of Heaven and Earth", the preeminent goddess in the Mesopotamian pantheon. Her consort was Dumuzi, a pastoral god. She had a voracious sexual appetite. She was worshiped in Sumer from around 4000 to 1000 BCE. Under her Akkadian name of Ishtar she was worshiped for another 1,000 years in Babylon into the Common Era.
- Enki (Ea in Akkadian) was the god of fresh water and "Manager of the Soil". His wife was Damgalnuna (or Damkina). They were the parents of Marduk, the chief god of Babylon.
- Nanna (or Sin in Akkadian) was the god of the moon and the god of the city of Ur. His consort was the

goddess Ningal, and together they were the parents of Utu, the sun god.
- Utu (Shamash in Akkadian), the sun god, drove his chariot across the sky daily and then went to the underworld through the night. Utu was also a human benefactor who was a god of truth and justice. His consort was Sherida, the goddess of light and also a goddess of fertility and sexual love. Their children included the goddess Kittu ("Truth") and the god Misharu ("Justice").
- Ishkur (Adad in Akkadian) was the Sumerian god of storms, hail and lightning.
- Ninurta, the son of Enki and Ninmah, was both a god of war and a god of agriculture.
- Nergal and his consort Ereshkigal were gods of the underworld and guardians over the realm of the dead.
- Asshur, a war god of Assyria identified with the city of that name, gained ascendancy when Assyria rose to power in the ninth century BCE.
- Marduk, the god of Babylon, eventually became head of the Mesopotamian pantheon. He was the patron god of Babylon during the Third Dynasty of Ur. He became more important when Babylon became the great power in the region. He subsumed attributes of the gods An and Enlil.

Worship and Sacrifice

The place of worship for the gods in Mesopotamia was the ziggurat. They were built from 2200 to 550, the time of the Persian conquest. They had temples at their summits dedicated to its primary god, although worship spaces for other gods were often incorporated along terraces. The ziggurat was the central and most important edifice in Mesopotamian cities. The temples employed many people including the chief priest or priestess, lower priests or priestesses, musicians, diviners, magicians, dream interpreters, cooks, and other workers. People would make food and monetary offerings to the temples which supported the personnel.

Glenn Holland (2009) has described the temple rituals. He said food offerings were made twice daily; in the morning when the temple doors were opened and last thing in the evening before the temple was closed for the night. The food was intended to be the best meat and produce available. Incense was burned, and musicians provided dinner music. After the gods had consumed the spiritual essence of the food, the meal would be cleared and then consumed by temple personnel.

In addition to offerings of food and money to the temple, Mesopotamians also offered hymns of praise to gods, primarily to elicit help in achieving some desired result. It was believed during this time period that all calamitous events were the result of displeasing gods, and all fortuitous events were the result of pleasing gods. It was not until the first millennium BCE that the idea of malevolent evil gods or demons causing woe came into prominence. Since pleasing the gods was of paramount importance, various methods were employed to determine the will of gods. This included divination; specialists were available who professed the ability to determine the will of gods. Methods included the casting of lots, examining the appearance of dregs in a cup of wine and extispicy, which is the examination of the viscera of sacrificed animals. Prophecy and dream interpretation were other methods employed.

The Epic of Gilgamesh

The earliest literature that is known in the world is the Epic of Gilgamesh, dated to 2100 BCE during the Third Dynasty of Ur. The stories are believed to have been around and passed by oral tradition for centuries prior to this. The earliest version is five Sumerian poems about "Bilgamesh", which is Sumerian for "Gilgamesh", the king of Uruk. They were considered to be distinct stories. Later they were combined into an epic. The earliest combined epic of Gilgamesh dates to 1800 BCE known as the Old Babylonian tablets. Akkadian versions were found around 1200 BCE; it is known as the "classical Epic of Gilgamesh" and was known to the Babylonians and Assyrians as "He who saw the Deep". There are many versions of this epic that have been discovered. More than 80 manuscripts of this epic poem have been discovered on cuneiform tablets. They have been discovered in Mesopotamia, the Levant and Anatolia.

The setting of the epic is the city-state of Uruk, the greatest city of its day. Gilgamesh was its tyrannical ruler. He was semi-divine; his mother was the goddess Ninsun. However, he himself was mortal. It is not known if there was an actual historical King Gilgamesh. He is listed on the list of Sumerian kings as the fifth ruler of the First Dynasty of Uruk. He thus would have lived around 2800 to 2700 BCE. His reign lasted a mythical 126 years.

The epic was popular for many centuries because it dealt with common and important universal human themes:

- Fear of death
- Acceptance of human limitations
- What it means to be a man

- Immortality through achievement
- Path to wisdom
- Duties of leadership
- Explanation of the natural world

The story begins with an introduction of King Gilgamesh, who was beautiful, strong, wise, but also cruel and dominating. Although he built magnificent ziggurats in Uruk, he took advantage of his subjects including raping any woman he desired. His subjects complained about his oppression of them, and the gods responded by creating a wild man named Enkidu, who was strong and very hairy. Enkidu lived in the wilderness with the wild animals until he was tamed by a temple prostitute. It was believed at that time that sex could calm men, and Enkidu and the prostitute copulated for a solid six days and seven nights. The prostitute told Enkidu about King Gilgamesh; Enkidu wanted to challenge him to see who was stronger. Enkidu traveled to Uruk and confronted Gilgamesh. They fought, and Gilgamesh prevailed. They then become friends.

The two of them looked for an adventure to share, and they decided to steal trees from a distant forest which was forbidden to mortals. The forest was guarded by a terrifying demon named Humbaba, the servant of the god Enlil (god of earth, wind and air). They confronted the monster and were able to kill it, with the assistance of the sun god, Shamash. They returned to Uruk. There the goddess, Ishtar, the very sexual goddess of fertility, made sexual advances toward Gilgamesh, who spurned her. She was furious. She asked her father, Anu, the god of the sky, to send the Bull of Heaven to punish him. The bull came to bring seven years of famine. Together Enkidu and Gilgamesh killed the bull.

The gods met in a council to decide what to do about this, and it was decided that one of the two must die for this transgression. Enkidu was the one who died, and Gilgamesh was heartbroken. Not only did he grieve for Enkidu, but he ruminated about eventually dying himself.

Gilgamesh decided to set off to find Utnapishtim, the one man who survived the great deluge that destroyed mankind. Utnapishtim had been made immortal, and Gilgamesh wanted to find out how he could become immortal himself. On the journey Gilgamesh met a tavern keeper, Siduri, who counseled Gilgamesh that seeking immortality was a useless and futile endeavor. Her advice was (Jacobsen's 1949 translation):

> "Fill your belly. Day and night make merry. Let days be full of joy, dance and make music day and night. And wear fresh clothes. And wash your head and bathe. Look at the child that is holding your hand, and let your wife delight in your embrace. These things alone are the concern of men."

This advice reminds one a great deal of the writer of the book of Ecclesiastes in the Bible, written many centuries later:

> "So I commend enjoyment, for there is nothing better for people under the sun than to eat, and drink, and enjoy themselves, for this will go with them in their toil through the days of life that God gives them under the sun." Ecclesiastes 8:15

Undaunted, Gilgamesh continued on his journey to find Utnapishtim and did find him. Utnapishtim tells him the story of the great flood. The gods had met in council and decided to destroy humankind with a deluge. However, Utnapishtim was warned by the god Ea of the plan and was advised to make a giant boat to house him and his family and also the seed of every living creature.

When the storm came the gods climbed as high as they could on mountains to escape the waters. Eventually the boat came to rest on a mountain top. After seven days Utnapishtim released a dove; because it could not find a place to alight it returned to the boat. Later Utnapishtim released a swallow; it too returned to the boat. Later he released a raven; it never returned. When Utnapishtim made it to dry land he made a sacrifice to the gods, and the famished gods came to the altar. The god, Enlil, was furious that anyone escaped death with the flood. The god, Ea, criticized Enlil for creating the flood in the first place and said all of humankind were not deserving of death. He suggested that plagues, wolves, and famine should be used to kill only people deserving of death rather than killing off the whole human race.

Obviously, there are many similarities in this story with the story of Noah in Genesis in the Bible, written many centuries later. God saw the wickedness of mankind and regretted that he ever created humans. He decided to destroy every living thing on earth. However, God found favor with Noah, a "righteous man, blameless in his generation". He told Noah to build a giant ship that would hold specimens of every species of animal on earth (in chapter 6 of Genesis his instructions are two of every kind, but in chapter 7 it is seven pairs of every kind). The flood came, and Noah, his family, and the animals were safe on the ark, but every other living creature was destroyed. When the flood waters subsided the ark came to rest on the mountains of Ararat. Noah sent out a raven; it had no place to alight. He then sent out a dove; it could find no place to alight and returned to the boat. Seven days later he sent out another dove; this dove returned with a freshly plucked olive leaf, and so Noah knew that the waters had subsided. Then seven days later he sent out another dove that did not return. When the earth was dry the ark was evacuated. Noah built an altar to God and offered sacrifices. God smelled the pleasing odor of the sacrifice and made the promise never to destroy the living world again.

Code of Hammurabi

Hammurabi (1792-1750) was the ruler of the city of Babylon, and he unified southern Mesopotamia under his central government. He is probably most famous for his legal code, known as the Code of Hammurabi. In the prologue to the code Hammurabi writes "Anu and Bel called me, Hammurabi, the exalted prince, a God-fearing man, by name, to cause justice to be practiced in the land, to destroy the wicked and the evil [alike], to prevent the strong from oppressing the weak, so that I might go forth like Shamash to rule over the Black-haired people, to give light to the land, and, like Anu and Bel, promote the welfare of mankind."

Hammurabi's code was written many centuries before the writing of Moses' law codes in the Torah. There are many similarities in the codes. In 1947 an even earlier law code promulgated by King Lipit-Ishtar came to light; this law code preceded Hammurabi's by 150 years. It was written in Sumerian, not the Semitic Babylonian language of Hammurabi. Just one year later, 1948, yet another law code was uncovered that was written even earlier (300 years prior to Hammurabi during the Third Dynasty of Ur. It was written in the Semitic Babylonian language.

I will cite a few examples from the Hammurabi code (Davies, 1905). In normal type I will cite the Hammurabi code, and in italics I will cite similar codes from the Torah.

If a man steal an ox, or sheep, or ass, or pig, or boat, from a temple or palace, he shall pay thirty-fold; if it be from a freeman, he shall pay tenfold. If the thief has nothing with which to pay, he shall be put to death. Code #8
If a man shall steal an ox or a sheep, and kill it, or sell it, he shall pay five oxen for an ox, and four sheep for a sheep...If the theft be found in his hand alive, whether it be ox, or ass, or sheep, he shall pay double. (Ex. 22:1 and 4)

If a shepherd, without the consent or permission of the owner of a field, have pastured his sheep upon the growing grain; the owner shall reap his field, and the shepherd, who without his permission has pastured his flock in the field, shall pay in addition [as damage] twenty GUR of grain for every ten GAN. Code #57
If a man shall cause a field or a vineyard to be eaten, and shall let his beast loose, and if it feed in another man's field; of the best of his own field and of the best of his vineyard shall he make restitution. Ex. 22:5

If a man incur a debt and sell his wife, son, or daughter for money, or bind them out to forced labor, three years shall they work in the house of their taskmaster; in the fourth year they shall be set free. Code #117

If thy brother, an Hebrew man, or an Hebrew woman, be sold unto thee, and serve thee six years: then in the seventh year thou shalt let him go free from thee. Deut. 15:12. See also Ex. 21:2

If a man's wife be caught lying with another man, both shall be bound and thrown into the water, unless the husband of that woman desire to pardon his wife, or the king his servant. Code #129

And the man that committeth adultery with another man's wife, even he that committeth adultery with his neighbor's wife, and adulterer and the adulteress shall surely be put to death. Lev. 20:10

If any one violate the wife [betrothed] of a man, who has not known a man, but who is still living in the house of her father, and he lie with her and be caught, he shall be put to death, but the woman shall go free. Code #130

But if the man find the damsel that is bethrothed in the field, and the man force her, and lie with her: then the man only that lay with her shall die: but unto the damsel they shall do nothing, there is in the damsel no sin worthy of death. Deut. 22:25

If a man have betrothed a girl to his son, and his son have known her, but he [the father] afterwards lie with her, and be caught with her, they shall bind him and throw him into the water. Code #155

And if a man lie with his daughter-in-law, both of them shall be surely put to death. Lev. 20:12

If a man have betrothed a bride to his son, and his son has not known her, but he [the father] afterwards lie with her, he shall pay one-half mina of silver, and return to her all she brought from her father's house. She may marry the man of her choice. Code #156

If a man finds a damsel that is a virgin, which is not betrothed, and lay hold on her, and lie with her, and they be found; then the man that lay with her shall give unto the damsel's father fifty shekels of silver, and she shall be his wife, because he hath humbled her. .Deut. 22:28

If a son strike his father, one shall cut off his hands. Code #195

He that striketh his father or his mother shall surely be put to death. Ex. 21:15

If he destroy the eye of a man's slave, or break the bone of a man's slave, he shall pay one-half his value. Code #199

If a man smite the eye of his servant or the eye of his maid, and destroy it, he shall let him go free for his eye's sake; if he smite out his man servant's tooth, he shall let him go free for his tooth's sake. Ex. 21:26

If a man strike a free-born woman, and produce a miscarriage, he shall pay ten shekels of silver for the loss [of that in her womb]. Code #209

If men strive, and hurt a woman with child, so that the fruit depart from her, and yet no mischief follow, he shall be surely punished, according as the woman's husband will lay upon him, and he shall pay as the judge determine. Ex. 21:22

If an ox, while passing through the streets [market] gore and kill a man, this case is not subject to litigation. Code #250
And if an ox gore a man or a woman, that they die, the ox shall be surely stoned, and its flesh shall not be eaten; but the owner of the ox shall be quit. Ex. 21:28

If a man's ox were known to gore, and he had been notified that it was a gorer, and he have not wound up its horns, and have not shut it up, and the ox gore a free-born man, and kill him, he shall pay one-half mina of silver. Code #251
But if the ox were wont to gore in time past, and it hath been testified to its owner, and he hath not kept him in, but that he hath killed a man or a woman; the ox shall be stoned and his owner also shall be put to death. Ex. 21:29

If it kill the slave of a man, he [the owner] shall pay one-third mina of silver. Code #252
If the ox gore a man-servant or a maid-servant; he shall give unto their master thirty shekels of silver, and the ox shall be stoned. Ex. 21:32

Atrahasis

Clay tablets inscribed with this epic have been dated to around 1700 BCE. Written on three tablets, it tells a story of creation and also a description of the great flood. Atrahasis is the name of the main character, the same character named Utnapishtim in the Epic of Gilgamesh. Likely the "standard" or Babylonian version of the Gilgamesh Epic took material from "Atrahasis" and incorporated it. Likely the story about the great flood was told by oral tradition for hundreds of years in Mesopotamia, and being dated at 1700, the Atrahasis epic predates the writing of the Noah story by a millennium.

Tablet I tells the story of the creation of humans. Junior divinities were doing menial labor but rebelled against doing this kind of work. Humans then were created to do these tasks. Tablet II discussed the overpopulation of humans. Famine and drought are first used to decrease the human population. Then Enlil decides to completely destroy humankind with a great flood. Tablet III contains the flood story which is primarily as it is in the Epic of Gilgamesh.

An even earlier version of the Mesopotamian deluge myth was found by Arno Poebel in 1914. It was of Sumerian origin. The protagonist in this version is named Ziusudra.

Enuma Elish

This creation epic, also known as "The Epic of Creation", perhaps dates to as early as the time of Hammurabi, but the cuneiform that was discovered in Nineveh in 1849 likely dates to the twelfth century BCE. The hero of the poem is

Marduk, the chief god of Babylon, who had over the years risen in importance in the Mesopotamian pantheon. The primary goal of the epic appears to be mainly the assertion of Marduk's supremacy in the Mesopotamian pantheon. The epic describes how everything came to be in the beginning. Some scholars have suggested that the myth might have had some influence on the writers of the Biblical creation story. In chapter one of Genesis God did not create the world *ex nihilo* (out of nothing) but rather "the earth was a formless void and darkness covered the face of the deep". God created light and separated the light from darkness. In the Enuma Elish the universe is also described in the beginning as being in this formless state.

In Genesis on day two God "separated the waters that were under the dome from the waters that were above the dome." Then God created dry land and vegetation. On the fourth day God created the sun, moon and stars. On the fifth day God created the sea creatures and birds, and on the sixth day God created the land animals, including humankind. On the seventh day God rested.

The Enuma Elish begins with a story about a conflict between the evil god Tiamat who is the goddess of salt water and Marduk, the good god who is the heaven god and storm god. Marduk killed Tiamat and created the world out of her body; the upper part of her body was used to create the vault of heaven, and the lower part to create the earth. The epic continues with the creation of the sun, moon, stars, and finishes with the creation of man. The epic ends with the construction of a temple to Marduk in Babylon. This is a polytheistic story, whereas in Genesis only the one God is responsible for creation.

Enki and Ninhursag

This Sumerian poem consists of 278 lines inscribed on a six-column tablet. It describes a garden paradise called Dilmun. In this paradise the mother-goddess of the Sumerians, Ninhursag, has eight plants sprout. The god, Enki, eats them, which angers Ninhursag; she puts a death curse on Enki, who gets ill. Eight of his organs become sick. Ninhursag is persuaded later to help cure Enki, and she brings into existence eight healing deities for each of the diseased organs, and Enki is brought back to health. The Sumerian scholar Samuel Noah Kramer (1956) notes that this has some parallels to the Biblical paradise story. First of all Kramer said the idea of a divine paradise is of Sumerian origin. The Biblical description of Eden is that it was east and was fed by four rivers including the Tigris and the Euphrates. Enki being cursed for eating forbidden plants reminds us of Adam and Eve's punishment for eating the forbidden fruit. Finally, Kramer said he had always wondered why of all the body parts to choose from, God had chosen a rib to make Eve. In this Sumerian story, one of the body parts that was affected on Enki was a rib. The Sumerian word for rib is *ti*. The word *ti* also means in Sumerian "to make live". The goddess who cured Enki's rib was called Nin-ti. So this goddess may have been both "the lady who makes live" and "the lady of the rib". This may be why a rib was chosen for Eve's origin in Genesis.

The Sumerian Job

A Sumerian poetic essay consisting of about 135 lines was the basis of a paper written by the Sumerian scholar Samuel Noah Kramer. The Sumerian fragments are all over a thousand years older than the written story of Job in the Bible. This was the story of a man who was wealthy, righteous and wise, or so it seemed. Sickness and suffering came upon him. He humbly prayed to his personal god who was moved to compassion and reversed his misfortunes. As I mentioned earlier in this chapter, it was believed by the Sumerians that all misfortunes were deserved. The Sumerians had developed a notion of a personal god, i.e. that each individual had an angel of sorts that they could pray and plead to.

Sumerian Proverbs

Older than the Book of Proverbs in the Old Testament were Egyptian proverbs, and even older were Sumerian proverbs, written down more than 3500 years ago. They are very similar to the proverbs in the Bible.

- A restless woman in the house adds ache to pain
- A scribe who does not know Sumerian, what kind of scribe is he!
- Friendship lasts a day, kinship endures forever.
- A joyful heart: the bride. A sorrowful heart: the groom.
- Can one conceive without intercourse, can one get fat without eating!

Lamentations

The Biblical book of "Lamentations" is a work of art that is in response to a historical disaster, the destruction of Jerusalem and the deportation of its citizens to Babylon. This is a genre of literature that has its origins in Mesopotamia. The genre is believed to have started in response to the conquest of Sumerian cities by Sargon and his successors, although we do not have these documents. We do have some later documents, however, including "Lamentation over the Destruction of Sumer and Ur" and "The Lamentation over the Destruction of Nippur."

Syncretism

"Religious Syncretism" refers to the fusion of religious beliefs and practices. Over time when different cultures came into contact with each other, ideas, beliefs, customs, stories and rituals become incorporated into each other's cultures. The cultures of Mesopotamia certainly likely had a great effect on the religion of the Hebrew people and the stories of the Torah.

The Tower of Babel
The story of the Tower of Babel ("a tower with its top in the heavens") in Genesis 11 is believed by scholars to have been based on the Mesopotamian ziggurats.

Law Codes
There were law codes in Mesopotamia similar to the "Law of Moses" many centuries before there even were a Hebrew people.

Creation myths
Mesopotamian creation myths, with some similarities to the myth in Genesis, predated the Hebrew writings by centuries.

Flood stories
Mesopotamian deluge myths predate the Hebrew writings by a millennium.

Beliefs about death
The Mesopotamians believed in an afterlife, although a dreary and shadowy existence. The later early Hebrew people also conceived of such a place and called it Sheol.

Sacrifices/Worship
The Mesopotamian people made sacrifices to the gods in order to try to curry favor from them. The later early Hebrew people also made sacrifices to Yahweh for the same reasons, e.g. health, safety, prosperity, or to make amends.

God's home
The Mesopotamian people believed that the gods resided in their temples. The later early Hebrew people believed that Yahweh resided in the portable tabernacle, and then later in the temple built by King Solomon.

Garden Paradise
The Sumerian poem "Enki and Ninhursag" describes a garden paradise called Dilmun. In this garden are forbidden plants; the god Enki eats them and is cursed. This story predates the Genesis story by many hundreds of years.

Snakes

A snake was a villain in the Epic of Gilgamesh as it was in the Genesis story of the Garden of Eden where the serpent tempts Eve to eat of the forbidden fruit. In the Epic of Gilgamesh the hero obtains a plant from the bottom of a sea that can restore youth and vigor. A serpent ends up stealing the plant.

Moses birth story

The beginnings of Moses are described in the Hebrew book of Exodus. Moses was born in secret and after three months was placed in a papyrus basket lined with pitch. The basket was placed among the reeds on the banks of a river. Moses was discovered by the pharaoh's daughter who raised him. Sargon was born in secret and placed in a basket of reeds which was sealed with pitch. The basket was set adrift in the Euphrates River. Sargon was raised by the king's gardener and achieved power by winning the favor of the goddess, Ishtar. The story of Sargon's beginning predates the story of Moses by almost a thousand years.

Wisdom literature

The Sumerians had wisdom literature similar to that found in the Hebrew book of Proverbs. The Sumerian literature predates the Hebrew literature by over a millennium.

Job

Again, more than a millennium before the book of Job was a Sumerian story about a righteous man who was afflicted with sickness and suffering. Like the book of Job the story is about the quandary of why bad things happen even to good people.

Ecclesiastes
Qoheleth in the Biblical book of Ecclesiastes advises people to "eat, and drink, and enjoy themselves", advice very similar to that given by Siduri in the Epic of Gilgamesh written many hundreds of years earlier.

Lamentation literature
The Hebrew book of Lamentations was in response to the grief over the destruction of Jerusalem and the deportation of the Jews (interestingly to Babylon). This type of literature was found in ancient Babylon (many hundreds of years earlier) in response to grief over the conquests of ancient cities.

Abraham

It was in Mesopotamia that the great patriarch, Abram, was born and raised. Genesis calls his birthplace Ur of the Chaldeans. As I mentioned previously in this chapter, there is some disagreement whether Abram's origins were in the great Sumerian city of Ur in southern Mesopotamia or the city of Urfa in northern Mesopotamia (present day Turkey). Also as I mentioned previously in this chapter, there is controversy about the time period in which Abram lived (anywhere from 2000 BCE to 1400 BCE). I think there is a compelling argument for the latter date of 1400 BCE if you do not take the reported life spans literally in the book of Genesis. However, tradition places Abraham at 2000 BCE.

In chapter 11 of Genesis we are told that Terah, the father of Abram, intended to migrate to the land of Canaan. He set off along with Abram, Abram's wife Sarai, and his grandson Lot for Canaan but ended up settling in Haran. This town was in Mesopotamia and present day Turkey. At the age of 75 Abram left Haran along with Sarai and Lot and set off for Canaan in response to a directive from God. They arrived in Canaan, which was inhabited by Canaanites. In Shechem, Abram built an altar to God before moving on to Bethel, where he also built an altar. For some reason they continued moving south to the Negeb, a desert region. Because of famine, he continued south farther to Egypt.

Before entering Egypt Abram told his wife Sarai to pretend to be his sister rather than his wife. Because Sarai was so beautiful, Abram was fearful that he would be killed in order that someone else could have Sarai. The pharaoh did become aware of Sarai and did take her into his house (presumably for sexual reasons). As punishment, God inflicted plagues upon the pharaoh. Somehow the pharaoh figured out that Abram had lied about Sarai not being his wife. The pharaoh chastised Abram for lying to him, and he set them on their way. (Later in Genesis Abraham again denies Sarai as his wife to King Abimelek of the Philistines for the same reason. Then incredulously in chapter 26 of Genesis Isaac does the same thing to King Abimelek, i.e. told the lie that Rebekah was his sister for fears of losing his life to men who are attracted to her). Abram travelled north and returned to the Negeb, and then from there he returned into the land of Canaan.

Both Abram and Lot had become very rich with much livestock as well as slaves. Abram figured they needed to separate, as the land where they were living could not support all of them. Lot moved into the plains of Jordan, and Abram settled in Canaan, specifically at Hebron. When Abram was 99 years old God appeared to him and said that Abram would be the ancestor of a multitude of nations. His name was to be changed to Abraham, and Sarai's name changed to Sarah. The practice of circumcision began at this time. Eventually Abram's elderly "barren" wife conceived a child, who they called Isaac.

Although Abraham had migrated out of Mesopotamia, it would not be the end of his or his descendant's contacts with that region. In chapter 24 of Genesis Abraham from Canaan requests his servant to travel to Aram, the family homeland in Mesopotamia, to secure a wife for his son, Isaac. He wanted Isaac's wife to be of Mesopotamian descent rather than Canaanite descent. Actually Abraham wanted Isaac's wife to be a relative. This appears not to have been uncommon during this time. Abraham himself was married to Sarah, his half-sister. A young woman was found for Isaac: Rebekah, Isaac's second cousin.

Isaac and Rebekah had twins: Jacob and Esau. When Jacob was older, Isaac told him to travel to Aram, their homeland in Mesopotamia, to obtain a wife and not to marry a Canaanite woman. Jacob was told to take a wife from among the daughters of Laban, who is Jacob's uncle. Jacob ends up marrying two of Laban's daughters (Rachel and Leah), who would be Jacob's first cousins. Jacob continued living in Mesopotamia for 20 years before deciding to return to Canaan. All of his children were born there, including his youngest, Joseph. Jacob's family packed up all their belongings for the move, and Rachel stole her father's household gods. As previously mentioned in this chapter it was customary in Mesopotamia to have "personal" gods or goddesses.

When they returned to Canaan in Shechem and on their way to Bethel, Jacob instructed his household to "put away the foreign gods that are among you, and purify yourselves, and change your clothes; then come, let us go up to Bethel, that I may make an altar there to the God who answered me in the day of my distress and has been with me wherever I have gone." (Gen. 35: 2-4). Jacob's household then gave up their gods. This would be the end of Abraham and his descendant's contact with their homeland, Mesopotamia, at least for many hundreds of years.

Chapter 3

Egypt

Jacob

"Jacob settled in the land where his father had lived as an alien, the land of Canaan." (Gen. 37:1) There his children grew up. When Joseph was 17, his brothers took the opportunity to sell him to a band of traders. They did this because of jealousy; Joseph was his father's favorite son. The traders took Joseph to Egypt. There he was sold to one of Pharaoh's officials, Potiphar. Jacob had been led to believe by his sons that Joseph had been killed and eaten by a wild animal. Joseph served Potiphar well and eventually became the head of his household, overseeing all that Potiphar had. However, because of rejecting sexual advances from Potiphar's wife, he was framed by her; she told Potiphar that it was Joseph who was making sexual advances toward her and not vice versa. Joseph was jailed by Potiphar. It was in prison that Joseph gained the reputation as a gifted interpreter of dreams.

After a couple years in prison the Pharaoh had a dream that the other dream interpreters of Egypt could not decipher. The Pharaoh sent for Joseph who successfully interpreted the dream. The Pharaoh was so pleased that he placed Joseph in second command of all that he had. At this point Joseph was 30 years old. The Pharaoh gave Joseph an Egyptian name: Zaphenath-paneah. He gave him an Egyptian wife: Asenath.

A famine came to the whole Middle East. Joseph had wisely stored up grain during the previous seven years of plenty, and so people from all over the Middle East came to Egypt because that was the only place where there was food. Jacob sent ten of his sons to Egypt to procure food. They met Joseph who recognized them, although they did not recognize Joseph (who spoke in the language of the land and to them only through an interpreter). Eventually, later on in the story, Joseph does reveal his identity to his brothers. Because the famine was to last yet another five years, the entire family was invited to live in Egypt, in the land of Goshen. Jacob, all of his children and their spouses, his grandchildren, their livestock and all their possessions moved from Canaan to Egypt.

"Thus Israel (Jacob) settled in the land of Egypt, in the region of Goshen; and they gained possessions in it, and were fruitful and multiplied exceedingly. Jacob lived in the land of Egypt seventeen years; so the days of Jacob, the years of his life, were one hundred forty-seven years." (Gen. 47: 27-28). After Jacob's death, he was embalmed, as was the manner of the Egyptians. Jacob's body then was brought out of Egypt to Canaan, where he was buried in the cave of the field bought by Abraham as a burial site. When Joseph was 110 years old he also died and was embalmed and placed in a coffin in Egypt.

The Pharaoh in the story of Joseph is unnamed in the Bible. Some scholars have suggested Senusret II (1897-1878) as theunnamed Pharaoh. Others have suggested a much later Pharaoh, e.g. Seti I (1308-1291). What I would like to do now is give the history of Egypt up to the Middle Kingdom, the earliest time period that the legendary Joseph may have lived.

History of Egypt: 5000 to 3000 BCE

The ancient Egyptians called their country the "Kingdom of the Two Lands"; these two lands first unified during this time period, although throughout history during periods of weakened government, the two areas (the delta of Lower Egypt and Upper Egypt) would split apart. The Egyptian civilization began as small agricultural settlements along the Nile River. Life in predynastic Egypt consisted of growing wheat and barley and raising sheep, goats and cattle (and pigs in the north). There also was fishing and hunting. There were chiefdoms; the country was divided up into *nomes* or districts. During this time period Egypt was much less developed and sophisticated than was Sumeria.

Chapter 3: Egypt

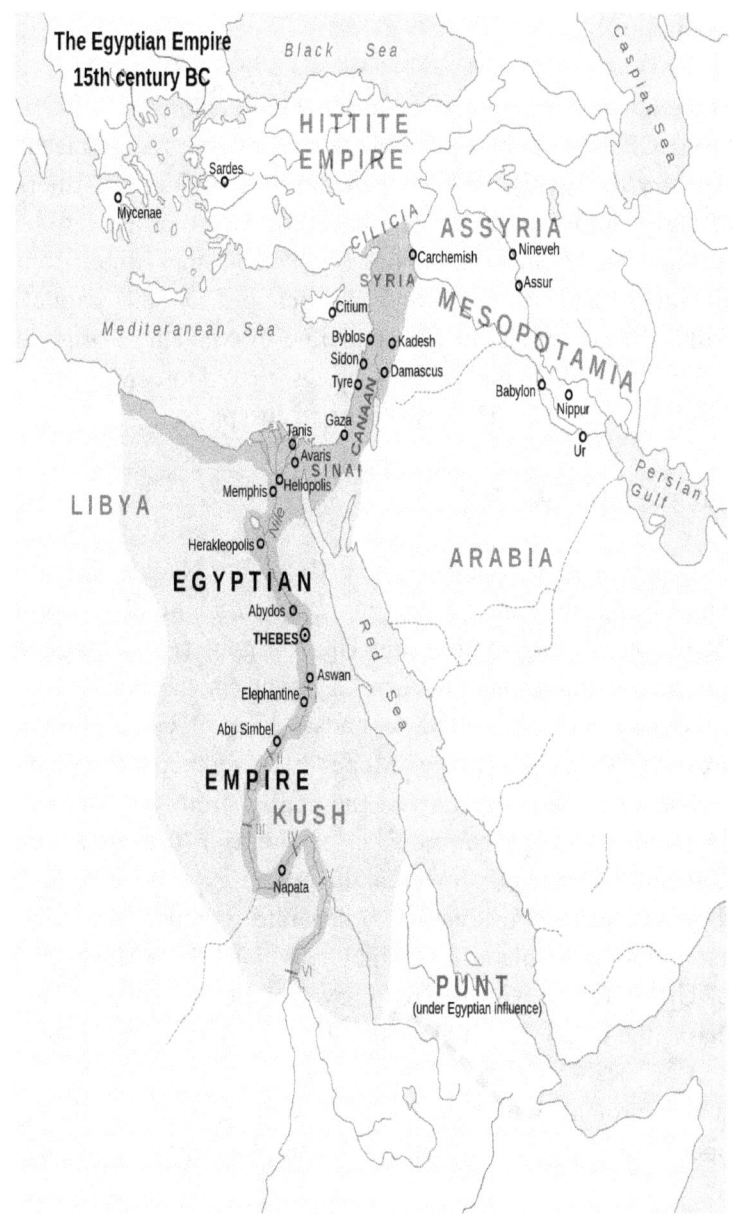

Manetho

Manetho was an Egyptian historian who lived in the 3rd century BCE, during the Ptolemaic era. He wrote "Aegyptiaca" (History of Egypt). It was Manetho who divided the rulers of Egypt into dynasties. The basis for dynastic distinctions included not only bloodlines but also other significant changes, such as a change in location for the capital. Although no copies are yet available of Manetho's original writing, we do have other writings that quote Manetho's work, including the Hebrew historian Josephus.

Dynasty 0 (3200-3000)

This period is also called phase III of the Naqada Period. The Naqada culture existed in Egypt from 4000 to 3000 BCE. According to tradition Upper Egypt (i n the south, contrary to intuition) and Lower Egypt (in the north) first combined under Menes, a legendary king of Upper Egypt, around 3000 BCE. Likely "Menes" was another name given to King Narmer. He moved the capital from the south to Memphis, a more centralized location for the combined kingdom. Although lower and upper Egypt were united, they still were considered two separate regions. The king even wore a double crown which combined the white crown of Upper Egypt with the red crown of Lower Egypt. This marks the beginning of "Dynasty 1".

It was around 3100 that Egyptian writing was first developed, "hieroglyphs", which combined pictographic and phonetic symbols.

Early Dynastic Period (3000-2686)

First Dynasty (3000-2890):

The kings of Dynasty 1 and 2 expanded the borders of Egypt by warring against the Nubians to the south and the Libyans west of the Delta. During this time period the kings presented themselves as being divine, specifically as incarnations of the god Horus, the chief god of Lower Egypt. When someone was crowned king, they would take a "Horus" name as their throne name.

Second Dynasty (2890-2686):

Not a lot is known about the period of time known as the Second Dynasty. For the kings that we do know from this period, we only have their "Horus" names.

Old Kingdom (Dynasties 3-6) (2686-2160)

The term "old kingdom" came from 19th century historians and is believed to be misleading in that the ancient Egyptians would not have recognized any differences from the previous Early Dynastic Period (3000-2686) and this period. What is remarkable in this period, however, is that the Egyptians (beginning with King Djoser) began using stone for life-sized statuary and monumental buildings.

Third Dynasty (2686-2613)

It was in this time period that the king, Djoser (2667-2648), is believed to have built the first pyramid. This was a step pyramid. "This first pyramid was apparently designed to replicate the primeval mound of earth on which the creator god stood while doing the work of creation." (Holland, 2009, p. 5).

Fourth Dynasty (2613-2494)

Sneferu (2613-2589) completed three large true pyramids that had the familiar smooth limestone surface. Khufu (2589-2566) (often known as Cheops) built the Great Pyramid at Giza. It was during this period that methods to mummify corpses were developed. Khufu's successor, Djedefra (2566-2558) called himself "The son of Ra", the Egyptian sun god. His successor, Khafra (2558-2532), was the model for the human head on the Great Sphinx of Giza. His successor,

Menkaura (2532-2503) built the last of the pyramids at Giza, for the most part using granite rather than limestone.

During this time period the king was believed to be the mediator between the gods and the populace, with allegiances to both. Not only did the kings take on a "Horus name", but from the reign of Khafra onward the kings were introduced with the title "son of Ra". Kings would have contact with gods through ritual, and it was their job to ensure the regular change of seasons, the annual flooding of the Nile, the movements of the stars, and protection from foreign enemies. The king's role did not end with death, and so that was the reason for the construction of the pyramids to be tombs for the kings. They were filled with rich and elaborate grave goods for the king's afterlife. Family members and court officials would be buried in tombs nearby.

The Great Pyramid at Giza

Great Sphinx of Giza

Fifth Dynasty (2494-2345)

The sun god Ra grew in prominence during this period; elaborate temples were built in dedication to Ra, who became somewhat of a state god. Also the god Osiris, god of the Underworld, grew in importance during this period. During this period Osiris developed from being a local god associated with agriculture and the annually recurring events of nature to a major god who ruled the kingdom of the dead. The widespread belief in deceased persons entering the kingdom of Osiris after death developed at this time.

Sixth Dynasty (2345-2181)

During this period central power began to erode. Egypt's longest ruling king lived during this period: Pepy II (2278-2184) (Horus Netjerkhau) who came to the throne at the age of 6 and reigned for 94 years. The kings of this dynasty built shrines to local gods all over Egypt. Practically every area of Egypt had a local god that was its most important deity (of greater importance than the state god, Ra).

Seventh and Eighth Dynasties (2181-2160)

In these periods there were 17 or more kings (and one queen) who ruled extremely briefly. We know little about them.

First Intermediate Period (Dynasties 9-11) (2160-2055)

During this time period there was no central figure to rule all of Upper and Lower Egypt. Egypt was controlled by various regional rulers. Egyptologists have divided major periods of Egyptian history as either "kingdoms" (periods of political unity) or "intermediate periods" in which various local rulers vied for power over various areas. The First Intermediate Period is considered a "dark age" that separates the two epochs of glory, the Old and the Middle Kingdoms.

Middle Kingdom (Dynasties 11-14) (2055-1650)

After two centuries of political chaos, Egypt was reunited by Nebhepetra Mentuhotep II (2055-2004) of Dynasty 11. The Thebans located at Thebes in the south pushed northward and conquered Herakleopolis and the delta in the north. Upper and Lower Egypt are now once again reunified under the rule of Mentuhotep, who ruled from Thebes. He appointed an overseer for the delta region.

Late Eleventh Dynasty (2055-1985)

Mentuhotep II had a 51 year reign. He initiated many building projects. Mentuhotep II stressed his self-deification. His Horus name of Netjeryhedjet meant "the divine one of the white crown". He described himself as "the son of Hathor", the Egyptian goddess. "Evidence from his Deir el-Bahri temple indicates that he intended to be worshiped as a god in his House of Millions of Years, thus pre-dating by hundreds of years ideas that became a central religious preoccupation of the New Kingdom. It is evident that he was reasserting the cult of the ruler." (Shaw, 2000, p. 141).

Twelfth Dynasty (1985-1773)

At the beginning of this dynasty the royal capital was moved from Thebes to a site south of Memphis by Amenemhat I (1985-1956). Successive rulers were Senusret I, Amenemhat II, Senusret II, Senusret III, Amenemhat III, Amenemhat IV, and Queen Sobekneferu. Territory was expanded during the 12th dynasty, and there was substantial building of shrines, temples and tombs. Slaves were imported from western Asia to serve as laborers for building projects.

Some Biblical scholars have dated the settlement of Jacob and his family in Egypt at 1876 BCE. This date is arrived at if we take the lifespans of Genesis literally and not mythically. Some have suggested that the pharaoh that Joseph served under was Senusret II.

Thirteenth and Fourteenth Dynasties (1773-1650)

These dynasties were made up of different lineages; it is not really known on what basis the kings during this period were chosen.

One of the important developments during the Middle Kingdom was the growth of the cult of Osiris. Whereas the idea of an afterlife had previously been stressed for just the kings, now ordinary citizens took part in the rites of Osiris, thus receiving the blessings that previously were reserved for kings. Funerary beliefs and rites of the entire population began to change. Also, previously it had been believed that only kings had *ba*, the spiritual force. Now it was believed that all people had this spirit or personality. I will speak more about *ba* later in this chapter.

There also was a growing emphasis during this period on personal piety, i.e. that ordinary individuals had access to the gods rather than needing to access the divine through priests or kings. This concept further grew later during the New Kingdom.

Also during the Middle Kingdom mummification became more widespread, although the technique during this time was nowhere near perfected.

Second Intermediate Period (Dynasties 15-17) (1650-1550)

This period is significant for the Hyksos, who founded Dynasty 15. The Hyksos were a dynasty of foreigners of Semitic descent who ruled Egypt for about a century. Semitic peoples had entered the Egyptian delta from Syria-Palestine and migrated south in Egypt. The Hyksos ruled Upper and Lower Egypt and parts of Syria-Palestine from their capital Avaris in the eastern Nile Delta. Farther south the people were ruled first by Dynasty 16 and then by Dynasty 17. Both of these dynasties ruled from Thebes.

Eventually the Theban rulers of Dynasty 17 went to war against the Hyksos and drove them out of Egypt. Once again Egypt was reunited under one ruler, King Ahmose, founder of Dynasty 18, the beginning of the "New Kingdom".

New Kingdom (Dynasties 18-20) (1550-1069)

This is the third great period of Egyptian culture. This was likely Egypt's most prosperous period, and they were likely at their military peak. Military campaigns during this period extended Egyptian influence throughout the Near East. The pharaohs during this period had vast wealth. The god, Amun-Re, gained in prominence. The period was known for monumental architecture which honored both gods and pharaohs, who were treated as gods. Also during this period, pyramids were replaced by tombs to house the mummies of deceased pharaohs. They were carved out in rock. Many were entombed in the area known as the "Valley of the Kings" which is situated in the Theban Hills, west of the Nile. The New Kingdom was a period of political stability and great prosperity.

Scholars believe that slavery was rare in Egypt up until the New Kingdom. The many military conquests created a large supply of prisoners that became slaves. Slaves could be owned by the pharaoh or by private individuals. Although they did have limited rights (e.g. to own property), they could be bought and sold and inherited. In addition to slaves, many people in Egypt were serfs who often would work only for food. The Egyptian government also at times would require citizens to provide labor for specific building projects. Just as in modern countries where during times of war there have been military conscriptions, there were times of forced labor in Egypt termed *corvee labor*. Monogamous nuclear families were likely the norm, although polygamy was legal for all and common for the pharaohs. Pharaohs also at times would marry sisters or other close female relatives, although this likely was not commonplace among the general population. Divorce and remarriage were believed to have been common for both men and women.

Karnak temple of Amun-Re

The Colossi of Memnon

Eighteenth Dynasty (1550-1295)

King Ahmose (1550-1525) brought peace and security to Egypt. He was the first king of the 18th dynasty. Ahmose venerated Egypt's deities, likely particularly the god, Amun, whose cult centered in Karnak. Ahmose's son, Amenhotep I, continued his father's policies and building projects and also was a devotee of the god, Amun. Amenhotep I also had a very successful reign and was deified and worshiped after his death at Thebes, as was his mother. Amenhotep I became a major god of the region, and there were festivals throughout the year to celebrate him and his mother.

The following are subsequent rulers in the 18th Dynasty:

Thutmose I (1504-1492)
Thutmose II (1492-1479)
Thutmose III (1479-1425)

Queen Hatshepsut (1473-1458)
Amenhotep II (1427-1400)
Thutmose IV (1400-1390)

Amenhotep III (1390-1352)
Some scholars believe that Amenhotep III was deified during his lifetime, which would have been quite unusual. Although Amen continued to be the supreme deity in Egypt, Amenhotep III also had association with another solar god, Aten. In Thebes his enormous palace was called "the gleaming Aten". The Colossi of Memnon were towering quartzite images of the king near his funerary temple. Amenhotep III's construction of tombs, statues and shrines were unrivaled from any of the other pharaohs.

Amenhotep IV/Akhenaten (1352-1336)
Amenhotep III left behind a very wealthy country when he died. Jacobus Van Dijk writes in "The Oxford History of Ancient Egypt" that "Amenhotep's court had become a diplomatic centre of international importance, and friendly contact with Egypt's neighbors had led to an atmosphere of openness towards foreign cultures. During the earlier part of the dynasty, immigrants had introduced their native gods into Egypt and some of these deities had become associated with the Egyptian king, especially in his warlike aspect, but now foreign peoples were themselves seen as part of god's creation, protected and sustained by the benevolent rule of the sun-god Ra and his early representative, the pharaoh." "The sun-god and the king lay at the heart of Egyptian theological thinking and cultic practice as they had developed over the previous centuries."

Van Dijk maintains that during Amenhotep III's reign there was growing evolution toward monotheism with all deities being aspects of a great solar god, a "primeval creator". "the sun-god is clearly set apart from the other gods- he is the supreme god who is alone, far away in the sky, whereas the other deities are part of his creation, alongside men and animals." The preeminent sun-god at times was known as Ra. During Amenhotep III's reign the city of Thebes' local god, Amun, had become associated with Ra. Amun was worshiped in every major temple in Egypt. "The king was publicly acclaimed as the early embodiment of Amun" who "became the most important god of the country." As you may have noticed, the god Amun's name was subsumed into the names of the pharaohs named "Amenhotep".

All of this changed with Amenhotep III's son, Amenhotep IV. Rather than worshiping the god Amun, Amenhotep IV worshiped a new sun-god whose official name was "The living one, Ra-Horus of the horizon who rejoices in the horizon in his identity of light which is in the sun-disc". This was shortened to the Egyptian word "Aten". The new pharaoh built temples to Aten throughout Egypt, including at the center of the cult of Amun, Karnak. Aten now replaced Amun as the supreme deity in which all other gods were subsumed. Amenhotep changed his name to Akhenaten to reflect this. The name "Akhenaten" means "he who acts effectively on behalf of the Aten" or maybe "creative manifestation of the Aten".

Akhenaten decided to build a new religious capital for Egypt devoted to the worship of Aten. The new city was called Akhetaten, meaning "Horizon of the Aten". It is now known as Amarna, and this was the beginning of what has become known as the Amarna Age. In the ninth year of his reign

Akhenaten made further religious reforms. The official name of Aten was changed somewhat to "the living one, Ra, ruler of the horizon who rejoices in the horizon in his identity of Ra the father who has returned as the sun-disc". The deified Amenhotep III is associated with the god Aten, which makes Akhenaten the son of god. The name of the god "Horus" is removed from Aten's formal name. Akhenaten began banning the historic traditional gods such as Horus, Osiris, and especially Amun. Their names were removed from monuments. This is believed by many scholars to be the first instance of monotheism, i.e. that there is only one god, the sun.

Aten was seen as the life-giving light. At night after the sun set, Aten was absent. The Egyptians had long believed in an eternal afterlife. During the Amarna Age it was taught that the way to attain life after death was to follow the teachings and be loyal to the pharaoh Akhenaten, the son of god. The Amarna Age ended with Akhenaten's death. Religion reverted back to what it had been prior to Akhenaten's reign. Thebes once again became the religious center of Egypt. The god Amun regained supremacy, and the god Osiris was once again seen as the nocturnal expression of Ra.

Tutankhamun (1336-1327)
As a child (perhaps around the age of 9), the next king Tutankhaten, the son of Akhenaten, ascended the throne. He abandoned the city founded by his father, and the seat of government moved back to Memphis. His name was changed from Tutankhaten (to praise Aten) to Tutankhamun (to praise Amun). His wife was his half-sister, and her name was also changed to reflect the religious shift (Ankhesenpaaten to Ankhesenamun). This king, often referred to today

at "King Tut" is well known because of the discovery of his non-plundered tomb in 1922. Most of the pharaohs' tombs had been discovered and plundered long ago, but this tomb was untouched. Its remarkable riches are on display in the Cairo Museum. King Tutankhamun died likely shy of the age of 20 and had a rather unremarkable reign. In considering the extravagant riches in his tomb, one can only wonder what the tombs of the more remarkable and important pharaohs might have held.

Gold death mask of Tutankhamun

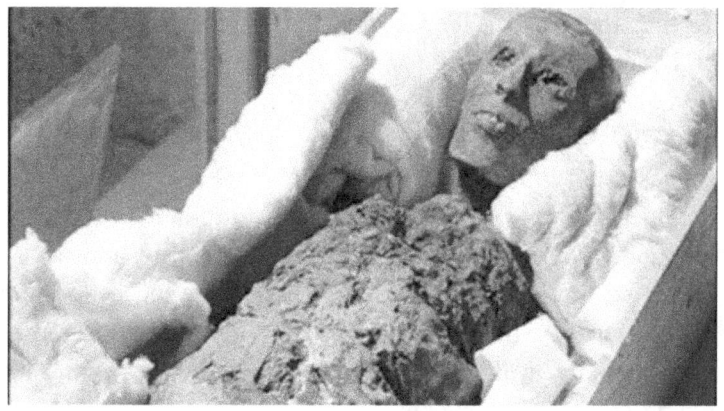

King Tutankhamun's mummy

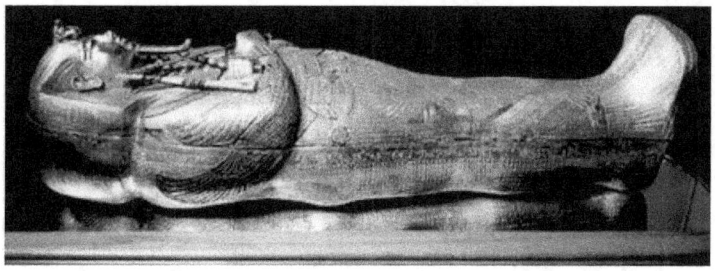

Ay (1327-1323)
Horemheb (1323-1295)

Nineteenth Dynasty (1295-1186)

Dynasty 19 was founded by Rameses I. This is the beginning of an age known as the Ramesside Period, a period of stability of succession of Rameses's heirs. There were eleven pharaohs who took the name "Rameses". This also was a period where there was destruction of statues representing the Amarna Period and the worship of the "false" god, Aten.

Rameses I (1295-1294)

Paramessu was a friend, vizier and confidant of Pharaoh Horemheb. Because Horemheb had no heirs, it appears he bestowed the succession to Paramessu who succeeded him as Rameses I. His son Sety was appointed vizier. Rameses was probably in his 50s when he became pharaoh, and his reign only lasted two years.

Seti I (1294-1279)

Seti continued with the restoration of the traditional temples to the traditional gods. He reinstated the name Amun where it had been destroyed during the Amarna Period. During his thirteen year reign Egyptian art and culture matured. His third son was named Rameses, after his grandfather, who was still living when he was born. During his reign territory was regained that had been lost in Syria and Nubia.

Rameses II (1279-1213)

Rameses II ruled Egypt for sixty-six years, the second longest reign of a pharaoh (Pepy I was the longest reign). He presided over a vast building program in the country. Perhaps more than any pharaoh, he filled the country with temples and statues. Perhaps his greatest monument was the huge temple carved from rock at Abu Simbel. He expanded the city of Avaris to build a new royal capital, Piramesse ("House of Rameses") in the eastern delta. This became an important international trading center. Because of increasing foreign influences, many foreign deities were worshiped in Piramesse, e.g. Baal, Anat, Astarte, etc.

Even earlier in his reign than Amenhotep III, Rameses II declared himself deified and had gigantic statues and temples built for his worship.

The Great Temple of Ramses II at Abu Simbel

Merenptah (1213-1203?)
About this time period "sea peoples", most notably the Philistines, became a major force in Syria-Palestine due to the collapse of the Hittite kingdom, Mycenaean Greece, and other kingdoms in the eastern Mediterranean. Merneptah battled against them in Nubia and Palestine.

Amenmessu (1203-1200?)
Sety II (1200-1194)
Saptah (1194-1188)
Queen Tausret (1188-1186)

Twentieth Dynasty (1186-1069)

Sethnakht (1186-1184)

Rameses III (1184-1153)
This was probably the truly last great pharaoh to be on the throne of Egypt. He led once again a battle against the "sea peoples" who invaded Egypt from the north. Because of a number of bad harvest years in the Levant, the sea peoples were likely intent on moving into and settling into Egypt. Rameses III's forces drove them back. Rameses III's reign lasted for 31 years.

Moses

The book of Exodus in the Bible tells us that since the days of Egypt the Israelites "multiplied and grew exceedingly strong, so that the land was filled with them." The pharaoh of the time forced them to do hard labor in service of Egypt. As I mentioned previously in this chapter, the Egyptian state not only had slave laborers, but also peasants were forced into labor on state building projects. The pharaoh of that time was concerned about the increasing numbers of the Hebrews and so for some reason told Egyptian midwives to kill any Israelite *males* that were born. One would think that the best way to restrict the population of a group of people would be to kill the *females* rather than the males. Also, since the Israelites were employed to do heavy physical labor, it would be more advantageous to have males rather than females.

A certain male baby was born to a Levite couple; the baby was hidden for three months at which point the mother placed him in a papyrus basket and placed it among the reeds in the river. The pharaoh's daughter saw the basket and had her servant bring it to her. "She took pity on him" and adopted the baby as her own son. The baby was named "Moses".

Moses grew up. One day he saw an Egyptian beating a Hebrew; in retaliation he killed the Egyptian. When he discovered that his crime was observed, he fled Egypt and settled in the land of Midian, where he remained for forty years. He married a Midianite woman. His father-in-law, Jethro, was a Midianite priest.

One day Moses was tending to Jethro's flock when an "angel of the Lord appeared to him in a flame of fire out of a bush." A voice said "I am the God of your father, the God of Abraham, the God of Isaac, and the God of Jacob". Exodus 12:40 tells us that the Israelites were in Egypt for 430 years. Now for the first time in four centuries this god reveals himself. Moses is told to lead the Israelite people out of Egypt and out of bondage to Pharaoh to the land of Canaan, which is the present home of the Hittites, the Amorites, the Perizzites, the Hivites and the Jebusites. God said his name was "I Am Who I Am" (Exodus 3:14). Later, God reveals his name as Yahweh (which is often translated in our Bibles as "The Lord").

"God also spoke to Moses and said to him: 'I am the Lord. I appeared to Abraham, Isaac, and Jacob as God Almighty, but by my name 'The Lord' I did not make myself known to them." (Exodus 6:2-3). In the King James version of Exodus "The Lord" is translated as "Jehovah".

Moses was reluctant to take on this task but agreed. He took his wife and sons to the land of Egypt. During the journey a very surprising event occurred: the "Lord" (God) tried to kill Moses because he was not circumcised. Moses' wife Zipporah quickly circumcised their son and touches her son's foreskin to Moses' genitals, which evidently appeased God.

In Egypt Moses and his right-hand man, Aaron, went to Pharaoh and relayed the message of the Hebrew god that Pharaoh should let the Israelite people go. Nobody had ever heard of this god, and so Pharaoh wondered why he should be heeded. He would not let the Israelites go. At this point Moses was 80 years old and Aaron age 83. In order to convince pharaoh of God's power, Aaron threw down his staff and it became a snake. The pharaoh's magicians replicated this feat, however. Then Aaron struck the river with his staff and it turned into blood. "The river stank so that the Egyptians could not drink its water, and there was blood throughout the whole land of Egypt." Egypt's magicians replicated this feat as well (although it is not explained how this could be replicated if all the water *already* had been turned to blood). Seven days passed. Then Aaron caused frogs to cover the land of Egypt. Again, Egyptian magicians also caused frogs to come up in Egypt. Pharaoh would not release the Israelites.

God caused further plagues to Egypt to try to change pharaoh's heart (although the Bible also states that god simultaneously, intentionally, and paradoxically hardens pharaoh's heart to not relent).

Third Plague: "gnats came on humans and animals alike".

Fourth Plague: "in all of Egypt the land was ruined because of flies", except in Goshen where the Israelites lived.

Fifth Plague: "all the livestock of the Egyptians died" but not of the Israelites.

Sixth Plague: "festering boils on humans and animals".

Seventh Plague: "the Lord sent thunder and hail, and fire came down on the earth." "The hail struck down everything that was in the open field throughout all the land of Egypt, both human and animal" except in the land of Goshen, where the Israelites lived.

Eighth Plague: "the Lord brought an east wind upon the land all that day and all that night; when morning came, the east wind had brought the locusts." "Nothing green was left, no tree, no plant in the field, in all the land of Egypt."

Ninth Plague: "dense darkness in all the land of Egypt for three days".

Final Plague: With the exception of the Israelites, "the Lord struck down all the firstborn in the land of Egypt, from the firstborn of Pharaoh who sat on his throne to the firstborn of the prisoner who was in the dungeon, and all the firstborn of the livestock." Finally Pharaoh relented and allowed the Israelites to leave Egypt.

God told Moses and Aaron that this event (the liberation of the Israelites from Egypt) should be commemorated as the Passover. In commemoration, only unleavened bread should be eaten during the seven-day festival. Foreigners in addition to Israelites could celebrate this festival, but only if they were circumcised. God also commanded that every first-born male of the Israelites from thence forth should be set apart for God (both humans and animals).

God led the Israelites out of Egypt but in a roundabout course in order to avoid an encounter with the Philistines. Pharaoh had a change of heart and regretted his decision to let the Israelites go. He pursued them. I assume all my readers at this point know what then happens: the Israelites cross the Red (or Reed) Sea, and the Egyptians are destroyed when the seas (which had been divided) crash in on them.

It is not known what pharaoh was in power at this time. The Bible when discussing pharaohs do not give their names. Some suggestions for pharaohs at the time of the Exodus include Ahmose I, Thutmose II, Amenhotep II, Rameses II, Merneptah, Setnakhte, and Ramses III.

Sigmund Freud (1939) theorizes that Moses was a follower of the pharaoh, Akhenaten and of the god, Aten. As previously mentioned in this chapter, Egypt's long history of polytheism was briefly interrupted by a new religion advocated by Pharaoh Akhenaten. This new religion promoted the worship of only one god, the sun-god Aten. The new religion also put less emphasis on an after-life, which the traditional Egyptian religion so emphasized. Freud notes that Akhenaten "worshiped the sun not as a material object, but as a symbol of a divine being whose energy was manifested in his rays." In one of Akhenaten's hymns to Aten he states

"O Thou only God, there is no other God than Thou." Akhenaten closed temples to other gods, particularly those to Amun. Inscriptions on monuments were changed so that the word "god" was no longer written in the plural.

After Akhenaten's death, Egypt reverted back to its polytheistic traditions. Freud believed that Moses was a prominent Egyptian. The Book of Exodus notes that "Moses himself was a man of great importance in the land of Egypt, in the sight of Pharaoh's officials and in the sight of the people" (Exodus 11:3). Moses was able to schedule audiences with the pharaoh apparently without difficulty. Freud believed Moses was a disciple of the god Aten and taught this religion to Semites living in Egypt. Freud speculated that perhaps Moses "was at the time governor of that border province (Goshen) in which-perhaps already in the 'Hyksos period'- certain Semitic tribes had settled. These he chose to be his new people. A historic decision!" "Moses' active nature conceived the plan of founding a new empire, of finding a new people, to whom he could give the religion that Egypt disdained."

Freud cites conclusions made by Herodotus, the Greek historian who lived in the fifth century BCE He is widely known as the "father of history". Herodotus reported that the ancient Egyptians were unique in practicing circumcision. The ancient Semites, Babylonians and Sumerians did not practice this. Also, interestingly, Herodotus reported that the ancient Egyptians had an aversion to swine.

Freud makes the startling hypothesis that after leading the Israelites out of Egypt Moses was later killed by his followers. Actually, this is not an original idea of Freud but actually comes from the German Protestant theologian Ernst

Sellin (1867-1946). In his *book Geschichte des israelitische-judischen Volkes* (1924) Sellin in his study of the Hebrew scriptures found suggestions that Moses might have been murdered, particularly in passages from the writings of the prophet, Hosea.

Freud further hypothesized that there were two different men who were "Moses". In addition to the Egyptian Moses, Freud believed that the son-in-law of the Midianite priest, Jethro, was a different person. Recall that the book of Exodus has Moses fleeing Egypt after killing a man and settling in "the land of Midian". There he married the daughter of a Midianite priest who is called both Jethro (Exodus 3:1) and "Reul" (Exodus 2:18) which in Hebrew means "friend of God". In the book of Judges this man is referred to as Hobab and is noted to be a Kenite (Judges 4:11). The terms "Midianite" and "Kenite" seem to be used interchangeably in the Hebrew scriptures.

The Hebrew scriptures have the Israelite people living in Egypt for 430 years. Their religion would have been Egyptian. There likely would have been no memories of a personal, unnamed god of Abraham. Moses lived in Midian for 40 years. Midian is believed to have been located near the Gulf of Aqaba. Moses was close to his father-in-law, a Midianite priest, considered a "friend of God". Many scholars, Freud included, believe that this is where the God, Yahweh, came from, i.e. the god worshiped by the Midianites. The book of Exodus has Moses meeting a god in Midian; "the Lord appeared to him in a flame of fire out of a bush". This god identified himself as "the God of Abraham, the God of Isaac, and the God of Jacob." This god identified himself as "I Am Who I Am". "Thus you shall say to the Israelites, 'I Am has sent me to you.'"

Freud believed that the religion of the Israelites was a conflation of the religion Moses brought from Egypt (the worship of Aten which rejected anthropomorphisms, magic, and focus on an afterlife) with the religion that Moses learned from the Midianites (the worship of Yahweh, a god probably not unlike the other gods of the middle east). Moses retained the ancient Egyptian custom of circumcision to set the Israelites apart from other cultures in the Levant.

Egyptian Religion

Egyptian culture and religion developed in relative isolation from the other cultures of the middle east. Its religious beliefs and practices were relatively stable through the centuries, although gods continued to be added through the centuries, including some foreign gods such as Astarte and Anat. Various myths continued to be added as well, and myths would merge with other myths. Deities did not become fixed at a particular time but developed and changed over thousands of years. Various gods would merge with other gods, and the importance of gods would rise and fall over the ages and in different localities (or nomes). However, although the gods varied from nome to nome, the essential religion remained basically the same. The Egyptians did not have a canon or holy book to refer to, as the Israelites would eventually have in the distant future. Therefore, there was no development of an "orthodoxy".

Initially gods were represented in animal form, often animal heads on human bodies. Gods were very anthropomorphic, just as the gods of Mesopotamia were. They basically were humans with supernatural powers. They had very human qualities; they loved, hated, got jealous, employed trickery, had sex, had regrets, etc. Gods and humans were created, although the creator god (which might be called Atum, Aten, Ra or Ptah) were thought to be either uncreated or self-created. Although gods like humans had finite lives, they might live for millions of years. The gods frequently had family relationships; they married and had children. The gods generally lived in the sky or in the Underworld. Generally, the Egyptians visualized also the gods as being located in the east where the sun arose. The Nile Valley was the land of the living, and the dead were visualized as being in the west, the land of the setting sun.

Gods also were believed to live within temples built for their worship. Inside the temples were shrines which contained a cultic statue of the temple's god. These statues were generally only a couple feet tall and could be made of wood, stone or metal. The statues were believed to be the abode of the god's *ba* and *ka* (see below). Rituals were performed in the hope of influencing the gods to do favors. Temple priests would clean and dress the cultic statues daily. Offerings would be presented to nourish them. Hymns were sung throughout the day. Temples also observed festivals throughout the year. Often these festivals involved the transportation of a cultic statue from one place to another so that one god could visit another god in commemoration of a mythic event. These festivals promoted community and a bond between the people and the religious culture.

In addition to the worship of the national gods, there also were local gods that were associated with specific regions. Gods also could be worshiped in individual homes. Prayers and offerings would be made to the gods, and ancestors would be commemorated.

There was much syncretism with the Egyptian gods; functions overlapped, myths merged, and gods rose and fell in importance. Solar deities were often identified as chief gods, and various solar gods have been identified as the initiators of creation. Ra was the dominant solar deity, particularly during the early dynasties of the Old Kingdom. Ra also was manifested as Atum. During Akhenaten's reign, Aten was the worshiped solar god (and only god).

Creation

Prior to creation there existed only the primordial sea. There are a number of Egyptian creation stories, and in most the creator god is uncreated and eternally existent. Like other ancient Middle East cultures, there are four means by which creation can occur:

1. Creation by making: through divine will the god brings order to the primordial matter.
2. Creation through conflict: the creator god has a conflict with an opponent, often some sort of sea monster, and from the defeated corpse the god turns this matter into the cosmos (creation by making).
3. Creation through sex: gods often had progeny.
4. Creation by word: when ideas come to mind, gods can make it happen by their word.

Holland (2009) summarizes: *"Despite the different versions of the Egyptian creation story, the dominant outline of the master creation narrative that appears to lie behind most of them is fairly clear. Before creation, there is only a primordial sea, the dark waters of the abyss. Out of the depths of the waters arises a hill of earth, and from this pyramid-shaped hill the process of creation is initiated by an act of a god or a group of gods. The process of creation moves from the creation of elemental gods Shu and Tefnut to their sexual generation of Geb and Nut, and the further generation of the gods of the political realm, Osiris, Isis, Seth, and Nephthys. These four divine couples, together with a creator god such as Atum or Amun, form the Ennead, the nine principal gods of Egypt, although in some cases, the ninth god is Horus, son of Osiris and Isis."*

Divinity of Kings

The king or pharaoh, as the leader of the Egyptian people, was seen as the intermediary between the people and the gods. They also were seen as being divine themselves, particularly upon their deaths. The kings of the Old Kingdom were called "Son of Ra", believed in a literal sense. It was believed that their mothers were impregnated by Ra, thus producing divine offspring. The kings were also known as a "Horus" and were given Horus names. The kings built temples to the gods, but they also built funerary temples for themselves, where they could be worshiped after their deaths.

Magic

Magic and Sorcery were part of Egyptian culture and religion. The Egyptians depended on science for the subjects that they knew about, for example pyramid building. But for problems that arose that they did not have knowledge, for example a mysterious disease, they often would rely on magic. The Bible shows us examples of this. When Moses and Aaron employ their own magic to turn a staff into a snake, to turn the river water into blood, and to cause frogs to cover the land, the pharaoh's magicians are able to replicate these feats. Priests were involved with dream interpretation and recitations of spells to help maintain order and to ward off disease and afflictions. People often wore magic amulets for protection.

Afterlife

The Egyptian culture and religion were unique in the middle east in regards to their emphasis on a glorious afterlife. All of the other cultures of the ancient world believed that upon death individuals would go to a dark, dreary netherworld where individuals would live in semi-consciousness for eternity. The Greeks called this place Hades, and the Hebrews called it Sheol. The Canaanites, Hittites and Babylonians also held this belief. This was a place for all people, whether good or evil.

The Egyptians, on the other hand, believed that the deceased continued on in a pleasurable physical afterlife. However, Egyptians believed in a personal judgment on how one lived their life. Paradise was reserved only for those whose character and life warranted it. This was a novel concept at this time. The idea of a personal judgment to get into heaven did not develop for the Israelites and Mesopotamians until many centuries later, and it never developed for the Babylonians and Assyrians. For this reason Egyptians built elaborate tombs for the pharaohs which were filled with all the necessities for a life in the next world, including furniture, luxuries accumulated in life, and reading materials.

During the Old Kingdom only kings were thought to have immortal spirits and were the only ones to have elaborate tombs, but later the "cult of the dead" was extended to the nobles. During the Middle and New Kingdoms everyone who could afford it would build and equip a tomb as it was then believed that everyone could expect to live after death in the land ruled by Osiris, the king of the dead. Mummification was developed to prevent the body from deteriorating and to preserve it for eternity. For the poor who could not afford formal mummification, bodies were buried in shallow graves in the desert where the hot, dry sand would naturally preserve the bodies from decay.

The Egyptian underworld, Duat, is ruled by Osiris. The deceased's tombs became their homes. For this reason they were lavishly decorated, sometimes even including gardens and lavatories. The dead were believed to have some influence on the living. They could move about as ghosts and could be either benevolent or malevolent. They could be solicited for assistance (as the dead prophet Samuel was solicited by King Saul in the Hebrew scriptures). The deceased were also believed to be among the stars in the sky.

The Egyptians believed that humans were composed of five parts, and burial practices took into account all five of these different aspects of the individual.

- Body
- Name: A person's name was considered an essential aspect of who they were. Pharaohs would have several names, including a "Horus name". To eradicate a name was to eradicate the essence of a person. To speak a name would animate their spirit. The ancient Israelites were not allowed to speak the name of Yahweh.
- Shadow: A person's shadow (in sunlight) was understood as the physical presence of a person that was distinct from their body.
- *Ba*: This is the persona of a person- what they project to others as their self. It also is one's self-consciousness.

- *Ka*: This is the life force of an individual. It remains with the body after entombment. It requires ongoing nourishment, which is provided by *ka*-priests.

Mummification

The Egyptians were unique in the middle east in regards to their practice of mummification of corpses. The Greek historian Herodotus wrote about the Egyptian process for mummification. He actually wrote about three different methods that differed due to expense. The most expensive process was obviously the best and involved drawing out part of the brain through the nostrils with an iron hook and then injecting certain drugs into the rest. Then a cut was made near the flank with a sharp knife of Ethiopian stone. Intestines were removed, and the belly would be cleaned with palm wine and bruised spices. The belly is then filled with pure ground myrrh, cassia and other spices (except frankincense), and then the belly is sewed shut. The body then is embalmed in saltpeter and concealed for seventy days. After that the body is washed and wrapped in bandages of fine linen cloth, then anointed with gum (which the Egyptians used instead of glue). Then the dead individual would be given to family or friends. The least expensive option involved cleansing the belly with a purge and then embalming the body for seventy days.

The book of Genesis tells us that both patriarchs, Jacob and Joseph, were mummified. Genesis 50:3 says in regards to Jacob "they spent forty days in doing this, for that is the time required for embalming. And the Egyptians wept for him seventy days." In regards to Joseph, Genesis 50:26 states

"And Joseph died, being one hundred ten years old; he was embalmed and placed in a coffin in Egypt."

Maat

Maat is a goddess, daughter of Ra, that personified righteousness, but the term *maat* also refers to order, truth, justice and righteousness. It was the duty of every Egyptian ruler to be the champion of *maat*. Osiris judged the deceased on their devotion to *maat*.

Egyptian Pantheon

The term, "Ennead", refers to the nine principal gods. The first two created gods were the "elemental gods" Shu and Tefnut. They were the first divine couple and were the offspring of the creator sun god (Atum or Ra-Atum). The creator god was said to have masturbated and then swallowed his own semen in order to reproduce himself. Shu was sneezed out, and Tefnut was spat out. These three gods were treated in the Coffin Texts, ancient Egyptian funeral writings, as a trinity: "the one who developed into three."

Shu was considered one of the creator gods. He separated the earth and sky creating a void which allowed the process of creation to begin. Shu was male and Tefnut female. Their sexual union produced offspring: the earth god Geb and the sky goddess Nut. Geb and Nut embraced passionately, and they were forced apart by their father, Shu. This had very important ramifications according to the Egyptian myth. Their separation allowed air and light to exist in the space that was now between them.

Geb and Nut were the parents of five children: Osiris, Horus the elder, Seth, Isis and Nephthys. Now Egyptian genealogy is confusing and often contradictory. Although following the above genealogy Geb would be the grandson of the creator sun-god, he was sometimes known as the father of the sun-god Ra. Horus "the elder" was the son of Geb and Nut in the above genealogy, but Horus was also the son of Osiris and Isis. Sometimes these "Horuses" were considered as separate gods, but also at times as separate aspects of the same deity. Confusing!

These four divine couples (Shu and Tefnut, Geb and Nut, Isis and Osiris, and Set and Nephthys), together with a creator god such as Atum or Amun, form the Ennead, the nine principal gods of Egypt, although in some cases, the ninth god is Horus, son of Osiris and Isis. The process of creation moves from the creation of elemental gods Shu and Tefnut to their sexual generation of Geb and Nut, and the further generation of the gods of the political realm, Osiris, Isis, Seth, and Nephthys. I will discuss these gods in more detail below as well as the sun-gods, although there are numerous other gods in the Egyptian pantheon.

Creator Sun-gods

Ra (or Re) was the source for light, energy and life. The name "ra" is the Egyptian word for the sun. The cult of Ra originated in the Egyptian town Iunu, which the Greeks referred to as Heliopolis ("city of the sun god"). From the fourth dynasty onward the Egyptian rulers referred to themselves as the Sons of Ra.

The god Amun's name means "hidden one". The origins of this god are unclear, but during the Middle Kingdom Amun became the chief god in the Theban area. In the New Kingdom Amun became combined with the god Ra. Amun-Ra was worshiped as the King of the Gods and creator of the world and its inhabitants. Amun was often depicted as a virile ram and was associated with male sexual power. He was said to unite with Egyptian queens to produce heirs to the Egyptian throne. Alexander the Great, the Macedonian conqueror, was said to have been sired by Amun.

Atum was the creator deity who began the world and from whom the other deities came. By inseminating himself he produced the gods Shu and Tefnut. According to Pinch (2002) "Atum and Ra were often regarded as the primordial and solar aspects of the creator." They coalesced into Ra-Atum.
I already have discussed the sun-god Aten in some detail. He was the god promoted by the pharaoh, Akhenaten. According to Pinch (2002) he was worshiped as the "sole god without equal" and the god of light who had made the world and sustained it every day. After Akhenaten's death, Amun-Ra once again became the chief deity of Egypt.

Other Egyptian gods

Osiris
Osiris was the eldest son of the gods Geb and Nut (who were both siblings and spouses), and his own spouse was Isis, his sister. The reader might have taken notice that this seems to be a common pattern in Egyptian mythology. This is suggested in Hebrew mythology as well, as it is assumed that

the offspring of Adam and Eve also coupled as siblings to produce progeny.

Osiris and Isis together ruled Egypt until Osiris was killed by his brother Seth. Osiris in death became inert, but Isis is still able to conceive the god, Horus, even without an active partner. Isis, Horus and other gods pleaded to the Divine Tribunal on Osiris' behalf. Because it was determined that Osiris was the possessor of *maat*, he was resurrected and made king to judge over the dead. The cult of Osiris became prominent during the Fifth Dynasty. Osiris became known as the just and fair savior of the dead.

Isis
Isis was the spouse of Osiris and the loving mother of Horus. She was known for her maternal love and perhaps was worshiped more than any other Egyptian deity. The cult of Isis became prominent in the first millennium BCE. Pinch (2002) notes "her promise to believers of a happy afterlife made the Isis cult the closest rival to Christianity in the early centuries of the first millennium CE."

Set (or Seth)
Seth is the god of disorder. He is the brother of Osiris and the rival of Horus, the god of order. He is one of the five offspring of Nut and Geb. He had a lustful nature and had a number of consorts including his own sister, Nephthys, and the foreign goddesses Anat and Astarte. Seth was represented as a human form with an animal head that had a long curved snout, long ears or horns, reddish skin, and sometimes with a forked tip on his tail. Seth was sometimes equated with the Palestinian god, Baal.

Nephthys
This god was the sister of Isis and Osiris and Seth. Although an unwilling consort of Seth, she seems to have lived with Osiris and Isis, to whom she was very devoted.

Horus
Horus was one of the earliest gods in the Egyptian pantheon, and he continued to be worshiped even into the Greek and Roman periods. He was the chief god of Lower Egypt. He was the son of the gods Osiris and Isis. As an infant, Horus was threatened by Seth and had to be hidden in the papyrus marshes by his mother, Isis. Isis is known for her love and devotion to Horus, who is completely dependent on her. They were often depicted together as divine mother and child, with Horus sitting on his mother's lap.

When Horus became a youth he approached the tribunal of the major gods, the Ennead led by Ra, and requested his rights as the legitimate heir of his father, Osiris, who had been murdered. Seth disputed this claim and wished to be the king himself. The tribunal mostly sided with Horus, except for Ra who sided with Seth. Seth and Horus had a number of contests, and Horus eventually prevailed and took his rightful place as king of the living. The cosmos was again in order, and *maat* returned.

D.M. Murdock (2009) in her research on the god, Horus, reported a remarkable biography:

- Horus was born on "December 25th" (winter solstice) in a manger.
- He was of royal descent, and his mother was the "virgin Isis-Mery".

- Horus's birth was announced by a star in the East and attended by three "wise men."
- At age 12, he was a child teacher in the Temple, and at 30, he was baptized.
- Horus was baptized by "Anup the Baptizer," who was decapitated.
- The Egyptian god had 12 companions, helpers or disciples.
- Horus performed miracles, exorcised demons and raised Osiris from the dead.
- The god walked on water.
- Horus was "crucified" between two "thieves."
- He (or Osiris) was buried for three days in a tomb and resurrected.
- Horus/Osiris was also the "Way, the Truth, the Life," "Messiah." the "Son of Man," the "Good Shepherd," the "Lamb of God," the "Word made flesh," the "Word of Truth," etc.
- Horus's personal epithet was "Iusa," the "ever-becoming son" of the Father. He was called "Holy Child," as well as "the Anointed One," while Osiris was the KRST.
- Horus battled with the "evil one," Set/Seth.
- Horus was to reign for one thousand years.

Chapter 4

Syria-Palestine

The Sinai

The Israelites left Egypt to go to Canaan, although according to Exodus they took a very round-a-bout route in order to avoid the Philistines.

"When Pharaoh let the people go, God did not lead them by way of the land of the Philistines, although that was nearer; for God thought, 'If the people face war, they may change their minds and return to Egypt'" (Exodus 13:17)

Instead of making their way north, they moved south from Rameses in the land of Goshen to Succoth. They then went south following the west coast of the Sinai Peninsula. Eventually they made their way to the wilderness of Sinai. The trip took about three months to get to Mt. Sinai (sometimes referred to as Mt. Horeb), which is where Moses presented to the Israelite people the Ten Commandments. Moses went up Mt. Sinai twice. The first time he came down with the Ten Commandments. On the second occasion Moses "was there with the Lord forty days and forty nights."

When Moses returned to the Israelite people the first time, he discovered that they had created a calf made of gold to worship. Aaron, Moses' right hand man, built an alter before it. The people offered burnt offerings and participated in a festival. Where did this idea of a golden calf come from? Perhaps from the Egyptians. The aurochs, a wild bull, were widely worshiped throughout the ancient world. One may recall from chapter one the many bulls heads that were excavated from Catal Huyuk during the Neolithic Age. In Egypt the bull was worshiped as "Apis".

According to Pinch (2002), "Apis was a bull kept at Memphis who was the most important of all sacred animals. In life, the Apis bull was honored as the physical manifestation of Ptah; in death he was worshiped as a form of Osiris. A festival called the Running of the Apis Bull is recorded as early as the First Dynasty. By the Late Period the Apis bull had become a kind of national mascot."

There is another story in the Hebrew scriptures where Israelite people worship golden calves. The first book of Kings (12:28-29) tells us that Rehoboam, the king of the northern kingdom of Judah, made two golden calves to be worshiped in the towns of Bethel and Dan. He did this to prevent the citizens of Judah from traveling to Jerusalem in the kingdom of Israel to worship God at the temple there.

When Moses descended the mountain and found that the Israelites had made the golden calves, he was very angry and actually broke the stone tablets that contained the Ten Commandments. I had grown up to believe that Moses was angry because the Israelites were worshiping idols and false gods. Actually, Exodus 32:4 quotes Aaron as saying "These are your gods, O Israel, who brought you up out of the land of Egypt." This is interesting for at least two reasons; first of all gods are mentioned in the plural, and second of all it is Aaron's understanding that this is a representation of the god(s) whom they were supposed to be following. Although the Ten Commandments specifically prohibit that making of graven images, at this point that law had not yet been given to the Israelite people.

From there the Israelite people went north along the east coast of the Sinai Peninsula. Across the Gulf of Aqaba was the land of Midian, where Moses previously lived. The book of Numbers in the Pentateuch tells the story of the Israelites' forty year journey in the wilderness. Chapters 1-10 describe being in the Sinai wilderness, chapters 10-22 describe the march through the wilderness to Transjordan, and chapters 22-36 describe being in the plains of Moab.

The map below shows the route the Israelites were believed to have taken from the Land of Goshen, south along the west coast of the Sinai peninsula to the believed site of "Mount Sinai" and then north along the eastern part of the Sinai peninsula to the Transjordan.

An Integral and Evolutionary World View: Evolution and Syncretism of Religion

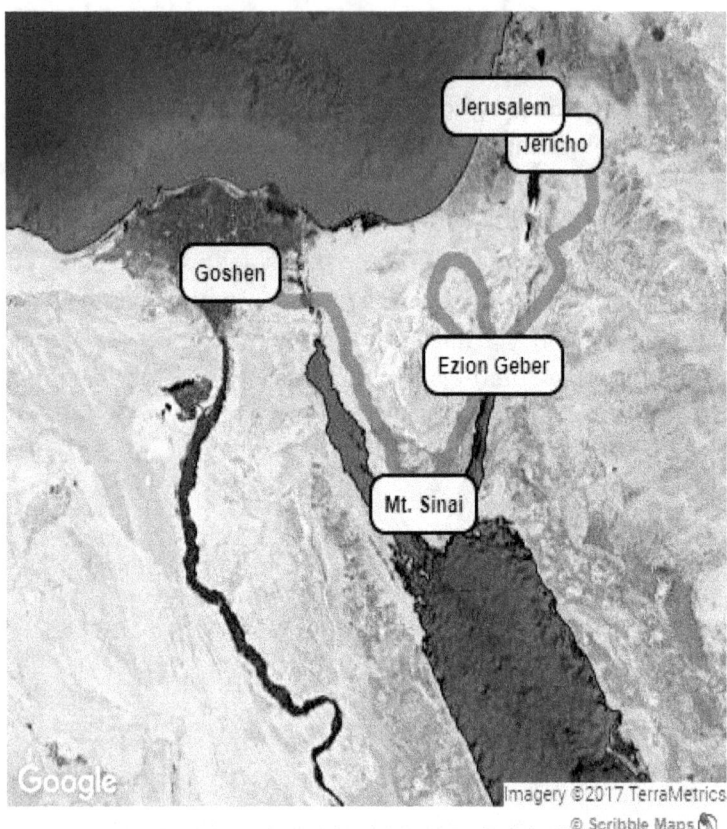

The Transjordan

The Jordan River runs between the Sea of Galilee and the Dead Sea. Today it divides the country of Israel and the West Bank from the country of Jordan. The term "transjordan" refers to the land east of the Jordan River. Numbers 13 tells us that from the wilderness of Paran (before getting to the transjordan) in the northern Sinai peninsula, Moses sent out spies to investigate the land of Canaan. They returned to report to Moses that the inhabitants of the land were strong and unlikely to be overcome by the Israelites. They reported that the inhabitants of the land included the Amalekites, the Hittites, the Jebusites, the Amorites, the Canaanites, and the Anakites who were reportedly descendents of the Nephilim. The Nephilim are mentioned in the book of Genesis: they were reported to be giants who were the products of the sexual union of "the sons of God and the daughters of humans" (Genesis 6:4). These groups of people were primarily tribes and chiefdoms. Tribes are groups of up to a few thousand people linked by ancestral ties that can be either settled farmers or nomadic herders. Chiefdoms are larger groups of typically 5,000 to 20,000 individuals led by a chief or king.

From Kadesh, which was just west of Edom, the Israelites asked the king of Edom whether they could pass through the kingdom. The king refused this, and so they had to travel the long way around Edom to the east.

An Integral and Evolutionary World View: Evolution and Syncretism of Religion

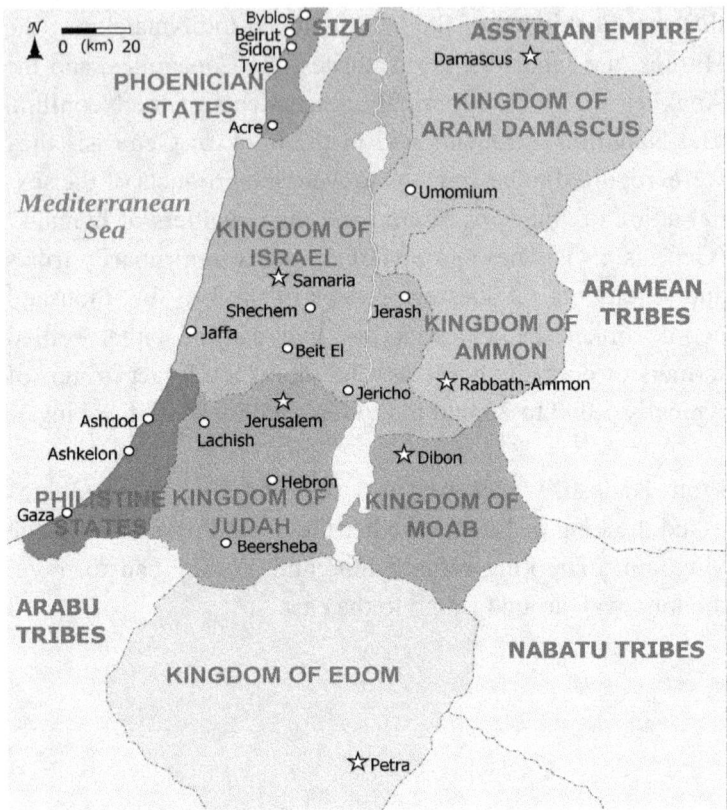

Courtesy of Wikimedia

The Israelites encountered a number of tribes on their journey. "When the Canaanite, the king of Arad, who lived in the Negeb, heard that Israel was coming by the way of Atharim, he fought against Israel and took some of them captive." The Israelites made a deal with God; if the people were returned, the Israelites would reciprocate by utterly destroying those Canaanites. That is what reportedly happened.

They arrived at the wilderness of Moab. They requested of King Sihon of the Amorites passage through their land. Sihon responded by attacking them, but Israel again prevailed and defeated the Amorites. Then King Og of Bashan fought against the Israelites which also ended badly for the aggressor: "So they killed him, his sons, and all his people, until there was no survivor left; and they took possession of his land. (Numbers 21: 35). Some of the Israelites settled there.

"The Israelites set out, and camped in the plains of Moab across the Jordan from Jericho." The king of Moab, Balak, was very fearful of the Israelites, as he heard what they had done to other peoples who went up against them. He sought out a prophet, Balaam, who was well known for his effectiveness in giving blessings and curses. Balak wanted Balaam to curse the Israelites. What I find extremely interesting is that Balaam was a Midianite; these were the people Moses previously lived with. Moses had married the daughter of a Midianite priest. It was in Midian that Yahweh was encountered for the first time.

The elders of both Moab and Midian came to Balaam with their request. Balaam said he wanted to consult with God about how to respond to the request. This was not a pagan god, but the same god that the Israelites worshiped! Balaam referred to the Lord as "my God". God told Balaam not to curse the people as they were "blessed". Balaam refused the job, but another delegation was sent by Balak to try again to solicit Balaam's help. This time God told Balaam to go with the delegation but "do only what I tell you to do."

The book of Numbers then relates a well-known and very strange story; on the journey Balaam's donkey began talking and told Balaam that there was an angel of the Lord blocking the road. The angel told Balaam to continue on the journey: "Go with the men; but speak only what I tell you to speak." Balaam reached Balak who was dismayed that instead of cursing the Israelites, they were blessed three times, since this was the will of God.

Although God showed favor to the Israelites, they continued in their unfaithfulness. They began having sexual relations with the women of Moab, and they began worshiping the Moabite gods. God was angry and sent a plague that killed twenty-four thousand. Midianites are blamed for contributing to Israelites' unfaithfulness, and God told Moses to wage battle against Midian. All of the Midianite males were killed, which was commanded by God. Even Balaam, who did only what was commanded by God, was killed. The women and children were taken captive. When the soldiers returned from the war, Moses was angry that the women were not also killed. "Now therefore, kill every male among the little ones, and kill every woman who has known a man by sleeping with him. But all the young girls who have not known a man by sleeping with him, keep alive for yourselves." (Numbers 31: 17-18). This is one of those Biblical passages that is highly disturbing and disappointing to many of us.

Three of the Israelite tribes had land allotted to them in the Transjordan (i.e. east of the Jordan River). Those tribes were Reuben, Gad and Manasseh. The book of Joshua takes up the story of the Israelite conquest of the "promised lands". In chapter one Joshua reminds the men of the three above tribes that they need to keep their obligation of helping the other tribes conquer the lands west of the Jordan River.

Chapter 4: Syria-Palestine

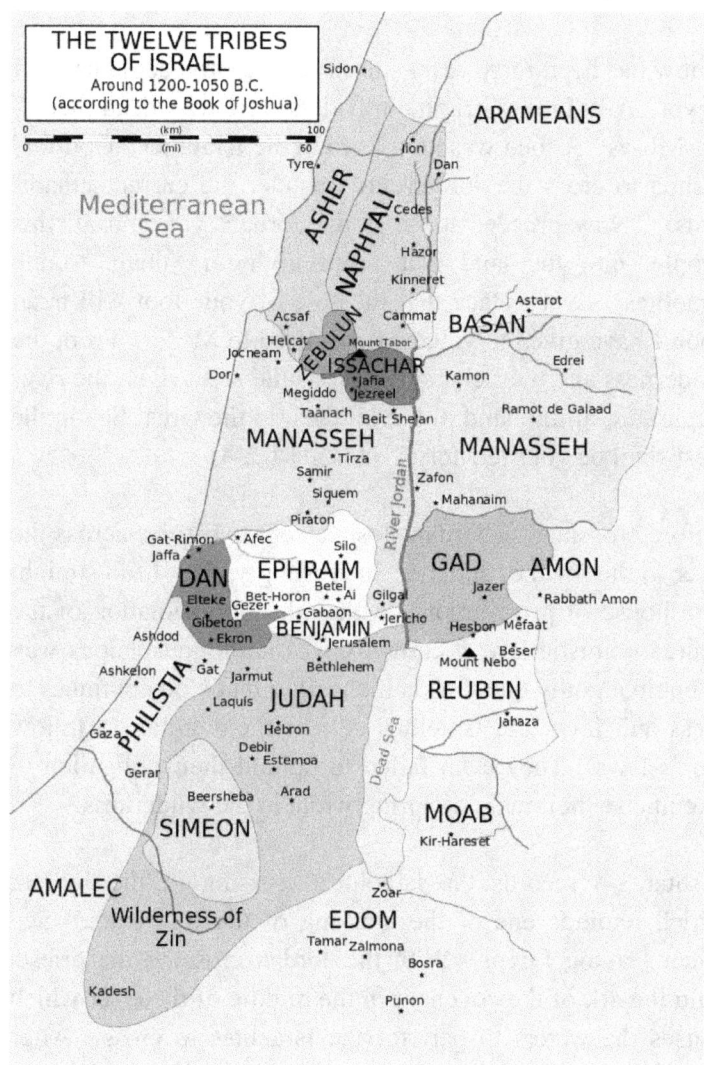

Courtesy of Wikimedia

Crossing the Jordan

It now has been forty years since the Israelite people had left Egypt. All of those original travelers were now dead including Moses. Joshua was now leading the Israelites. God told Joshua to cross the Jordan and conquer the current inhabitants. "Now proceed to cross the Jordan, you and all this people, into the land that I am giving to them, to the Israelites. Every place that the sole of your foot will tread upon I have given to you, as I promised to Moses. From the wilderness and the Lebanon as far as the great river, the river Euphrates, all the land of the Hittites, to the Great Sea in the west shall be your territory." (Joshua 1:2-4)

Before crossing the Jordan, Joshua sent two spies across the river to the town of Jericho. Interestingly, they head straight to a house of prostitution. Although not a violation of the deuteronomistic law, it certainly was not an auspicious way to begin a godly quest. It is interesting that God continues to bless and favor the Israelites despite their failure to follow God's laws. They even failed to uphold their obligation to circumcise their male offspring while in the wilderness.

Joshua 3-4 records the Israelite's crossing of the Jordan, which reminds one of the crossing of the Red (Reed) Sea when leaving Egypt. With the Jordan crossing the priests hold the ark of the covenant in the middle of the river which causes the waters to part for the Israelites to cross. After reaching the other side, the Israelites proceeded to conquer Jericho. Then the Israelites proceeded to conquer the rest of Canaan. Chapter 12 of the Book of Joshua lists the defeated kings. The suggestion was made that most of Canaan was now occupied by the Israelites. "So Joshua defeated the whole land, the hill country and the Negeb and the lowland

and the slopes, and all their kings; he left no one remaining, but utterly destroyed all that breathed, as the Lord God of Israel commanded." (Joshua 10: 40)

The conquered territories were divided among the tribes and decided by lot. Thus, by casting lots, God was the one to decide which tribe got what. (See the above map.) The book of Judges, however, which follows the book of Joshua in the Hebrew scriptures, suggests that there was not a complete conquest of Canaan by the Israelites. Nor does archaeology suggest widespread destruction and genocide.

Just as the Israelites were conceived of as various tribes, the "Canaanites" also were a diverse group of tribes. "Canaanite" is a generic term for the West Semitic peoples of the Levant. The Hebrew scriptures name a number of different ethnic groups:

- Amalekites (Gen, 14:7; Exodus 17:8-13; 1 Sam. 15:2; Deut. 25:17; Num. 13:29)
- Amorites (Josh. 3:10; 9:1; 11:3; 12:8)
- Canaanites (Josh. 3:10; 9:1; 11:3; 12:8)
- Gibeonites (2 Sam. 21)
- Girgashites (Josh. 3:10)
- Hittites (Josh. 3:10; 9:1; 11:3; 12:8)
- Hivites (Josh. 3:10; 9:1; 11:3; 12:8)
- Jebusites (Josh. 3:10; 9:1; 11:3; 12:8). Interestingly, this is the Canaanite tribe that built and inhabited Jerusalem prior to King David conquering it and making it his capital city.
- Jerahmeelites (1 Sam. 27:10; 30:29)
- Kenizzites (Josh. 14:13-14; 30:29)
- Perizzites (Josh. 3:10; 9:1; 11:3; 12:8)

Archaeology

"History" in the ancient world was conceived of somewhat differently than it is today where the emphasis is on factual correctness. I am not suggesting that ancient historians wrote fiction, but the emphasis was on conveying a political, theological or social agenda. Because of this, caution needs to be taken when reading ancient "historical" writings, particularly when the subject matter happened centuries prior to their having been written about. This is the case with many writings in the Hebrew scriptures. The exodus is believed to have occurred between the 16th and the 13th centuries BCE The writings that described these events were not composed until centuries later (the earliest, the "J" source was believed to have been from the ninth or tenth centuries BCE). They were not fused into their current form until after the Babylonian exile. The Hebrew canon did not take shape until the second century CE.

A relevant field of scientific study is archaeology, which has been able to shed light on the historical facts of the exodus story. Thus far, according to archaeologist William Dever (2003), no archaeological evidence has been found for the exodus from Egypt, including in the dry desert sands of the Sinai, where physical evidence would have been well preserved. Despite the fact that we have possession of many writings from ancient Egypt, there has been found no reference to Israelites or Hebrews in Egypt, and no mention of a mass exodus. The only reference to "Israel" found from ancient Egypt was a stele (a stone slab) known as the Merenptah Stele (Pharaoh Merneptah was the son of Ramses II). The stele lists Israel as one of the peoples defeated by the Egyptians in Canaan.

Early in the exodus story in the book of Exodus, the Israelites take a circuitous route in order to avoid the Philistines. However, archaeological evidence has shown that the Philistines, a "sea peoples" did not enter the Levant until the time of Ramses III, ca. 1180 BCE The Philistines were there at the time the exodus story was *written*, and so it would appear the writers assumed that the Philistines had existed there centuries earlier when the exodus was purported to have happened. The book of Numbers also reports that the King of Edom refused passage of the Israelites through that kingdom; however, archaeological evidence demonstrates that Edom did not achieve statehood until the 7th century BCE and prior to that was largely nomadic. Midian, Moab and other areas of the Transjordan as described in the book of Numbers also reflect conditions in the 8th to 7th centuries BCE, not the conditions of 1600 to 1300 BCE when the exodus was purported to have taken place.

In regards to Jericho, archaeology demonstrates that Jericho was completely abandoned at the time period of the exodus. "Simply put, archaeology tells us that the biblical story of the fall of Jericho, miraculous elements aside, cannot have been founded on genuine historical sources. It seems invented out of whole cloth." (Dever, 2003)

Dever said archaeologists now predominantly agree that the Israelites developed from within Canaanite society and that there was not a widespread foreign invasion in which the indigenous peoples were destroyed. Biblical Hebrew is a Canaanite dialect. Even the prophet Ezekiel wrote about Israel's Canaanite roots: "Your origin and your birth are of the Canaanites; your father was an Amorite, and your mother a Hittite" (Ezekiel 16:3).

Archaeologists Israel Finkelstein and Neil Asher Silberman (2001) put it this way: "the emergence of early Israel was an outcome of the collapse of the Canaanite culture, not its cause. And most of the Israelites did not come from outside Canaan- they emerged from within it. There was no mass Exodus from Egypt. There was no violent conquest of Canaan. Most of the people who formed early Israel were local people- the same people whom we see in the highlands throughout the Bronze and Iron Ages. The early Israelites were-irony of ironies- themselves originally Canaanites!"

Dever concludes from the Merneptah Stele:

1. There existed in Canaan by 1210 BCE a cultural and probably political entity that called itself "Israel" and was known to the Egyptians by that name.
2. This Israel was well enough established by that time among the other peoples of Canaan to have been perceived by Egyptian intelligence as a possible challenge to Egyptian hegemony.
3. This Israel did not comprise an organized state like others in Canaan, but consisted rather of loosely affiliated peoples- that is, an ethnic group.
4. This Israel was not located in the lowlands, under Egyptian domination, but in the more remote central hill country, on the frontier.

History of Syria-Palestine

I will describe the history of this area in each of the following archaeological time periods:

Neolithic Period	8000 BCE to 3500 BCE
Early Bronze Age	3500 BCE to 2200 BCE
Middle Bronze Age	2200 BCE to 1550 BCE
Late Bronze Age	1550 BCE to 1150 BCE
Iron Age I	1150 BCE to 900 BCE
Iron Age II	900 BCE to 586 BCE

Neolithic: I described the Levant in this time period in the first chapter of this book. Prior to the Neolithic period there existed a culture known as Natufian (12,000 to 8500 BCE). Jericho was one of the world's first towns. By 8000 BCE it had around 2,000 residents of Natufian descent. Toward the end of the millennium it was deserted for a while and then repopulated around 6,800 BCE

Early Bronze Age: From about 2850 to 2200 BCE what is termed "Canaanite material culture" first appeared in Palestine west of the Jordan, in what is now Lebanon, and in southern coastal Syria. From about 2500 a number of large cities appeared in northern Syria, but these disappeared as a result of political and economic collapse around 2300 BCE

Middle Bronze Age: This era was initially characterized by semi-nomadic life, but by around 2000 cities began to reappear. Various Palestinian ethnic groups migrated southward into Egypt and founded cities in the Nile Delta, including the important city of Avaris. This city was the Egyptian capital under the Hyksos, a Semitic people who ruled Lower Egypt briefly. When the Hyksos were eventually expelled, Egyptian domination over Canaan was reestablished.

Late Bronze Age: In this period Syria-Palestine was influenced by both Egypt in the south and by new powers in the north. First it was the Hurrian kingdom of Mitanni. Around 1341 Mitanni submitted to the Hittite state of Hatti. Around 1200 BCE the eastern Mediterranean basin had an economic collapse that was perhaps caused by severe droughts. This led to the fall of the kingdoms of Mycenaean Greece, Minoan Crete, and the Hittite empire. At this time the "sea peoples" migrated into the area. This included the Philistines. These people probably migrated from the Aegean Sea and were probably refugees from the collapsed Mycenaean, Minoan and Hittite kingdoms. The Philistines founded five major cities: Ashdod, Ashkelon, Ekron, Gaza and Gath. They were not Semitic and culturally were very different from the other peoples in Canaan. As previously mentioned, the Merneptah stele (1213-1203) had among other writings on it "Israel lies desolate". And so in this time period there were a group of people in Canaan known as "Israelites".

Iron Age I: In this period Canaan was made up of loose tribal confederations and royal city-states. They all shared a common language and culture; they were all Semitic. To the east of Israel and Judah were Ammon, Moab and Edom, territories that had not yet coalesced into kingdoms. Northeast of Israel were the Aramaeans, with Damascus their most important city.

<u>Iron Age II</u>: These various states at times fought with each other, and at other times formed alliances against other enemies. This continued for a couple of centuries into Iron Age II. This continued until the development of empires, the topic of the next chapter of this book.

Ugarit

Unlike Mesopotamia and Egypt, extensive writings have not been recovered from Canaan. An exception to this have been writings uncovered from the ancient city-state Ugarit, which was located on the north Syrian coast of the Mediterranean, north of Lebanon. Scholars are able to decipher their language, Ugaritic, a Semitic language, which is closely related to Biblical Hebrew and other ancient Semitic languages such as Aramaic and Phoenician.

Syria-Palestine was populated by a number of different peoples who shared a similar language, culture, and genetic background. Collectively they are called Semitic. The Israelites were a Semitic group. Most of Syria-Palestine was populated by Semites; an exception were the Philistines. Much of Mesopotamia were populated by Semites; an exception there were the Sumerians.

Coogan and Smith (2012) write that the "term 'Canaanite' requires explanation. The Canaanites were a group of

Semitic peoples who during the third and second millennia BCE occupied parts of what is today Syria, Lebanon, Israel, Palestine, and Jordan. They were never organized into a single political unit; nevertheless, the relatively independent city-states such as Ugarit, Byblos, Sidon, Tyre, Shechem, and Jerusalem had a common language and culture (with local idiosyncrasies), which we call Canaanite."

Since 1929 there have been ongoing excavations near Ugarit, and thousands of texts have been found on tablets of baked clay. From these writings scholars have learned much about Canaanite culture and religion.

Religion of Syria-Palestine

Like Mesopotamia and Egypt, religion in Canaan was polytheistic, i.e. the worship of multiple gods. The gods were in a hierarchy, usually with a chief god. The various city-states had their own hierarchies of gods, but the close proximity of the various city-states of Canaan with each other led to syncretism, i.e. the merging of myths and beliefs with one another. As new gods, myths, and rituals became known, they were assimilated. Pantheons continued to evolve. This syncretism affected the Israelite's religion as it did the other Canaanite religions. The early Israelite religion was different in one important aspect, however, from the other religions in the region. It was "henotheistic" rather than polytheistic.

Henotheism means the worship of only one god from a multitude of gods. It is not that there *is* only one god (which would be "monotheism"), but that there exists many gods and our tribe only worships the one god, which in the case of the Israelites would be Yahweh. In the Ten Commandments is the decree "you shall have no other gods before me". It is not that there isn't other gods; it is that Yahweh needs to be first and foremost. Monotheism eventually developed among the Israelites, but it took centuries.

At this point I would like to make the distinction between the terms "monotheism" and "monolatry". The former means a *belief* in one god. The latter refers to the *worship* of only one god. Modern Christians know that their religion stresses belief rather than actions. That was not true of ancient religions of the near east, including Judaism, where what was important was practices. It did not matter what one believed; what mattered was rituals, such as making sacrifices.

When man was first created, Genesis 1:26 tells us that God said "Let *us* make humankind in *our* image, according to *our* likeness". Mankind is made in the likeness of *gods*, not just the one god. After Adam eats of the forbidden tree God said "See, the man has become like one of *us*, knowing good and evil; and now, he might reach out his hand and take also from the tree of life, and eat, and live forever." (Genesis 3:22). Man, like the *gods*, now knows the difference between good and evil and could also potentially live forever, like the *gods*. In the story of the Tower of Babel, God said "Come, let *us* go down, and confuse their language there, so that they will not understand one another's speech." (Genesis 11:7). Again Yahweh is part of a group of *gods*.

Psalm 82 of the Hebrew scriptures says "God has taken his place in the divine council; in the midst of the gods he holds judgment." A heavenly council is also presented in the book of Job: "One day the heavenly beings came to present themselves before the Lord, and Satan also came among them"

(Job 1:6). The concept of a divine council was prevalent throughout Canaan and Mesopotamia.

Although we do not have stories about the creative activities of the god, El, we do know his epithet included "El, creator of Earth". Presumably much of creation was the result of his sexual activity with his consort, Asherah, known as "Creatress of the gods". El was the father of Baal. El and Baal also were known as divine warriors, and it was through battles that order was imposed on the cosmos. Stories of giant sea serpents are common in ancient near eastern creation myths. In Mesopotamia there is the myth of the god Marduk defeating the serpent Tiamat whose body was used to create the heavens and the earth. Similarly there is a Canaanite myth of the gods Baal and Anat defeating the sea monster Lothan. There are similar references in the Hebrew scriptures to a sea monster named Leviathan, who was defeated by Yahweh.

Canaanites, including Israelites, believed that after death one went to the underworld. They believed in the same type of semiconscious existence as did the Mesopotamians. In Judaism this place was called "Sheol". For many of the Canaanites that underworld was ruled by a god named Mot. For those in Mesopotamia as well as those in Syria-Palestine, it did not matter what kind of a life one lived; all ended up in the underworld upon death. After King David of Israel died, 1 Kings 2:10 tells us "Then David slept with his ancestors".

Although it was believed that everyone ended up in the same place after death no matter if one did good or evil, it was believed that it made a difference in this life. Sacrifices were made to gods to make atonement or to seek favors. The focus was for assistance in *this* life.

There has been some attestation in Ugaritic texts of offerings being made to the dead. There also is evidence of necromancy, the practice of mediums consulting the dead. The prophet Isaiah refers to this practice (chapter 8: 19-20), and despite banning the practice in Israel, King Saul himself consulted a medium to raise up the dead prophet Samuel (1 Samuel 28).

The worship of the gods in Syria-Palestine primarily happened in temples and at shrines. There were a number of both men and women who were employed in temples besides the priests who performed ritual sacrifices. Other vocations included butchers, bakers, maintenance people, temple prophets and diviners, and sacred prostitutes (both male and female). The Hebrew book of Deuteronomy condemns the practice of temple prostitution: "None of the daughters of Israel shall be a temple prostitute; none of the sons of Israel shall be a temple prostitute. You shall not bring the fee of a prostitute or the wages of a male prostitute into the house of the Lord your God in payment for any vow, for both of these are abhorrent to the Lord your God (Deut. 23: 17-18).

Gods were worshiped not only at official temples but also at sacred shrines and altars. When Judah and Israel became separate kingdoms many centuries later, not only did they have the temple of Yahweh in Jerusalem, but they also had officially sanctioned altars and shrines, most notably in Bethel and Dan.

Sacrifice

In order to gain favor from the gods or to make amends, sacrifices were offered. Almost anything of value could be offered to the gods. Common offerings were animals, grains and vegetables, and libations such as oils, beer and wine. Although it was forbidden to make representations of Yahweh, images of other gods likely were present in various temples. Holland (2009) states that Hebrew covenantal law required that every adult male was required to make offerings to Yahweh three times per year at festivals: early spring during Passover, late spring during the festival of Weeks, and in fall as part of the festival of Booths or Tabernacles.

The term "offering" can refer to any gift presented to a god, i.e. not only animal sacrifices but also grains, vegetables or beverage. The term "sacrifice" usually refers to animal offerings. The term "burnt offering" also refers to *animal* offerings. Offerings and sacrifices were prevalent among all the religions of the near east including the Israelites. The Israelite's religious practices and rituals were quite typical of all the religions in the near east with the exception of their not making graven images of their god, Yahweh.

According to Hebrew mythology, the concept of making sacrifices to God goes all the way back to Cain and Abel, the sons of Adam and Eve. Genesis 4 tells us that "Cain brought to the Lord an offering of the fruit of the ground, and Abel for his part brought of the firstlings of his flock, their fat portions. And the Lord had regard for Abel and his offering, but for Cain and his offering he had no regard" (v. 3-5). Why was God pleased with Abel's offering and not with Cain's? Was it because Abel presented a burnt offering of meat and Cain only presented grain? Perhaps. It also could be because of the quality of the sacrifice: Abel presented the fat portions (the choicest cuts) of the *firstlings* of his flock. Cain presented an agricultural offering, but not necessarily the best he had to offer, the "*firstfruits*".

The Torah does stress the importance of the quality of one's sacrifice. The Torah also stresses that what Yahweh finds most appealing about burnt offerings is the "pleasing odor" it produces. There is no indication in the Hebrew scriptures that Yahweh eats the offerings presented, but that Yahweh enjoys the pleasing odors of the burning fat. The following are just a few of the verses in the Hebrew scriptures that stress the importance of a "pleasing odor".

- Genesis 8:20-21 "Then Noah built an altar to the Lord, and took of every clean animal and of every clean bird, and offered burnt offerings on the altar. And when the Lord smelled the pleasing odor, the Lord said in his heart, 'I will never again curse the ground because of humankind, for the inclination of the human heart is evil from youth; nor will I ever again destroy every living creature as I have done.'"

- Leviticus 1:9b "Then the priest shall turn the whole into smoke on the altar as a burnt offering, an offering by fire of pleasing odor to the Lord."

- Numbers 29:2 "and you shall offer a burnt offering, a pleasing odor to the Lord: one young bull, one ram, seven male lambs a year old without blemish."

- Leviticus 3:3-5 "You shall offer from the sacrifice of well-being, as an offering by fire to the Lord, the fat that covers the entrails and all the fat that is around the entrails; the two kidneys with the fat that is on them at the loins, and the appendage of the liver, which he shall remove with the kidneys. Then Aaron's sons shall turn these into smoke on the altar, with the burnt offering that is on the wood on the fire, as an offering by fire of pleasing odor to the Lord."

In Exodus 20:23-24 Yahweh gives Moses directions for altars and burnt offerings. "You need make for me only an altar of earth and sacrifice on it your burnt offerings and your offerings of well-being, your sheep and your oxen; in every place where I cause my name to be remembered I will come to you and bless you." Even after formal places of sacrifice and worship were created (first the tabernacle and then later the temple), the practice of building private altars for the worship of Yahweh continued. From these individual altars sacrifices were made. Sacrifices also were made at altars associated with the tabernacle and temple, but these formal "sanctuaries" were also known to be the residence of Yahweh.

The book of Leviticus, arguably the most boring and least read of the books in the Bible, goes into a tremendous amount of detail in describing procedures for sacrifice. If the offering is of cattle or of sheep/goats, it should be a male "without blemish". If individuals are poor and cannot afford to sacrifice cattle or sheep, then they can sacrifice birds (which should be either a turtledove or pigeon). If they cannot afford a bird, they can offer grain; it should be *choice* flour with oil and frankincense put on it.

For animal offerings, "You shall lay your hand on the head of the burnt offering, and it shall be acceptable in your behalf as atonement for you" (Lev. 1:4). If offerings are made for the atonement of sin, there are specific sacrificial requirements depending on who is doing the sinning, e.g. an anointed priest, the whole congregation of Israel, a ruler, or ordinary individuals. "Sin" includes not only moral failings but also physical impurities such as leprosy or bodily discharges. After childbirth a mother is "ceremonially unclean" for seven days if she gives birth to a son and is unclean for two weeks if she bears a female child. "When the days of her purification are completed, whether for a son or for a daughter, she shall bring to the priest at the entrance of the tent of meeting a lamb in its first year for a burnt offering, and a pigeon or a turtledove for a sin offering" (Lev. 12:6).

Human Sacrifice

The ideology behind sacrifice is that the greater the sin, the greater the requirement for atonement. If we really want to impress a god, we will give a gift that is as grand as possible. What greater sacrifice is there than giving a human life, particularly the life of one's eldest son. This is the ideology behind a mainstream Christian idea, i.e. that the life of the one and only son of God was the necessary requirement to pay for the sins of all of mankind.

The primary way for worshiping gods and atoning for sins in the ancient near east was with sacrifice. Did it go so far as human sacrifice? There is evidence that there was human sacrifice in the near east. The most disturbing evidence of this to date has been found in Carthage in North Africa (near present day Tunis, Tunisia). Carthage was founded by the

Phoenicians around 800 BCE Phoenicia was located on the Mediterranean coast in northern Canaan in what is present day Lebanon. Phoenicia was made up of various city-states such as Tyre and Sidon. They spoke Phoenician, a Canaanite language. Baal-Hammon and Tanit-Ashtarte were well known gods in Phoenicia. King Hiram of Tyre was a friend and ally of Kings David and Solomon. King Hiram was instrumental in helping Solomon build his great temple (I Kings 5)

Carthage was a Phoenician settlement, that as I said was founded around 800 BCE, became independent of the motherland around 6oo BCE, and emerged as a major power in the Mediterranean world in the third and second centuries BCE. Archeologists Lawrence Stager and Samuel R. Wolff have excavated an area in Carthage that they conclude is "the largest cemetery of sacrificed humans ever discovered." As many as 20,000 urns have been deposited there between 400 and 200 BCE. The urns contain the charred remains of children. In the lower layers of the cemetery, where the earliest "deposits" were made, were remains of both humans and animals. Higher layers contained a greater proportion of humans to animals, suggesting that animal sacrifice was more common earlier than later when the human sacrifices increased.

Why would people sacrifice their children? Likely it was a great sacrifice (a supreme gesture) in order to achieve what they perceived as a much greater good, e.g. to achieve success in war, to stave off epidemics, to ward off famine, and ironically for fertility. Scholars think a widespread belief was that by sacrificing the first born the gods would reward a couple with increased offspring. Individuals also were sacrificed for the sake of new building projects; adults or children were often interred in the foundations of new buildings or under gates and bridges.

Philo of Byblos, who wrote a history of the Phoenicians, said "Among ancient peoples in critically dangerous situations it was customary for the rulers of a city or nation, rather than lose everyone, to provide the dearest of children as a propitiatory sacrifice to the avenging deities. The children thus given up were slaughtered according to a secret ritual." Smith (2002) reported that burned bones of infants also have been found from Amman from the late bronze age.

When the Israelites were in the Sinai God gave them commandments through Moses. One commandment was: "The firstborn of your sons you shall give to me. You shall do the same with your oxen and with your sheep: seven days it shall remain with its mother; on the eighth day you shall give it to me" (Ex. 22:29b-30). Does this mean what it sounds like it means, i.e. that the first born child and first born animals should be sacrificed to Yahweh?

In the book of Numbers (3:13) "for all the firstborn are mine; when I killed all the firstborn in the land of Egypt, I consecrated for my own all the firstborn in Israel, both human and animal; they shall be mine. I am the Lord." In chapter 8, verses 17-18 the same thing is written with the addition of "but I have taken the Levites in place of all the firstborn among the Israelites."

The book of Ezekiel (20:25-26) gives an explanation for human sacrifice: "Moreover I gave them statutes that were not good and ordinances by which they could not live. I defiled them through their very gifts, in their offering up all their firstborn, in order that I might horrify them, so that they might know that I am the Lord."

Davies (1981) who completed a comprehensive study of human sacrifice concluded "The early Hebrews probably did sacrifice humans on a limited scale when they came out of Egypt and entered the Promised Land, but once they had settled there, ritual killing, far from dying out, reached new heights as they adopted the child burnings of their Canaanite neighbours, an abomination against which the great prophets never ceased to rail." Smith (2002) writes "that in the seventh century child sacrifice was a Judean practice performed in the name of Yahweh." Smith said that "in Moab, Judah, and Phoenicia, child sacrifice was a form of *mlk* sacrifice, performed primarily in times of national crisis". There will be an explanation of *"mlk"* later in this chapter.

Perhaps the most well-known story in the Hebrew scriptures is the story of Abraham and Isaac. God said to Abraham "Take your son, your only son Isaac, whom you love, and go to the land of Moriah, and offer him there as a burnt offering on one of the mountains that I shall show you" (Genesis 22:1-2). Abraham unquestionably obeys. Just before he puts the knife to his son, God stops him. Traditionally this is seen as a story about Abraham's unquestioning obedience to God. However, it also implies that the concept of child sacrifice was part of that culture.

In chapter 32 of Exodus in response to the sin of the Israelite people in making the golden calf, Moses offers to sacrifice himself to save the Israelite people. "But now, if you will only forgive their sin- but if not, blot me out of the book that you have written" (v. 32). God will not accept that sacrifice.

Joshua in leading the Israelites into Canaan and destroying the city of Jericho killed everything there: the elderly, the children, men and woman, oxen, sheep and donkeys. Was it for punishment? Did the children do evil? No, it was human sacrifice for Yahweh. In First Samuel 15, King Saul is told: "Now go and attack Amalek, and utterly destroy all that they have; do not spare them, but kill both man and woman, child and infant, ox and sheep, camel and donkey." Again, most of us probably interpreted this as passage as an example of divine punishment, but did infants and cattle really do evil? I think a more likely interpretation is that they were to be sacrifices for the glory of Yahweh. Tierney (1989) writes "This kind of ritual killing 'before the Lord' was typical for all peoples of Palestine of 1000 BCE. A Moabite stele from about 830 BCE tells how, when a Moabite king captured the Israelite town of Nebo, he killed seven thousand men, women and children as a holocaust dedicated to Astarte-Chemosh."

In 2 Samuel 21 we are told that there was a three-year famine in Israel caused by drought. Despite normal sacrifices, Yahweh did not send rain. Yahweh told King David that the cause of the drought was King Saul, who had been dead for decades. "There is bloodguilt on Saul and on his house, because he put the Gibeonites to death" (2 Sam. 21:1). King David asked the Gibeonites what it would take to make things right. The Gibeonites demanded seven of Saul's male descendants, which David agreed to. "They were put to death in the first days of harvest, at the beginning of barley harvest." This ended the famine.

In the book of Judges is the story of a great warrior known as Jephthah; the Jewish elders offered to make him a judge of Israel if he could defeat the Ammonites, who were making war against the Israelites. "And Jephthah made a vow to the lord, and said, 'If you will give the Ammonites into my hand, then whoever comes out of the doors of my house to meet me, when I return victorious from the Ammonites, shall be the Lord's, to be offered up by me as a burnt offering" (Judges 11:30-31). Jephthah won the victory over the Ammonites. When he returned home, it was his daughter who greeted him. He kept his vow and sacrificed her to Yahweh.

The sacrifice of children for military success was apparently not uncommon in Iron Age Palestine. 2 Kings 3 tells us that King Mesha of Moab made a burnt offering of his firstborn son (and successor) for this reason. Mesha's sacrifice apparently worked; the tide of battle turned, and the Israelites were forced to retreat. King Ahaz of Judah (during the period of the divided kingdoms) sacrificed two of his sons: "He even made cast images for the Baals, and he made offerings in the valley of the son of Hinnom, and made his sons pass through fire, according to the abominable practices of the nations whom the Lord drove out before the people of Israel. He sacrificed and made offerings on the high places, on the hills, and under every green tree" (2 Chron. 28:2-4). King Manasseh of Judah did likewise: "He made his son pass through fire" (2 Kings 21:6).

1 Kings tells the story of another long drought in Israel. This is also the famous story of the contest between the Prophet Elijah and the priests of Baal. Both Elijah and the priests of Baal made full sacrifices to their respective gods. This did not end the drought. Elijah then took 450 priests of Baal and "brought them down to the Wadi Kishon, and killed them there." Wadis were gorges and traditional places of human

offerings, according to Tierney (1989). This ended the drought.

The prophet Jeremiah describes a place on the outskirts of Jerusalem known as the "Tophet", or "Valley of the son of Hinnom", or "Valley of Slaughter" (Jer. 19:6). "For the people of Judah have done evil in my sight, says the Lord, they have set their abominations in the house that is called by my name, defiling it. And they go on building the high place of Topheth, which is in the valley of the son of Hinnom, to burn their sons and their daughters in the fire- which I did not command, nor did it come into my mind" (Jer. 7:30-31). Apparently it *did* actually enter Yahweh's mind in the past though; it was his suggestion to Abraham to sacrifice the son, Isaac.

Davies (1981) said it was so named (tophet) "because a great din was made with drums (tophim) to prevent the father hearing the cries of his child as it was burnt." This is where Kings Ahaz and Manasseh, described above, made the burnt offerings of their children.

It would appear that child sacrifice in Judah were ordered to end with the reformations made by King Josiah. Josiah removed from the temple all the vessels made for Baal and Asherah and burned them. He deposed the idolatrous priests. He removed the image of Asherah from the temple and burned it at the Wadi Kidron. He "broke down the houses of the male temple prostitutes that were in the house of the Lord." He "defiled the high places where the priests had made offerings." "He defiled Topheth, which is in the valley of Ben-hinnom, so that no one would make a son or a daughter pass through fire as an offering to Molech." The

Valley of Hinnom became known as Gehenna, the Hebrew word for "hell".

Although Josiah decreed an end to child sacrifice, the writings of both Ezekiel and Jeremiah would suggest that it did not end, as they condemned their contemporaries for the practice. Even after the Babylonian exile there is suggestion that the practice continued for at least a brief time (Isaiah 57: 5-9).

Child sacrifice has been associated with a god by the name of "Molech". However, there is some controversy among scholars about whether the term "*mlk*" refers to a god or whether the term means to "donate for immolation". Otto Eissfeldt and P.G. Mosca advocate for the latter. Levenson (1993) is one who concludes "that the biblical Molech was a chthonic deity honored through the sacrifice of little boys and girls." It could be that the term can mean both, i.e. the specific deity Molech and a general term for human sacrifice.

Although it appears clear that some Israelites made child sacrifices, what isn't clear is whether sacrifices were made only to pagan gods or whether human sacrifices also were made to Yahweh. As I cited previously, Smith (2002) is of the opinion that sacrifices were made in the name of Yahweh.

I mentioned the passage from Exodus 22 earlier that said "The firstborn of your sons you shall give to me". Levenson (1993) suggests some rituals used as substitutions for literally sacrificing as a burnt offering one's firstborn son. He believed the call for "child sacrifice" was not eradicated but was transformed. The substitution rituals were the paschal lamb, Levitical service, monetary ransom, Naziritehood, and perhaps circumcision.

The story of the Passover involves the Israelites slaughtering lambs and applying the blood of the lambs to their doorposts so that their households would be passed over by "the Destroyer" who came to kill the firstborn of the Egyptians. The Israelite's firstborn sons were spared as a result of the sacrifice of the sheep. This animal substitution is also seen in "The Aqedah", the story of Abraham's almost execution of his son, Isaac. Abraham is allowed to substitute a ram in place of his son, Isaac.

The book of Numbers (8:17-18) says the following in regards to Levitical service: "For all the firstborn among the Israelites are mine, both human and animal. On the day that I struck down all the firstborn in the land of Egypt I consecrated them for myself, but I have taken the Levites in place of all the firstborn among the Israelites."

In Numbers 3 it is reported that there are 273 Israelite firstborns who are over and above the number of qualified Levites. These individuals are required to pay money to fulfill their sacrifice. "As the price of redemption of the two hundred seventy-three of the firstborn of the Israelites, over and above the number of the Levites, you shall accept five shekels apiece, reckoning by the shekel of the sanctuary, a shekel of twenty gerahs" (v. 46-47).

Numbers 6 describes special vows men or women may make in order to be a Nazirite. They vow to avoid alcoholic beverage, to not cut their hair or beards, and to avoid corpses. Samson, Samuel and John the Baptist were Nazirites. Levenson (1993) believes that Naziritehood might have functioned as a suitable sacrificial substitution.

Levenson also believed that circumcision may have had some role as a substitution ritual for child sacrifice. "Though I know of no indication that circumcision was ever restricted to the first-born son, this circumstantial evidence that the rite may have once functioned as a substitution ritual for child sacrifice, averting the death of the son, should not be ignored."

Gods of Syria-Palestine

The main gods of the land of Canaan were the creator god and head of the pantheon, El, his sister and mistress Astarte, El's consort Asherah, El's sons Baal and Mot, and El's daughter Anat.

El
El was the father of the gods, the oldest of the gods, "father of mankind," and the head of the "divine council". In texts uncovered at Ugarit, El is portrayed as a benevolent deity, and also one of great power and strength, including sexually. El has many mistresses, but his main consort is Asherah. His sister, Astarte, is also one of El's mistresses. Such incestuous relationships among the gods were common in the myths of the middle east.

More than five hundred references to El have been found in Ugaritic texts. El is said to reside on a sacred mountain, and he is depicted as an aged male with a grey beard. A frequently employed epithet was "the benevolent, good-natured

El". "To El was attributed the kind of wisdom that made him judge everything rightly" (Van Der Toorn, Becking and Van Der Horst, 1999).

El is mentioned 230 times in the Old Testament. Genesis 33: 20 in speaking about Jacob says "There he erected an altar and called it El-Elohe-Israel" (which means "El, the God of Israel"). Unlike the other Canaanite gods such as Baal, El is never spoken of disparagingly in the Old Testament.

Baal
The name "Baal" is mentioned 90 times in the Old Testament, and in contrast to El is portrayed most negatively. Ugaritic texts portray Baal as a divine warrior who sits at El's right hand in council as his chief advisor. Baal is a son of El. The name "Baal" means "Lord" or "Master".

Van Der Toorn et al (1999) write "The worship of Baal demonstrably pervaded the entire area inhabited by the Canaanites. During the period of the Middle Kingdom, if not earlier, the cult was adopted by the Egyptians, along with the cult of other Canaanite gods. In the wake of the Phoenician colonization it eventually spread all over the Mediterranean region."

Baal was both a storm god and a god of fertility. Baal is responsible for bringing forth the rains that nourish the vegetation. When fall comes he disappears to the underworld; the vegetation dies with him. Both are resuscitated in the spring.

Baal

Mot

Mot, another son of El, is god of sterility and the ruler of the Underworld. Although El favored Mot over Baal, Mot was not a god who was worshiped in Canaan. He is to be "regarded as a demonic figure, wholly evil and without redeeming features" (Van Der Toorn et al, 1999). He "dwells in the underworld, which is an unpleasant (muddy) place of decay and destruction."

"Mot is the enemy of Baal in so far as he is the representative of all that is contrary to Baal's nature. Baal represents principally the life-giving fertility associated with essential autumnal rainfall. Mot represents the death-dealing sterility associated, at least in part, with the summer heat and drought" (Van Der Toorn et al, 1999).

Asherah

Asherah is the consort of El and was known also as Athirat (in Ugaritic texts). The name is mentioned forty times in the Old Testament, although most of the references are to a cult object rather than to the goddess herself. Asherah was a fertility goddess and was the mother of minor gods in the Canaanite pantheon. Very interestingly, some scholars (e.g. Israel Finkelstein and Neil Asher Silberman) think that Asherah may have been considered to be a consort of Yahweh as well as El. "She is frequently seen in the position of the tree of life, giving sustenance to animals on either side of her. It is for this reason that the stylized tree of life referred to in the Old Testament is called the 'asherah'" (Tubb, 1998).

The asherah or "asherah pole" was a wooden item that honored the goddess, Asherah and was erected next to the altar of a god. Smith (2002) writes "the asherah was acceptable in both the northern and southern Jewish kingdoms, both outside (see 1 Kings 14:23; 2 Kings 17:10, 16; Jer. 17:2) and inside the royal cults of Samaria (1 Kings 16:33; 2 Kings 13:6) and Jerusalem (2 Kings 21:7; 23:6, 2 Chron. 24:18). Besides Samaria and Jerusalem, devotion to the asherah is attested in Ophrah (Judges 6:25) and Bethel (2 Kings 23:15). From this information, it would appear that the symbol of the asherah was a general feature of Israelite religion." Saul Olyan (1988) notes that the asherah was associated historically with Yahweh, not Baal, and it was not opposed by prophets until the eighth century.

Astarte and Anat

Astarte was the sister of El as well as one of El's mistresses. Astarte was popular in Phoenician cities, particularly Sidon. She was known as a goddess of war. Anat was Baal's consort, a fertility goddess, and the mother of Baal's offspring. She was originally a north-west Semitic goddess. "Anat is depicted in the Ugaritic mythological texts as a volatile, independent, adolescent warrior and hunter" (Van Der Toorn et al, 1999).

Yahweh

Yahweh is not mentioned at all in Ugaritic texts and prior to 1200 BCE the name was not found in any Semitic texts. "The absence of references to a Syrian or Palestinian cult of Yahweh outside Israel suggests that the god does not belong to the traditional circle of West Semitic deities. The origins of his veneration must be sought for elsewhere. A number of texts suggest that Yahweh was worshiped in southern Edom and Midian before his cult spread to Palestine" (Van Der Toorn et al, 1999).

In Exodus 2 we have the story of Moses killing an Egyptian who he found beating a Hebrew. After the crime, Moses fled from the authorities and "settled in the land of Midian". This area is believed to have been in present day Jordan, east of the Gulf of Aqaba. There Moses was given a woman by the name of Zipporah to marry; she was the daughter of a Midianite priest by the name of Jethro. Who was the god that Moses' father-in-law, Jethro, was the priest for?

In chapter 3 of Exodus we have the story of a god speaking to Moses through a burning bush. The god gives himself the cryptic name of "I Am Who I Am" and said he was the god of Moses' ancestors: Abraham, Isaac and Jacob. These patriarchs came out of Mesopotamia and presumably worshiped an unnamed Mesopotamian god, likely a personal or "house god" which was common in Mesopotamia. Exodus 6:2-3 states "God also spoke to Moses and said to him: 'I am the Lord.' I appeared to Abraham, Isaac, and Jacob as God Almighty (or *El Shaddai*), but by my name 'The Lord' (or *Yahweh*) I did not make myself known to them."

It might be noted here that the patriarch, Joseph, son of Jacob, is not mentioned here. It could be that Joseph worshiped the Egyptian deities. The progeny of the patriarchs and their servants were in Egypt for 400 years. In all likelihood they were fully integrated into Egyptian culture including Egyptian religious beliefs.

There are a few passages in the Hebrew scriptures that suggest that Yahweh originated in Edom and Midian:

Deut. 33:2 "The Lord (*Yahweh*) came from Sinai, and dawned from Seir upon us; he shone forth from Mount Paran."

Judges 5:4-5 "Lord (*Yahweh*), when you went out from Seir, when you marched from the region of Edom, the earth trembled, and the heavens poured, the clouds indeed poured water. The mountains quaked before the Lord (*Yahweh*), the One of Sinai, before the Lord (*Yahweh*), the God of Israel."

Hab. 3:3 "God came from Teman, the Holy One from Mount Paran."

- "Seir" is believed to have been located on the east side of the Arabah (the land between the tip of the Gulf of Aqaba and the bottom of the Dead Sea) where the Edomites originally settled.
- "Mount Paran" was believed to be near the "Wilderness of Paran", west of the Arabah.
- Mount Sinai was believed to be either in the south of the Sinai Peninsula or on the other side of the Gulf of Aqaba in the land of Midian.
- "Teman" is on the western edge of the Arabah.

And so all of these Biblical passages suggest the origin of Yahweh to be in the lands of Midian and Edom.

"If Yahweh was at home in the south, then, how did he make his way to the north? According to a widely accepted theory, the Kenites (a branch of the Midianites) were the mediators of the Yahwistic cult. One of the first to advance the Kenite hypothesis was the Dutch historian of religion Cornelis P. Tiele. In 1872 Tiele characterized Yahweh historically as 'the god of the desert, worshiped by the Kenites and their close relatives before the Israelites'. The idea was adopted and elaborated by B. Stade, and it gained considerable support ever since" (Van Der Toorn et al, 1999).

The name "YHWH" appears in the Hebrew scriptures over 6000 times, and it's pronunciation guess is "yahweh". "YHWH" is known as the Tetragrammaton. In Hebrew it is written with four Hebrew letters: *yod*, *he*, *waw*, and *he*. For this reason it is referred as the tetragrammaton, which means "the four letters". Not only is the name also known as Yahweh, but it is also translated to Jehovah, the name used in many of our great hymns.

When you look in many English translations of the Bible, however, you do not always find the name "YHWH". In many early English translations "YHWH" is written as Jehovah. Take for example Exodus 6:2-3 in the King James Version:

- ²And God spake unto Moses, and said unto him, I am the LORD: ³And I appeared unto Abraham, unto Isaac, and unto Jacob, by the name of God Almighty, but by my name JEHOVAH was I not known to them.

In the Douay-Rheims Bible "Jehovah" in this particular passage is written as "Adonai", and in other English versions of the Bible (e.g. NASB, RSV, NRSV) the name is written as "Lord" or "The Lord".

In the third century C.E. Jewish people stopped pronouncing the name of God "YHWH" out loud for fear of violating the 3rd of the Ten Commandments:

- You shall not make wrongful use of the name of the LORD your God, for the LORD will not acquit anyone who misuses his name. (Exodus 20:7)

Henry O. Thompson writes in the Anchor Bible Dictionary (1992): "In antiquity, the significance of a name goes far beyond a mere label. In ancient times, the name held magical power. One who knew the name of the deity could wield power over the deity and summon him to his/her aid. e.g., against one's enemies. The importance of the name is underscored by the story of Jacob wrestling with a divine being who was reticent to reveal his name to Jacob."

Syncretism in the Religion of the Israelites

In my first book of this series, "Evolution of the Bible", I wrote about the "documentary hypothesis", first articulated by the German historian, Julius Wellhausen. Most Biblical scholars do not accept the traditional belief that Moses wrote the Torah. Many believe the Torah are a combination of writings from four principal authors: the Yahwist source (J), the Elohist source (E), the Deuteronomist (D), and the Priestly source (P). The two earliest sources were "E" and "J". The Yahwist source is signified with a "J" because in German Yahweh is spelled with a "J", i.e. Jahwe.

The Yahwist source is believed to have been the earliest and is believed to have come from the southern kingdom of Judah and was written in the ninth or tenth centuries BCE. It is called the "Yahwist source" because god is referred to as "YHWH". The god they describe is very human-like: he walks and talks, enjoys pleasing odors, and has quite a temper. The Elohist source is believed to have come from the northern part of Israel and was believed to have been written in the ninth or eighth centuries BCE. Their god is called "Elohim" and is more benevolent and less anthropomorphic. Van Der Toorn et al (1999) report that the noun "El" occurs in the Old Testament 230 times.

Smith (2002) believes that El was the original god of Israel, as evidenced in part by the name Isra*el* which is an El name and not a Yahwistic name. "This fact would suggest that El was the original chief god of the group named Israel" (Smith, 2002). In the various pantheons of deities in the middle east was the concept of a chief god who ruled over a divine council. This was previously discussed in the chapters of this book on Mesopotamia and Egypt. The same was true in Canaan, where the god El was at least initially seen as the chief god (later writings suggested that his son, Baal, supplanted El in this role). I also might mention here that the noun "El" was used as both a general name for "god" as well as the proper name for the god, El. For example, one might say that "El was an el." It is believed that the specific deity El developed first, and it was only over time that the word became a generic noun for god. I also might add here that English Biblical translations do not make clear the distinctions between Yahweh and El. The Hebrew "YHWH" is probably most often translated into English as "Lord". El may be translated into English as "Most High" or "God".

Psalms 82 speaks of a divine council. "God has taken his place in the divine council; in the midst of the gods he holds judgment" (v. 1). Deuteronomy 32:8-9 describes a distinction between Yahweh and El (Hebrew words in parentheses). The distinction is also made in Exodus 5:2-3.

"When the Most High (elyon) apportioned the nations, when he divided humankind, he fixed the boundaries of the peoples according to the number of the gods; the LORD's (YHWH's) own portion was his people, Jacob his allotted share" (Deut. 32:8-9).

"God also spoke to Moses and said to him: 'I am the Lord. I appeared to Abraham, Isaac, and Jacob as God Almighty (El Shaddai), but by my name 'The Lord' (YHWH) I did not make myself known to them" (Exodus 5:2-3).

"This passage [Deut. 32:8-9] presents an order in which each deity received its own nation. Israel was the nation that Yahweh received. It also suggests that Yahweh, originally a warrior-god from Sinai/Paran/Edom/Teiman, was known separately from El at an early point in early Israel. Perhaps due to trade with Edom/Midian, Yahweh entered secondarily into the Israelite highland religion. Passages such as Deuteronomy 32:8-9 suggest a literary vestige of the initial assimilation of Yahweh, the southern warrior-god, into the larger highland pantheism, headed by El; other texts point to Asherah (El's consort) and to Baal and other deities as members of this pantheon. In time, El and Yahweh were identified, while Yahweh and Baal co-existed and later competed as warrior-gods" (Smith, 2002).

It would seem that the eventual god of Israel was a merger of Yahweh, a god imported into the southern region of Israel with El, the primary Canaanite deity. Although a Canaanite deity, the Hebrew scriptures have no condemnations of El, such as there are of the god, Baal. Baal was an adversary; El was not. Yahweh eventually took on many characteristics of El, i.e. an aged patriarchal god who was merciful, kind and gracious.

My earlier life conception of Israel was of a people generally devoted to the god Yahweh. The worship of other gods such as Baal I had once thought to be aberrations. Actually, evidence suggests that throughout Israel's history up until the Babylonian exile the worship of many gods other than Yahweh was commonplace. Joshua attests to this: "Now therefore revere the Lord, and serve him in sincerity and in faithfulness; put away the gods that your ancestors served beyond the River and in Egypt, and serve the Lord" (Josh. 24:14). Despite this exhortation, the Israelites continued to worship on a large scale other gods besides Yahweh.

"Sacrifices were offered at shrines within domestic compounds, at family tombs, and at open altars throughout the countryside. These places of worship were rarely disturbed, even by the most 'pious' and aggressive of kings. Thus it is no wonder that the Bible repeatedly notes that 'the high places were not taken away" (Finkelstein and Silberman, 2001).

"The existence of high places and other forms of ancestral and household god worship was not - as the books of Kings imply- apostasy from an earlier, purer faith. It was part of the timeless tradition of the hill country settlers of Judah, who worshiped YHWH along with a variety of gods and goddesses known or adapted from the cults of neighboring peoples. YHWH, in short, was worshiped in a wide variety of ways- and sometimes pictured as having a heavenly entourage. From the indirect (and pointedly negative) evidence of the books of Kings, we learn that priests in the countryside also regularly burned incense on the high places to the sun, the moon, and the stars" (Finkelstein and Silberman, 2001).

Another source of evidence for syncretism and Hebrew polytheism is the examination of theophoric names in the Hebrew scriptures. The word "theophoric" means "bearing the name of a god". This was very common in the ancient Near East and Mesopotamia, and many names theophoric for Yahweh included Isaiah, Jeremiah, Joshua and Zechariah. There were many names theophoric for El as well, though, other than Isra*el*. These include Dani*el*, Immanu*el*, Gabri*el*, Ishma*el*, Micha*el*, Nathani*el*, Rapha*el* and Samu*el*. There also were theophoric names for Baal, including King Saul's son Esh-*baal* and Saul's grandson (the son of Jonathan) Merib-*baal* (1 Chron. 8:33-34)

Chapter 5

Ancient Empires

Judges

The book of Judges in the Hebrew scriptures tell us:

"The people worshiped the LORD all the days of Joshua, and all the days of the elders who outlived Joshua, who had seen all the great work that the LORD had done for Israel" (Judges 2:7).

Then Joshua died.

"Then the Israelites did what was evil in the sight of the LORD and worshiped the Baals; and they abandoned the LORD, the God of their ancestors, who had brought them out of the land of Egypt; they followed other gods, from among the gods of the peoples who were all around them, and bowed down to them, and they provoked the LORD to anger. They abandoned the LORD, and worshiped Baal and the Astartes. So the anger of the LORD was kindled against Israel, and he gave them over to plunderers who plundered them, and he sold them into the power of their enemies all around, so that they could no longer withstand their enemies" (Judges 2:11-14).

"Then the LORD raised up judges, who delivered them out of the power of those who plundered them" (Judges 2:16).

This was an ongoing pattern throughout the book of Judges: the Israelites live peacefully until they turn to evil ways, they are then oppressed by others in the land, they cry for deliverance from Yahweh, and then Yahweh sends another "judge" to deliver them. The term "judge" does not refer to the modern day profession of judging guilt and innocence of people. The "judges" in the Old Testament were military heroes.

The period of the judges is often referred to as the "Tribal Period" because this was a confederation of twelve tribes rather than a united nation. Tribes of other Canaanites also lived in the land. And as many archaeologists point out (Finkelstein, Dever), the Israelites were likely for the most part not immigrants or invaders but Canaanites themselves, i.e. native peoples.

The period of the judges lasted approximately from 1200 to 1000 BCE.

In chapter eight of First Samuel, the people of Israel expressed concerns to Samuel about his advanced age and also expressed concerns that Samuel's sons "do not follow in your ways". "Appoint for us, then, a king to govern us, like other nations" (1 Sam. 8:6). Although Samuel was against this idea, God agreed to give the people a king.

The first king was Saul (1025-1005), followed by David (1005-965), followed by Solomon (968-928). This period of these three kings is commonly known as a golden age for a unified Judah. Archaeologists Israel Finkelstein and Neil Asher Silberman (2001) disagree with this assessment. "It is now clear that Iron Age Judah enjoyed no precocious golden age. David and his son Solomon and the subsequent members of the Davidic dynasty ruled over a marginal, isolated, rural region, with no signs of great wealth or centralized administration. It did not suddenly decline into weakness and misfortune from an era of unparalleled prosperity. Instead it underwent a long and gradual development over hundreds of years. David and Solomon's Jerusalem was only one of a number of religious centers within the land of Israel; it was surely not acknowledged as a spiritual center of the entire people of Israel initially."

After Solomon's death, his son, Rehoboam, succeeded him. King Rehoboam made the mistake of listening to his buddies, rather than the experienced court advisers, and decided to take a hard-line approach with his subjects. The people of the northern tribes complained about the use of corvée labor (which is a form of unpaid temporary forced labor) to complete royal building projects. Rehoboam responded to the complaints with "Now, whereas my father laid on you a heavy yoke, I will add to your yoke. My father disciplined you with whips, but I will discipline you with scorpions" (1 Kings 12:11).

As a result, Jeroboam led the northern tribes in a rebellion, and they seceded from the unified kingdom. Jeroboam then reigned over the northern tribes called Israel, and Rehoboam continued to reign over the southern kingdom, Judah. Israel and Judah continued as two separate kingdoms until 722 (for Israel) and 597 (for Judah). The books of First and Second Kings portray *all* the rulers of the northern kingdom of Israel as being evil due to their apostasy. The rulers of the southern kingdom of Judah were presented as evil 60% of the time (twelve out of the twenty rulers).

In reading the two books of Kings, one might get the impression that Judah (which contained the holy city of Jerusalem) was the more important of the two kingdoms. Archaeologists Finkelstein and Silberman (2001) disagree: "In a sense, Judah was little more than Israel's rural hinterland." They also say "There is no doubt that the two Iron Age states- Israel and Judah- had much in common. Both worshiped YHWH (among other deities). Their peoples shared many legends, heroes, and tales about events in the distant past. They also spoke similar languages or dialects of Hebrew."

In 722 the northern kingdom of Israel was conquered by the Assyrian army. The citizens of Israel were dispersed throughout the Assyrian empire to be absorbed into the Assyrian population. This was their method to eliminate nationalistic aspirations by various peoples they conquered. The dispersed Israelites were the "ten lost tribes of Israel". They truly were never heard from again.

Assyrian Empire

Assyria was at a very low point at the end of the tenth century BCE. The kingdom's territory consisted of a narrow strip of land 1,600 kilometers long and 800 kilometers wide. The same family had ruled the land for more than two centuries. It remained a very militaristic society, and one of the king's main duties was to conduct war for the benefit of the state and the god, Assur.

Things started to change around 911 BCE. King Adad-nirari II (911-891 BCE) waged war against the Aramaeans who were driven out of the Tigris valley. Adad-nirari and his son, Ashurnasirpal II to some extent, substantially enlarged the territory of Assyria.

The kingdom of Assyria was greatly expanded under the rule of the cruel and despicable King Ashurnasirpal II (883-859). Although barbarity and terroristic acts were the norm in warfare in those days, Ashurnasirpal II was known to be unsurpassed in this regard. Rebellious leaders of enemy nations were killed, flayed, and had their skin "spread over the walls of their city". Innocent civilians were tortured. Ashurnasirpal II himself wrote:

"Many captives from among them I burned with fire, and many I took as living captives. From some I cut off their noses, their ears and their fingers, of many I put out the eyes. I made one pillar of the living and another of heads, and I bound their heads to tree trunks round about the city. Their young men and maidens I burned in the fire."

One reason for this behavior was to frighten nations into submission rather than attempting to defend themselves and resisting. After submission or military defeat, the foreign states were required to pay an annual tribute. Tribute was made in money or else in specialties of regions, e.g. Phoenicians had to provide cedar logs and purple cloth, the Zagros people had to provide horses, etc. At the end of Ashurnasirpal's reign the boundaries of Assyria were back to where they were in the late second millennium.

Ashurnasirpal's son, Shalmaneser III (858-824), had a thirty-five-year reign that continued military campaigns. Out of the thirty-five years, thirty-one were devoted to war. However, Shalmaneser III did not try to extend the boundaries of Assyria; rather the goal was to protect the borders of Assyria established by his father and to obtain tribute and booty. There were thus two types of territories; those of the land of Assur and those under the *yoke* of Assur.

Assur (also spelled Ashur) was the primary god of the Neo-Assyrian empire. Assur had subsumed all of the qualities of the god Enlil, the previous head of the Mesopotamian pantheon. Assur is also the name of the Assyrian city, the main center of the cult of this god. Assur and the god Marduk (the Babylonian major god) were relatively unknown in the third millennium. Assur became the major god of Assyria in the north, and Marduk became the major god of Babylon in the south. "As Assyria grew in military and political power, so too did their deity. When the Assyrian kings moved their capital to Calah (Nimrud) and then Nineveh, Assur maintained his status as deity of the expanded state" (Schneider, 2011).

"The gods of Assyria benefited from the empire in that their cults were well provided with tribute and booty. As main priest of the god Assur the king supported that cult, and other temples were probably also entirely dependent on the state for their maintenance. Provincial taxes were often collected as temple offerings. There is no evidence, however, that Assyrian cults were imposed upon conquered populations, certainly not at the expense of existing religions. Foreign temples were sacked for their treasuries. There was no religious intolerance and vassal treaties, for instance, were sworn in the names of the vassal's gods as well as those of Assyria" (Van De Mieroop, 2004).

Assyria did not become an "empire" until the reign of Tiglathileser III (744-727). This ruler continued military campaigns and incorporated new lands as part of Assyria proper, not just as vassal states. Assyria had been a landlocked kingdom, and now under Tiglathileser III they gained access to the Mediterranean Sea.

A significant policy of Tiglathileser III was the practice of mass-deportations. The purposes of this practice was to punish rebels, to prevent rebellions, to minimize nationalistic feelings, to populate new border towns in conquered countries, to repopulate abandoned regions, and to provide Assyria with needed workers, i.e. soldiers, laborers, and skilled trades such as craftsmen, artists and scholars. Foreign deportees were subsumed into the Assyrian population;

they were then considered "Assyrian". The number of people forcibly removed from their homes during the reign of Tiglathileser III and his successors over three centuries is estimated at four and a half million.

The book of Second Kings (chapter 16) informs us that Judah's king, Ahaz, had fears of attack from Aram (Syria) and Israel. He sought help from Tiglathileser III who subjugated Damascus, the capital of Syria. Judah becomes a vassal state. Ahaz had an altar built in the Jerusalem temple to the Assyrian god, presumably Assur.

Chapter 17 of Second Kings describes the relationship between King Hoshea of Judah and King Shalmaneser V, Tiglathpileser's son and successor. "Hoshea became his vassal, and paid him tribute. But the king of Assyria found treachery in Hoshea; for he had sent messengers to King So of Egypt, and offered no tribute to the king of Assyria, as he had done year by year; therefore the king of Assyria confined him and imprisoned him. Then the king of Assyria invaded all the land and came to Samaria; for three years he besieged it. In the ninth year of Hoshea the king of Assyria captured Samaria; he carried the Israelites away to Assyria. He placed them in Halah, on the Habor, the river of Gozan, and in the cities of the Medes" (2 Kings 17:3-6).

There is some debate about whether the Assyrian king who actually captured Samaria and dispersed its people was Shalmaneser V or his successor, Sargon II. "The king of Assyria brought people from Babylon, Cuthah, Avva, Hamath, and Sepharvaim, and placed them in the cities of Samaria in place of the people of Israel; they took possession of Samaria, and settled in its cities" (2 Kings 17:24). This was the end of the Kingdom of Israel.

The kingdom of Judah continued on as a vassal of Assyria. Sargon's descendants, known as the "Sargonids", governed Assyria for almost a century (704-609 BCE) and brought the empire to its pinnacle. The kingdom now had access to both the Mediterranean and the Persian Gulf and controlled the entire course of the Tigris and the Euphrates rivers.

Sargon's son, Sennacherib, succeeded him. King Hezekiah of Judah, who was praised in the Hebrew scriptures for attempting to eliminate the worship of gods other than Yahweh in his kingdom, sought also to reverse the policy of his predecessor, King Ahaz, of aligning themselves and paying tribute to Assyria. King Sennacherib responded with an invasion on "all the fortified cities of Judah and captured them." Hezekiah responded to Sennacherib with "I have done wrong; withdraw from me; whatever you impose on me I will bear." Hezekiah paid a mighty ransom, but still Sennacherib was intent on taking Jerusalem and deporting its citizens. According to Second Kings, Yahweh responded by killing 185,000 Assyrian soldiers in the middle of the night. Sennacherib withdrew to his home in Nineveh.

Sennacherib was also known for destroying the illustrious city of Babylon. One must remember that the northern and southern kingdoms in Mesopotamia had a shared culture and language, and Babylon had always been treated with the utmost respect. It is not known whether this is the reason, but Sennacherib was murdered by one or two of his sons. The books of 2 Kings report that his sons Adrammelech and Sharezer killed him.

A third son, Esarhaddon (680-669), succeeded Sennacherib. Esarhaddon's first act was to rebuild Babylon bigger and better than it had been even before. Esarhaddon was succeeded by his son, Ashurbanipal (668-627). Another of his sons, Shamash-shum-ukin, was appointed viceroy in Babylonia. After sixteen years, Shamash-shum-ukin led Babylonia and a coalition of Phoenicia, the Philistines, Judah, the Arabs of the Syrian desert, the Chaldaeans of southern Iraq, the Elamites, Lydia and Egypt against Assyria. War ensued for three years until Assyria prevailed.

It was during this time period that King Josiah (640-609) ruled over Judah. Josiah was reported to be the most righteous king to ever rule over Judah, and some might say that it was his reforms that led to the beginnings of Judaism. It was reported in the book of Second Kings that Josiah found in the Jerusalem Temple a book of law; this was most likely the core laws that are presented in Deuteronomy 12-26. Where did this come from? Nobody knows for sure. Perhaps the laws had been written during the reign of Hezekiah a century earlier, or perhaps they were written during Josiah's reign and only were reported to have been "found".

Josiah destroyed the idols to the various gods, deposed "idolatrous priests", destroyed the asherah which he removed from the Temple, broke down the houses of male prostitution, "defiled Topheth" (the place where human offerings were made), and destroyed the other "high places" and altars. Josiah commanded that the Jerusalem Temple be the only place where Yahweh was to be worshiped, and he demanded that Yahweh was the only god to be worshiped. He also established the observance of Passover which was outlined in the book of law. "Moreover Josiah put away the mediums, wizards, teraphim, idols, and all the abominations that were seen in the land of Judah and in Jerusalem, so that he established the words of the law that were written in the book that the priest Hilkiah had found in the house of the LORD" (2 Kings 23:24).

King Josiah was killed by King Neco of Egypt. Judah was a vassal state of Egypt. Josiah's son, Jehoahaz, took the throne briefly until he was removed from the throne by King Neco and replaced with another of Josiah's sons, Jehoiakim. His reign was followed by Jehoiachin (a confusingly similar name). It is implied that the reforms of Josiah went by the wayside after his death, and the people resumed the worship of many gods other than Yahweh.

During the reign of Ashurbanipal (668-627) Assyria was at the height of its powers and controlled a vast area of land from western Iran to Egypt. Assyria was also much more than just a militaristic society. The Assyrian kings' duties were more than just administrative and militaristic (they fought personally in battles); they also had religious duties. The king was the main priest and earthly representative of the god, Assur, and was responsible for bringing order to Assyria and the entire world.

The Assyrians had strong interest in literature and scholarship. Ashurbanipal had an extensive palace library; many of the literary texts in the library had a history of more than a thousand years. The Assyrians made significant strides in astronomy, mathematics, and medicine.

Babylonian Empire

The Assyrian empire came to an abrupt end around 610 BCE due to conquest by Babylonia and the Medes. The Medes were people from Media in northwestern Iran. In 615 they attacked cities in the heartland of Assyria and formed an alliance with the Babylonians. Together in 612 they sacked the Assyrian capital city of Nineveh. "By the end of 612 BCE the three capital cities of Assyria- Assur, the religious metropolis, Nineveh, the administrative center, and probably Nimrud, the military headquarters- as well as all the main Assyrian towns had been destroyed" (Roux, 1992). "Babylonia took over control of Assyrian territories in Mesopotamia, Syria, and Palestine, while the peoples of the Zagros Mountains, western Iran, and Anatolia regained their independence" (Van De Mieroop, 2004). This was the end of Assyria forever.

The Babylonian ruler was Nabopolassar and he came to power in 626 BCE. His reign was considered the beginning of the last Babylonian dynasty, often referred to as the "Neo-Babylonian Dynasty" or the "Chaldean Dynasty" or "Dynasty XI of Babylon". Babylonia took over most of the territories that Assyria had controlled. Nabopolassar reigned until 605 when he was succeeded by his son, Nebuchadnezzar II (604-562), the greatest military leader of the Neo-Babylonian Dynasty.

Judah became a vassal state of Babylon who took control over the area from Egypt. King Jehoiakim of Judah loyally paid the required tribute for three years but then rebelled. It was in the reign of his son, Jehoiachin, that King Nebuchadnezzar retaliated for this (597 BCE). Jehoiachin was taken prisoner. Nebuchadnezzar "carried off all the treasure of the house of the LORD, and the treasures of the king's house; he cut in pieces all the vessels of gold in the temple of the LORD, which King Solomon of Israel had made, all this as the LORD had foretold. He carried away all Jerusalem, all the officials, all the warriors, ten thousand captives, all the artisans and the smiths; no one remained, except the poorest people of the land" (2 Kings 24:13-14).

Nebuchadnezzar installed 21-year-old Zedekiah to reign over Judah. After several years this king also rebelled against Nebuchadnezzar, who responded with another siege of Jerusalem. Zedekiah was not as fortunate as Jehoiachin, who was treated kindly in Babylon. All of Zedekiah's sons were slaughtered before his eyes. Zedekiah himself had his eyes put out and was blinded. He was then taken in fetters to Babylon. In 587 BCE the city of Jerusalem was again besieged. More of the population were removed by force and taken into exile. Only the poorest of the population were left. Solomon's temple was looted and then destroyed along with most of Jerusalem.

In 582 BCE the governor that was appointed by Nebuchadnezzar was assassinated during a rebellion. Babylonian forces again intervened, and for a third time Judean people were taken into exile. In contrast to the Assyrians, the Babylonians did not repopulate or rebuild territories that they conquered and destroyed. The city of Babylon, in contrast, was continually developed to be the epitome of splendor. Its city-walls and hanging gardens were among the "seven wonders of the ancient world".

Babylon and other cities of Babylonia, due to various deportations of foreign peoples, became multi-ethnic; in these cities people from Syria-Palestine, Phoenicia, Elam, Persia, Media, Ionia, Cilicia, and Egypt lived in close proximity to each other. Aramaic became *lingua franca*, i.e. the language that became the main vernacular. Deportees were influenced by Babylonian culture. "In just one generation, Babylonian personal names, some including the names of Babylonian deities, were adopted by the exiles; even among the family of the Davidides, one finds names like Zerubbabel ("seed of Babylon") and Shenazzar ("the god Sin protects")" (Coogan, 1998), although that "fashion" appeared to be short-lived.

Prior to the Babylonian exile and during the period of the divided kingdoms, the following books of the Hebrew scripture were written:

Genesis	Judges, Ruth	Amos
Exodus	1, 2 Samuel	Micah
Leviticus	1, 2 Kings	Nahum
Numbers	Isaiah	Habakkuk
Deuteronomy	Jeremiah	Zephaniah
Joshua	Hosea	

During the Babylonian exile, the books of Lamentations and Ezekiel were written.

Nebuchadnezzar reigned until 562 BCE. Following his death, three kings ruled in the span of just six years; two of them were assassinated. Nabonidus (555-539) then took the throne; he was well-known for following his mother's devotion to the moon god, Sin, rather than having primary allegiance to Babylon's main god, Marduk.

Marduk's beginning can be found in the Old Babylonian period (and even earlier) when he was considered a son of Enki. He was a god initially associated with thunderstorms. He also was a god associated with the city of Babylon. "As Babylon developed, so did the god. Beginning as the local god and patron of Babylon, Marduk became the god and master of the Babylonia national state and the supreme god and absolute ruler of the universe" (Van Der Toorn et al, 1999). His elevation seems to have been first articulated during the reign of Nebuchadnezzar I (1125-1104) and became the supreme ruler of a universal empire during the Neo-Babylonia empire.

Cosmic Religion, Solar Deities and Astrology

Nabonidus (and his mother in particular) were devotees of the moon god, Sin. In Sumerian the god was known as "Nanna". Nabonidus infuriated the Murduk priesthood by giving special attention to the temples of Sin in Harran and Ur, moving from Babylon to the oasis of Teima in the Arabian Desert (where the cult of the moon god was prominent), and turning several of Marduk's temples in Babylon into sanctuaries for Sin.

Thus far in this book I have not spoken much about solar deities. It makes intuitive sense to me that the sun was something to be worshiped, considering that it is the source of light, heat and life. The sun was represented in Babylonia as the god Shamash (or Utu), who had the power of light over darkness and evil. He was known as the son of Sin, the moon god. The sun, moon, and the planet Venus (represented by the goddess Ishtar or Inanna) formed the great trinity of Babylonian astral religion. Ishtar was the goddess of love, war, fertility and sex.

Hawkes (1962) believes that the sun was worshiped from the early days of farming, and that solar worship was widespread. "There is hardly a region of the world that did not know it at some time and in some form." Some cultures that had solar deities included the Aztecs, the Incans, the Greeks, the Persians, the Romans, the Aborigines, the Chinese, Great Britain (Stonehenge), and the Egyptians. Egyptian gods associated with the sun include Ra, Amun, Aten and Horus.

You might recall King Akhenaten from our chapter on Egypt. He worshiped only one god, Aten, whom he believed was the sole deity. Aten was a sun god. Note Akhenaten's words about Aten in the hymn he wrote glorifying the deity:

"When you shone from the eastern horizon
You filled every land with your beauty.
You are lovely, great and glittering,
You go high above the lands you have made,
Embracing them with your rays,
Holding them fast for your beloved son."

The entire hymn to Aten can be found in Appendix A in this book.

Mesopotamian astrology arose out of astral religion. It was believed that the gods placed signs in the heavens which foretold events to come, both good and evil. By deciphering these signs, people had the opportunity to influence the future. The "ummanu" were specialists in this society who scanned nature for omens. Anything perceived as out of the ordinary, such as eclipses, carried special meanings for the king, the gods' representative on earth.

"The classical planets now familiar to us all had identifications with Babylonian deities, although their attributes were not always identical with the Greco-Roman gods. Marduk was the planet Jupiter, creator and ruler of the heavens, and also the god of life and justice. Nergal was Mars, god of war but also the ruler of the underworld. Nabu was Mercury, god of writing and of all intellectual pursuits. Ninib or Ninurta was the god Saturn, but without sharing Saturn's role as ruler of time; instead he was the god of the hunt. This view that the planets were manifestations of personal deities was one of the motives behind the development of Babylonian astronomy; if the planetary gods were responsible for determining what happened in love or war, in the harvest or the hunt, then the ability to predict celestial positions became tantamount to divining the gods' intentions" (Whitfield, 2001).

In Mesopotamia the planets were known as "the gods of the night". The planets' movements were perceived as having meanings for mankind. The Babylonian astronomers were knowledgeable about the regular patterns of celestial bodies, and any unusual events such as eclipses, comets or even unusual atmospheric events were interpreted as being signs from the gods.

Astrology, the belief in the influence of celestial bodies on humans and human events, gave rise to the science of *astronomy*, which used mathematics to describe the movements of celestial bodies. It was the belief in the celestial bodies' influence on people that proceeded the scientific study of the heavens.

Astrology spread throughout the Mediterranean world. It is mentioned in the Hebrew scriptures (in derogatory terms). A description of King Josiah's reforms within Judah included:

"He deposed the idolatrous priests whom the kings of Judah had ordained to make offerings in the high places at the cities of Judah and around Jerusalem; those also who made offerings to Baal, to the sun, the moon, the constellations, and all the host of the heavens" (2 Kings 23:5).

Isaiah (47:13-14) warns:

You are wearied with your many consultations;
  let those who study the heavens
stand up and save you,
  those who gaze at the stars,
and at each new moon predict
  what shall befall you.
See, they are like stubble,
  the fire consumes them;
they cannot deliver themselves
  from the power of the flame.

The prophet Jeremiah (10:2-3) also preaches:

Thus says the LORD:
Do not learn the way of the nations,
  or be dismayed at the signs of the heavens;
  for the nations are dismayed at them.
For the customs of the peoples are false

Whitfield (2001) concluded "that before 1000 BC the Babylonians had identified several dozen individual stars and had charted their yearly progress across the sky. They had recognized the more complex paths of the planets and, for some of them, had mastered the periodicity of their movements, their risings, settings and times of invisibility. They had begun the process of zoning the sky into three latitudinal bands, which they termed the paths of Anu, Ea and Enlil, after the three great gods of sky, water and air."

"We do know that astrology evolved into a systematized science- in the sense of an elaborate rule-based system with its own internal logic- by 1000 BCE. By then it covered nearly all observable celestial phenomena, permitting detailed predictions of unanticipated events and giving detailed answers to precise questions" (Campion, 2008),

Between the seventh and the fifth centuries BCE the path of the sun was divided into twelve zones or units. Let me take a moment here to review the astronomical basis for the calendar. A day lasts for 24 hours because that is the length of time it takes for the earth to revolve on its axis. The length of time of a year is based on the time it takes for the earth to make one revolution around the sun. A month is based on the time it takes for the moon to make one revolution around the earth.

The term *ecliptic* refers to an imaginary line that marks the earth's revolution around the sun during the course of one year. *Ecliptic* gets its name because eclipses can occur along this line. A *solar* eclipse happens when the moon is directly between the earth and the sun, blocking out the sunlight on the earth from the sun. A *lunar* eclipse happens when the earth is directly between the sun and the moon which blocks light onto the moon.

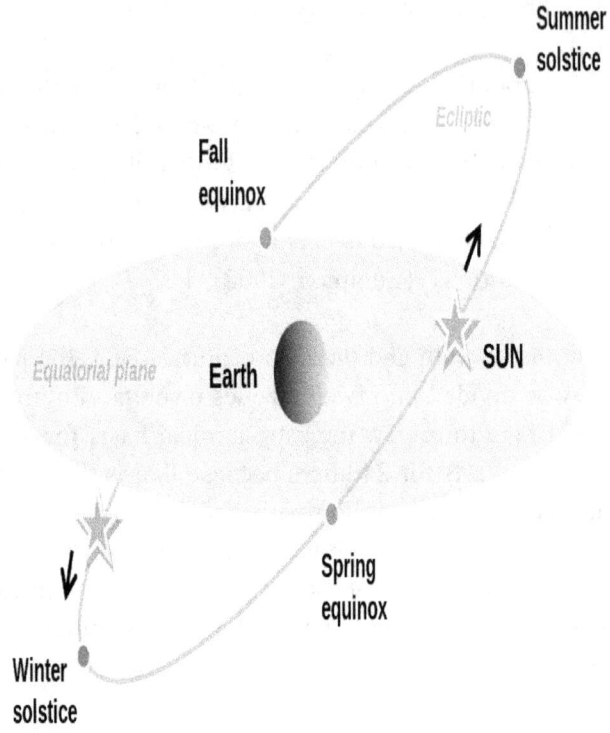

Courtesy of Wikimedia

Although we all know now that the earth revolves around the sun and not vice-versa, the Babylonians believed the sun, moon and planets revolved around the earth. Certainly through observation it does appear that the sun revolves around the earth. It rises in the east, sets in the west, and remains within a ribbon of space. That strip of sky is the *ecliptic*.

The ecliptic is a circle and thus has 360°. This is divided into twelve equal parts, each of 30°. The band of space surrounding the ecliptic (8° on each side) is the *zodiac*. So there are twelve signs of the zodiac. The stars that exist along the length of the ecliptic form the constellations of the zodiac. When the Babylonians were establishing the principles of astrology the constellations and the signs of the zodiac matched; they no longer do due to a process known as *precession of the equinoxes*, which is a 26,000 cycle. In the year 2380 the signs and constellations of the zodiac will again be at the position where they were for the ancient Babylonians.

The Babylonians believed that the various zodiac signs and planets were entities that had various qualities and powers. Also during this time period there was a belief in *hemerologies*, i.e. belief in lucky and unlucky days. The linking of the ideas of lucky/unlucky days with the observation of celestial omens led to the development of personal horoscopes.

The Babylonians believed that by knowing an individual's exact moment of birth we could mathematically figure out the positions of the sun, moon and planets within the zodiac at that moment. That then would tell us that individual's horoscope and the ability to predict events in the future for that individual.

On what basis did the Babylonians develop these ideas? What was the basis for their predictions? Did they gather any data to support their theories? We have absolutely no idea. There are no documents found from that time period to explain why they thought what they thought. Even today astrologers admit that they have no idea why astrology works, only (they maintain) that it does work. Actually, there is no scientific evidence that it does work.

Persian Empire

The Achaemenid (Persian) Empire began during the rule of Cyrus who rose to power in 559 BCE. The history of Persia/Iran stretches back millennia. Early inhabitants of the land were the Elamites. Their civilization can be traced back to the fourth millennium BCE, contemporary to the Sumerians. Aryan tribes moved into the area in the second millennium, and the Persians are believed to be descendants of them. Unfortunately written records from the Elamites and the early Persians are scarce.

There were a number of tribes that lived throughout Iran: Medes, Parthians, Hyrcanians, Areians, and Scythians. The heartland was located in the south-west of Iran, the region that today is called Fars. "Starting in the early sixth century, a local dynasty traced its ancestry back to a man called Achaemenes, and the term Achaemenids is often used to refer to the Persians. In 559 Cyrus came to power, and in 550 he defeated the Median ruler Ishtumegu" (Van De Mieroop, 2004).

With this military victory, Cyrus took over the entire area that had been controlled by the Medes. In 547 Cyrus defeated King Croesus of Lydia. In 539 he marched against Babylonia and defeated them. With this he took over the entire Neo-Babylonian empire.

One result of Cyrus' conquest of Babylonia was the return of the peoples that the Babylonians deported (including the

Jewish exiles) to their homelands. Cyrus is quoted in Ezra 1:2-4:

The LORD, the God of heaven, has given me all the kingdoms of the earth, and he has charged me to build him a house at Jerusalem in Judah. Any of those among you who are of his people—may their God be with them!—are now permitted to go up to Jerusalem in Judah, and rebuild the house of the LORD, the God of Israel—he is the God who is in Jerusalem; and let all survivors, in whatever place they reside, be assisted by the people of their place with silver and gold, with goods and with animals, besides freewill offerings for the house of God in Jerusalem."

Cyrus certainly had a different policy than the Babylonian King Nebuchadnezzar, who deported peoples of conquered lands to prevent nationalistic uprisings. Cyrus showed respect to these peoples and their customs and religions. Likely this was done in self-interest though, i.e. to gain these people's favor and allegiance. Indeed Deutero-Isaiah (45:1) refers to Cyrus as the Lord's anointed and as Yahweh's shepherd (44:28). Many, but not all Israelites, returned to their homeland from Babylon and other places.

The prophet Ezra decreed that the Israelite men who returned from the Diaspora should divorce their foreign wives and send their children away to ensure purity of the Israelite community. In Nehemiah 8 we are told that Ezra recited out loud from the Torah for the people to hear. This is the first time we hear of there being written scripture. Scholars believe the Pentateuch (writings from "P", "J", "E" and "D" as described in my own first book) came together during the Babylonian captivity, which would have been important to preserve Jewish traditions and to keep cohesiveness in the Jewish community in Babylon.

It was during the Persian Period that the following books of the Hebrew scriptures were written:

1, 2 Chronicles	Obadiah
Ezra	Jonah
Nehemiah	Haggai
Esther	Zechariah
Job	Malachi
Psalms	Ecclesiastes
Proverbs	Song of Solomon
Joel	

Astrology was prevalent in Persia as it was in Babylonia and Assyria. "It is also at this time that a new class of astrologers emerged into the historical record, in addition to the temple scribes of Mesopotamia. These were the magi, who arrived in Babylon with the city's Persian conqueror, Cyrus (559-530). These new astrologers' fame is attested by the well-known version of Christ's nativity recorded in Matthew's Gospel, in which the first individuals to venerate Christ, were Persian priest-astrologers. The Gospel writer's clear intent was to gain credibility for Christ's claim to be the son of God by linking it with the most renowned astrologers of the time, who would surely have known the mind of heaven" (Campion, 2008).

Zoroastrianism

The primary religion of the Persian Empire was Zoroastrianism. It is founded on the teachings of the prophet Zoroaster, also known as Zarausthra. Scholars are not sure when Zoroaster lived. Estimates range anywhere from 1800 BCE to the sixth century BCE. Some scholars believe he was a mythical figure who actually never lived.

Boyce (1979) maintains that Zoroastrianism is "the oldest of the revealed credal religions" and "some of its leading doctrines were adopted by Judaism, Christianity and Islam, as well as by a host of Gnostic faiths." Boyce reports that the religion (as well as Brahmanism) contain elements from the very ancient religion of the Proto-Indo-Iranians, i.e. the common ancestors of the Iranians and the Indians.

Zoroaster was said to have been a priest for the old Indo-Iranian religion. He composed seventeen hymns, called the Gathas, which were said to have been inspired by God. This special revelation was said to have occurred when Zoroaster was thirty. The Gathas were handed down orally from generation to generation until they were finally written down during the Sasanian Empire, perhaps the third or fourth century C.E

The prophet saw Ahura Mazda and six other radiant beings (the *heptad* or "seven") in a vision. Ahura Mazda was one of three great Ahuras (divinities) of the old religion. The other two ahuras were Mithra and Varuna. Zoroaster made the startling proclamation that Mazda was "the one uncreated God, existing eternally, and Creator of all else that is good, including all other beneficent divinities" (Boyce, 1979). This was perhaps the first statement of monotheism, predating perhaps even Akhenaten of Egypt. Zoroaster came to believe that all other divinities were manifestations of the one true god, Mazda, and he wanted Mazda to be worshiped as the foremost deity.

Zoroaster believed that Mazda created the world in seven stages. Mazda's first act was to evoke six lesser divinities, who together with Mazda made up the heptad. These six divinities in turn created other beneficent divinities, the gods of the pagan Iranian pantheon. Zoroaster taught also that there was an evil chief god, called Ahriman. It is not clear where this evil chief god came from; was Ahriman created by Mazda? Ahriman was the leaders of other evil gods, known as *daevas*, among them a relatively popular god among the warrior caste, known as Indra. The good gods (*ahuras*) were in battle with the evil gods (*daevas*). It is up to humans to choose either good or evil, and we will be judged when we die on our choices.

This teaching, that people would be judged on their behavior while alive, was revolutionary at this time. The belief of religions at this time was that gods, who were very human-like with both good and bad qualities, needed to be appeased so that rewards could be reaped in this life on earth. Early religion did not emphasize the importance of morality. There was no concept of a final judgment by God. There was no belief in a heaven or a hell, which Zoroaster in fact introduced.

"Many of Zoroaster's fundamental doctrines became disseminated throughout the region, from Egypt to the Black Sea; namely that there is a supreme God who is the Creator; that an evil power exists which is opposed to him, and not under his control; that he has emanated many lesser divinities to help combat this power; that he has created this world for a purpose, and that in its present state it will have an end; that this end will be heralded by the coming of a cosmic Saviour, who will help to bring it about; that meantime heaven and hell exist, with an individual judgment to decide the fate of each soul at death; that at the end of time there will be a resurrection of the dead and a Last Judgment, with annihilation of the wicked; and that thereafter the kingdom of God will come upon earth, and the righteous will enter into it as into a garden (a Persian word for which is 'paradise'), and be happy there in the presence of God for ever, immortal themselves in body as well as soul" (Boyce, 1979).

"These doctrines all came to be adopted by various Jewish schools in the post-Exilic period, for the Jews were one of the peoples, it seems, most open to Zoroastrian influences, a tiny minority, holding staunchly to their own beliefs, but evidently admiring their Persian benefactors, and finding congenial elements in their faith" (Boyce, 1979).

It was after the Persian Period and in the Greek Period that the last book of the Hebrew canon was written: the book of Daniel. It is not until this writing (and another of the latest writings of the Hebrew canon, Ecclesiastes), that the idea of a Day of Judgment appeared in Judaism. Also in the book of Daniel is the Zoroastrian themes of an apocalyptic end to the world, resurrection of the deceased, and judgment of individuals based on the moral quality of their lives. The concept of resurrection of the dead was also found in another writing of this time period, Second Maccabees, although an Apocryphal book. Another Apocryphal book of this time period, Wisdom of Solomon, is one of the earliest Jewish writings to present a doctrine of the immortality of the soul with the righteous being rewarded and the wicked going to Hades.

Another noteworthy writing of this time period is 1 Enoch, although it is not part of the Jewish canon or the Apocrypha. It is mentioned, however, in the canonical book of Jude. This writing discusses the origins of evil (fallen angels, Satan) and a day of judgment in which the righteous will be granted peace and the wicked will be destroyed.

The Axial Age

"Big History" is a term used to refer to the study of history from the beginning of time to now and interweaving information from diverse disciplines of study into a single story. It seeks to describe the big picture of history; a focus with a wide angle lens rather than the use of a telescope or microscope, which is the goal of many scientific disciplines. Many in western civilization perceive human history as being centered around the life of Jesus Christ. Our modern calendars reflect this; all history before Christ is designated *BC* or *BCE*, and all history after Christ is designated *AD* or *CE*. The German philosopher Hegel, as quoted by Karl Jaspers (1953), said that all history goes toward and comes from Christ.

Others believe that there was another time period that was crucial in man's history, particularly for spiritual development. That time period was termed *The Axial Age* by German philosopher and psychiatrist Karl Jaspers. This is the period of time from 800 BCE and 200 BCE. "The most extraordinary events are concentrated in this period. Confucius and Lao-tse were living in China, all the schools of Chinese philosophy came into being, including those of Mo-ti, Chuang-tse, Lieh-tsu and a host of others; India produced the Upanishads and Buddha and, like China, ran the whole gamut of philosophical possibilities down to skepticism, to materialism, sophism and nihilism; in Iran Zarathustra taught a challenging view of the world as a struggle between good and evil; in Palestine the prophets made their appearance, from Elijah, by way of Isaiah and Jeremiah to Deutero-Isaiah; Greece witnessed the appearance of Homer, of the philosophers- Parmenides, Heraclitus and Plato- of the tragedians, Thucydides and Archimedes. Everything implied by these names developed during these few centuries almost simultaneously in China, India, and the West, without any one of these regions knowing of the others" (Jaspers, 1953).

Jaspers said others before him discussed the Axial Period. He quotes philosopher Ernst von Lasaulx: "It cannot possibly be an accident that, six hundred years before Christ, Zarathustra in Persia, Gautama Buddha in India, Confucius in China, the prophets in Israel, King Numa in Rome and the first philosophers- Ionians, Dorians and Eleatics- in Hellas, all made their appearance pretty well simultaneously as reformers of the national religion."

Jaspers also quotes Viktor von Strauss: "During the centuries when Lao-tse and Confucius were living in China, a strange movement of the spirit passed through all civilised peoples. In Israel Jeremiah, Habakkuk, Daniel and Ezekiel were prophesying and in a renewed generation (521-516) the second temple was erected in Jerusalem. Among the Greeks Thales was still living, Anaximander, Pythagoras, Heraclitus and Xenopohanes appeared and Parmenides was born. In Persia an important reformation of Zarathustra's ancient teaching seems to have been carried through, and India produced Sakyamuni, the founder of Buddhism."

The Axial Age was the time period for the beginnings of the world religions. Jaspers sees this period as the third of four critical stages in the evolution of man.

1. The genesis of speech, the use of tools, and the use of fire "through which he first became man".
2. The establishment of the first ancient civilizations.
3. The Axial Period "through which, spiritually, he [man] unfolded his full human potentialities".
4. The scientific-technological age.

Prior to the Axial Age, the purpose of religion was for *cosmic maintenance,* using the terminology of theologian John Hick (1991). Humans completed various rituals, including making sacrifices and having festivals, to appease various gods. The goal was to make amends for mistakes or sins, or to entreat gods for favors such as rain, cure from disease, victory in battle, etc. During the Axial Age the purpose of religion shifted to *personal transformation*, again using Hick's terminology. Individuals began working on making personal changes in order to achieve greater happiness or the possibility of immortality or a glorious afterlife. There was expansion of the notion of goodness from the flourishing of one's self, family or tribe to an ever widening circle.

During this period of time there was greater self-reflection, self-awareness, and self-consciousness. Philosophers, ascetics, wandering thinkers, and prophets began to appear. There was increasing contemplation and fear about death. Associated with this growing concern about death was a growing concern about ethics and morality. We can see this shift in the religion of the Hebrews. It was not until the prophets that we saw an emphasis on justice issues rather than on just appeasing God. Prior to Moses religion involved for Abraham and his offspring primarily circumcision and making burnt offerings. With Moses we have the addition of various laws to keep, with the purpose again being of appeasing God or for keeping law and order in the Israelite community. There was no concept for a heavenly reward or an emphasis on helping the downtrodden for justice's sake.

With the Hebrew prophets there now was an emphasis on helping the poor, children, widows, the downtrodden. These prophets included Amos, Micah, Isaiah, Jeremiah, and Trito-Isaiah.

Amos in chapters 5-6 strongly condemns religious hypocrisy and economic inequality. The following is from Chapter 5: 21-24:

[21] I hate, I despise your festivals,
   and I take no delight in your solemn assemblies.
[22] Even though you offer me your burnt offerings and grain offerings,
   I will not accept them;
and the offerings of well-being of your fatted animals
   I will not look upon.
[23] Take away from me the noise of your songs;
   I will not listen to the melody of your harps.
[24] But let justice roll down like waters,
   and righteousness like an ever-flowing stream.

Micah decries the "rulers of the house of Jacob and chiefs of the house of Israel, who abhor justice and pervert all equity" (Micah 3:9).

Isaiah said "Wash yourselves; make yourselves clean; remove the evil of your doings from before my eyes; cease to do evil, learn to do good; seek justice, rescue the oppressed, defend the orphan, plead for the widow." (Isa 1:16-17). In chapter 10: "Ah, you who make iniquitous decrees, who write oppressive statutes, to turn aside the needy from justice and to rob the poor of my people of their right, that widows may be your spoil, and that you may make the orphans your prey!" (vs. 1-2).

Jeremiah exhorts in chapter 22: "Act with justice and righteousness, and deliver from the hand of the oppressor anyone who has been robbed. And do no wrong or violence to the alien, the orphan, and the widow, or shed innocent blood in this place." (v. 3).

Trito-Isaiah in chapter 58:6-7:

[6] Is not this the fast that I choose:
   to loose the bonds of injustice,
   to undo the thongs of the yoke,
to let the oppressed go free,
   and to break every yoke?
[7] Is it not to share your bread with the hungry,
   and bring the homeless poor into your house;
when you see the naked, to cover them,
   and not to hide yourself from your own kin?

The Axial Age was the beginning of the end of the mythical age; rationality now was integrated into religions, i.e. *logos* instead of *mythos*. With this change came more transcendent conceptualizations of God. According to Jaspers "This overall modification of humanity may be termed *spiritualisa-*

tion." Jaspers believed the changes that happened in the Axial Age were due to biological evolution.

Karen Armstrong (2006) also wrote about this pivotal age and termed it "the great transformation". "Before the Axial Age, ritual and animal sacrifice had been central to the religious quest. You experienced the divine in sacred dramas that, like a great theatrical experience today, introduced you to another level of existence. The Axial sages changed this; they still valued ritual, but gave it a new ethical significance and put morality at the heart of the spiritual life. The only way you could encounter what they called 'God,' 'Nirvana,' 'Brahman,' or the 'Way' was to live a compassionate life." "All the sages preached a spirituality of empathy and compassion; they insisted that people must abandon their egotism and greed, their violence and unkindness."

Chapter 6

Greco-Roman Age

Greek Empire

Cyrus "the Great" died in battle in 530. He was succeeded by his son, Cambyses (529-22). Cambyses was able to conquer Egypt in 525. Rather than just raiding and plundering Egypt and making it a vassal, Egypt was incorporated into the Persian Empire. Cambyses became king of Egypt and actually resided there until 522. Darius I ruled from 521-486 and was able to conquer Libya and to exact tribute from Nubia. Western India also was annexed. (Van De Mieroop, 2004). From that point on until the end of the Persian Empire the King of Persia also became the Pharaoh of Egypt. The Achaemenid Empire remained vital for over 200 years (550-330 BCE).

Alexander III (who was to become "Alexander the Great"), the son of Macedonian King Philip II, was born in 356 BCE. In his youth he was tutored by the philosopher Aristotle. His father, Philip, was assassinated in 336, and Alexander then assumed the throne. Alexander had military ambitions and invaded the Achaemenid Empire in 334. In 332 he became the Pharaoh of Egypt, replacing Darius III. In 330 he became the King of Persia, again replacing Darius III. In 331 he became known as the King of Asia, a title previously unknown. Alexander became known as one of the greatest military commanders to have ever lived.

With Alexander's conquests, Judea too came under Greek rule. Alexander died at the young age of 33 in 323 BCE. At that point the empire was divided into three parts; The Ptolemaic Empire in Egypt, the Seleucid Empire in Asia, and the Antigonid Dynasty in Greece itself. Initially Judea was under the control of the Ptolemies and were given significant independence. As a result of war at the end of the third century, Judea went under Syrian Seleucid control.

The Seleucids were more oppressive than the Ptolemaics. Jews were prohibited from practicing their religion, and the temple was desecrated by having a foreign deity's statue installed. The Jewish people revolted and took control over Jerusalem. They purified and rededicated the temple, an event now commemorated as Hanukkah.

A very important consequence of the Greek conquests was the concept of *hellenization*. Greek culture and language spread throughout the territories that were conquered by the Greeks. Ancient Greece is often considered the birthplace of western culture and of democracy. Of most importance, I believe, was the development and reliance on logic and rational thinking. The Greeks were pioneers in many scientific disciplines including geometry, history, biology, physics, medicine and philosophy. They also were proficient in various art forms and introduced epic and lyric poetry, tragedies and comedies.

Philo was an exemplary example of a Hellenistic Jew. Philo was a member of a prominent Jewish family who lived in Alexandria. Although the city was in Egypt, it was founded by Alexander the Great and was a center of Hellenistic culture. Philo was roughly a contemporary of Jesus, and Alexandria was under the rule of the Roman Empire. Philo sought to find a synthesis between the Jewish religion and Greek philosophy; between faith and reason.

Philo interpreted the Hebrew scriptures allegorically in many instances. He perceived God as being much more transcendent and ineffable than the anthropomorphic god often portrayed in the earliest written scriptures. He conceived of God as having a *logos*, which was a divine order to the universe. Before the world was created there was the *logos*, the divine animating algorithm that mediated between the transcendent God and the material world. Living over two thousand years ago, Philo was a very progressive thinker.

The major deities of the Greek pantheon were known as The *Twelve Olympians*; they were said to reside on Mount Olympus. These gods were basically flawed human beings who had superhuman powers. They could be cruel, jealous, insecure, passionate or petty. The Greeks, as with other ancient religions, were unconcerned about religious beliefs. The concern was to appease the gods with sacrifices, ritual dances and prayers. A body of rules developed to govern the proper performance of rituals. The following are the major Greek gods:

Zeus was the king of the gods and ruler of Mount Olympus. He came to power by overthrowing his father, Cronus, king of the Titans. The new pantheon he ruled was made up primarily of his siblings and children. His wife and sister was Hera, although he had other lovers. He was the god of the sky, lightning/thunder, and order/justice.

Hera, the wife of Zeus, was the queen of the gods. She was the goddess of marriage and family and was very jealous and vindictive of her husband Zeus's affairs.

Poseidon was the god of the seas and also of earthquakes. He was the middle son of Cronus and Rhea.

Demeter was the goddess of agriculture, the seasons, and fertility. She was the middle daughter of Cronus and Rhea.

Athena was the goddess of reason, wisdom and warfare. She was the daughter of Zeus.

Apollo, the twin brother of Artemis and son of Zeus and Leto, was the god of light, prophecy, the arts and medicine.

Artemis, twin sister of Apollo, was the goddess of hunting.

Ares was god of bloodlust and war. He was despised by the other gods. He was a son of Zeus and Hera.

Aphrodite was goddess of love, sex and beauty.

Hephaestus was the god of fire and blacksmiths. He was the son of Hera and Zeus.

Hermes was the messenger of the gods and was a pastoral figure responsible for protecting livestock. He was the son of Zeus and the nymph Maia.

Hestia was the eldest child of Cronus and Rhea. She was goddess of the hearth and domesticity.

Dionysus was a son of Zeus and born to a mortal mother. He was god of wine, intoxication and debauchery.

Hades was the god of the underworld, also known as Hades. He was the oldest son of Cronus and Rhea.

Astrology spread throughout the ancient near east including Egypt, Persia and also to Greece. Astronomy, the science of celestial objects and the physical universe, further developed with the Greeks due to the work of Eudoxus, Apollonius, Hipparchus and especially Ptolemy. "Celestial geometry achieved the power to predict the position of any star or planet in any epoch, past, present or future" (Whitfield, 2001).

The Greeks did not worship heavenly bodies as deities, as did the Babylonians, so why did astrology become popular amongst the Greeks? Whitfield believes the eastern religions held some appeal to them and led them to an interest in astrology. "By around 400 BCE, the era of Plato, the Greeks had re-named the five planets as the stars of Zeus, Kronos, Ares, Aphrodite and Hermes, corresponding directly to Babylonian gods Marduk, Ninib, Nergal, Ishtar and Nabu. The Greek names became, in their Latin equivalents, Jupiter, Saturn, Mars, Venus and Mercury."

Whitfield (2001) gives a nice summary of the development of astrology in the Greek world:

"First, a mature form of astronomy had been learned from Babylonia, central to which was the mathematical description of the movements of the heavens, but which also involved the firm belief that what happened in the heavens foretold in some way what was to happen on earth

Second, a more elevated and spiritual philosophy of man was evolving, drawn from eastern sources, in which man's soul was linked to transcendent powers which dwelled in the heavens. These ideas were articulated by the leading thinkers of the Greek world, Plato and Aristotle.

Third, the Stoic school of philosophy sought to show that the processes of nature and history were not the result of blind chance but were the workings of a divine reason which shaped human destiny and which man must learn to accept.

All these intellectual movements, in their different ways, carried with them a powerful motive to study the heavens in an attempt to uncover the link between man and the stars. If there was a divine reason shaping the destiny of man and the universe, how exactly could the heavens be read so as to make it accessible? Was there a code, a scientific language, which could unlock these secrets? This was the essential background to the development of astrology in the Greek world."

Philosophy as Religion

Greek mythology was at odds with the developing emphasis on rational thought. Myths began to be thought of as stories or legends to explain the past and they were often derided by philosophers as superstitions. Philosophy strived for the pursuit of knowledge and virtue by using reason and discouraging emotions as a ruling force for behaviors. The philosophies promised followers "self-sufficient, imperturbable tranquility that provided protection from the miseries and vicissitudes of life" (Tripolitis, 2002).

Various philosophical schools developed in classical Greece, and most of these schools were influenced in some way by the philosopher, Socrates. We do not have any actual writings of Socrates; we know about him through writings of his student, Plato. Socrates said that his own wisdom came from realizing how much ignorance he had. His mission then became to ask searching questions and to dialogue with others in the quest for discerning truth.

Plato (427-347 BCE),

Socrates' student, wrote about Socrates' philosophies but even more so about his own philosophy. Like Socrates he emphasized the benefits of questioning and contemplation. He founded Greece's first university, the Academy, and became very influential to subsequent Greek philosophers as well as to Judaism and Christianity. Plato wrote often about the soul; he drew a rather sharp distinction between the immortal, divine soul and the mortal, corrupt body. He believed souls were immortal, could be reincarnated, and could be rewarded or punished for behaviors in previous lives.

Plato believed emotions and "appetites" needed to be controlled by reason. He also taught that what is perceived in the physical world is only a shadow of that which is real, which can only be perceived through abstract reasoning. One of the writings that explains this is the "Myth of the Cave" from the *Republic*. Everett Ferguson (2003) wrote a nice summary of this story:

"Human beings, according to the myth, live in a cave, where from birth they are chained facing the inside wall. Outside the mouth of the cave a fire is burning. Between the fire and the entrance to the cave other beings pass by and cast their shadows on the inside wall. We never see anything but the shadows, hence we mistake that for reality. We know only shadows of reality and shadows of ourselves. We cannot turn around to look at each other. To 'know thyself' is to get out of the cave. Some break their chain and turn around. The light from outside after the darkness of the cave is dazzling. Those who cannot stand the light prefer to remain in

the cave. A few overcome the initial dazzlement and march out past the fire. These climb a steep hill and finally reach the top where they can see the sun. After an experience of ecstasy they return to the cave, because they have a duty to their fellow prisoners. As they return, they experience a second bewilderment. Accustomed to the light, they stumble in the darkness of the cave. Those who remained in the cave laugh at them and are so impatient with their stumbling that they may put them to death.

The meaning of the allegory is that the philosopher who has seen the world of ideas can explain the realities better than those who know only this shadowy world of sense. Some who have seen the light, however, cannot stand the truth. But those who know only darkness treat harshly those who have come from the world of light. The chains that blind people are their prejudices and appetites. The real truth is represented by the sun, not by man-made fire. The highest life is a combination of contemplation (the mountaintop) and action (returning to instruct others), of theory and practice."

Pythagoras

One of the earliest philosophers who lived in the sixth century BCE, he believed that the *psyche* (the soul or human essence) was a spark of divine reason that was trapped in the body. It is the goal of humans to purify the soul by acquiring knowledge that would enable one to lead a virtuous life. This process could take several lifetimes. Upon death the soul leaves the body and transfers to another body in a process known as *metempsychosis*. We know about Pythagoras's ideas only from later followers of his from his "school" of learning. Pythagoras was said to have worked miracles. He advocated a disciplined life including abstention from the use of animal products. He believed the cosmos could be understood through mathematics. He is probably best known now for his Pythagorean theorem in geometry.

Epicurus (341-270 BCE)

He founded the Epicurean school of philosophy. Epicurus intended that his philosophy would be an alternative to the superstitions of Greek mythology which created anxieties due to concerns about offending the various gods. Epicurus taught that the gods did not care about human behaviors, and that human existence ended with death. Thus one should focus on living a pleasurable life "of prudence, virtue, and justice and being in complete control of all the physical pleasures, the passions, desires, and needs that might be a hindrance to the tranquility of the soul" (Tripolitis, 2002). The philosophy does not seem dissimilar to me than the philosophy of the author of the Hebrew book of Ecclesiastes. The Epicureans called the process of controlling emotions and eliminating fear *ataraxia*.

Zeno (335-265 BCE)

He founded the school of Stoicism. Tripolitis (2002) characterizes this school as "the most popular and influential philosophical system from the 3rd century BCE to the early 2nd century CE. It was both metaphysical and a system of ethics with the primary interest and emphasis on ethics." The stoics were *pantheistic*, i.e. they believed that everything is a part of God. "The stoics claimed that the universe is a single ordered whole, a perfect organism that unites within itself all that exists in the world. It is ruled by a supreme cosmic power, a fiery substance that the Stoics called Logos, Divine Reason, or God. The Logos is the organizing, integrating, and energizing principle of the whole universe" (Tripolitis, 2002).

Each individual soul is but a part of this Logos (God). It should be the goal of each individual to pursue *Virtue*, which is to live in harmony with God. We do this by controlling passions and emotions. Since everyone is an equal part of the Logos or universal brotherhood, we should treat each other with love. Public service was encouraged. These ideas would have a significant impact on Judaism and Christianity, particularly the writings of Philo of Alexandria and the writer of the Gospel of John and the Johannine School. This philosophy also influenced another Greek group known as the Cynics. These individuals strove to live in accord with nature and to live an ascetic lifestyle, denouncing worldly pleasures.

Middle-Platonism, Neoplatonism and the Trinity

"The Platonic revival, which had begun on a modest scale in the latter part of the 1st century BCE, developed by the 2nd century CE into a philosophical movement known as Middle Platonism" (Tripolitis, 2002). Philosophers such as Numenius and Albinus combined ideas of Plato, Aristotle, the Stoics and Pythagoras into a philosophy that was known as *Middle Platonism*. A core belief was that human souls are part of the divine that have descended into the material world of matter. These philosophers postulated three divine beings: the supreme God called "The One" or "The Good" who is unchanging and transcendent (Plato's concept of *forms* is part of this supreme god), a lesser creator God who governs the world, and human souls which are also part of the divine. Human souls have descended from the divine and have become embodied in the material world. The goal then is to leave the evil material world and return to the divine. Albinus wrote that the aim for individuals was to become as much like god as possible. This was accomplished through knowledge of god (Tripolitis, 2002).

These ideas remind one of an early Christian group known as the *Marcionites*, whom I wrote about in volume one of this series. These devotees of the apostle Paul believed there were two gods: the wrathful, creator god of the Hebrew scriptures, and the loving, supreme god talked about by Jesus.

Middle Platonism was succeeded by *Neoplatonism*. Plotinus (204-270 CE) is generally considered its founder. Plotinus also taught that there was a supreme and totally transcendent "One". Emanating from the "One" is the Divine Mind or *Nous* which is a mediation of the Unknowable One. Emanating from the *Nous* is the Soul of the All. From the World Soul emanates the individual human souls.

The teachings of the middle Platonists and the Neo-Platonist might remind one of the Christian trinity. Where did the idea of the Christian trinity come from? It is not taught in the Hebrew scriptures, and it is not explicitly taught in the Christian New Testament. There are two verses in the New Testament that are used to support a Trinitarian view: 1 John 5:7-8

The King James version (KJV) of the Bible translates the passage from Greek as thus:

7 For there are three that bear record in heaven, the Father, the Word, and the Holy Ghost: and these three are one.

8 And there are three that bear witness in earth, the Spirit, and the water, and the blood: and these three agree in one.

The New Revised Standard Version (NRSV) translates the passage thus:

7 There are three that testify:[a] 8 the Spirit and the water and the blood, and these three agree.

Very interestingly, it is not found in any early Greek manuscripts of the Bible. It was found only in later Latin manuscripts. It is believed by scholars that the verses were added by later scribes to manuscripts to help support a Trinitarian doctrine (Ehrman, 2012).

I already mentioned earlier in this book the Egyptian trinity of Atun, Shu and Tefnut and the Babylonian trinity of the sun, moon and Venus. The idea of divine threesomes was common in ancient Europe, Egypt, the near east and Asia. In Hinduism the three gods of Brahma, Vishnu and Siva make up the *Trimurti*, where they are of inseparable unity but are three in form.

It is believed that pagan thought particularly Platonic and Neo-Platonic ideas had great impact on early church fathers, including Augustine. The historian Will Durant said "Christianity did not destroy paganism; it adopted it" and "While Christianity converted the world, the world converted Christianity" (1944). "Many thinkers influential in the development of trinitarian doctrines were steeped in the thought not only of Middle Platonism and Neoplatonism, but also the Stoics, Aristotle, and other currents in Greek Philosophy"

Mystery Religions

Hellenistic culture had tremendous influence on diverse peoples throughout the Mediterranean world and the Near East. "The Hellenistic-Roman age was an era of insecurity and anxiety. The shift from nationalism to cosmopolitanism, from the secure isolated city-state to the *oikoumene*, gave people a greater sense of individualism, but at the same time provided many with a feeling of alienation and insecurity. As people became more mobile and individualistic, old traditions and values were steadily being uprooted, static class structures began to disappear, past certitudes were questioned, and the future became uncertain" (Tripolitis, 2002).

Tripolitis (2002) goes on to say "The unsettling conditions of the time led people to long and search for *soteria*, salvation, a release from the burdens of finitude, the misery and failure of human life. People everywhere were keenly awake to every new message of hope and eagerly prospecting for a personal savior, someone who would bring salvation, i.e., deliverance or protection from the vicissitudes of this life and the perils of the afterlife. This they found in the mystery cults that had penetrated the Greek world." These religions were called "mystery" religions because the initiation rites, practices and knowledge about God were kept secret among the members.

Tripolitis maintains that although mystery religions had diverse rites and beliefs, they all shared three essential characteristics:

1. They all have purification rites which allow the initiates to participate in the activities of the cult.
2. They all promote a communion or a sense of a personal relationship with the worshiped deity.
3. They all promise a blessed, glorious life after earthly death.

Angus (1925) said that many of the mystery cults had congregational worship services, that there was a strong bond of fellowship between the congregants, and that the guilds were supported by free-will offerings. They sometimes had burial grounds for its members. Angus believed the religions probably began as religions of primitive agricultural peoples that were not restricted to "initiates" and without secrets that they kept to themselves.

Angus wrote about a number of characteristics of mystery religions:

- "A Mystery-Religion was a religion of redemption which professed to remove estrangement between man and God, to procure forgiveness of sins, to furnish mediation."
- The mystery religions imparted a secret knowledge about the deity and means of union with God that "rendered men superior to all the trials of life and ensured salvation." It was knowledge that ensured salvation, not faith.

- "A Mystery-Religion was a sacramental drama which appealed primarily to the emotions and aimed at producing psychic and mystic effects by which the neophyte might experience the exaltation of a new life."
- "The mysteries were eschatological religions having to do with the interests and issues of life and death."
- "A Mystery-Religion was a personal religion to which membership was open not by the accident of birth but by a religious rebirth."

There were a number of requirements in order to become a member of a mystery religion, and although there were some differences between the various cults, Angus (1925) said the following were common:

- Initiates were considered for membership on evidence of their sincerely and their fitness for inclusion. Not all who desired membership were granted it. Initiates took a vow of secrecy; "it was a crime of the most heinous character to divulge the mystery-secrets".
- Some sort of confession of sin was required.
- Baptisms were required. Angus (1925) reported that according to the Christian theologian Tertullian who wrote about the mysteries, "In certain Mysteries, e.g. of Isis and Mithra, it is by baptism that members are initiated...in the Apollinarian and Eleusinian rites they are baptized, and they imagine that the result of this baptism is regeneration and the remission of the penalties of their sins." According to Angus "In Gnosticism baptism was more important than even in orthodox Christianity. For the highest Mysteries a

threefold baptism was required, of Water, Fire, and Spirit."
- The beliefs and practices of the various mystery religions also had some variability, but the following were common:
- "Sacrifices were not overlooked in the Mysteries. In spite of the philosophic protest against bloody sacrifices, the prevailing view in the theology of antiquity was that 'without shedding of blood there is no remission of sin.'"
- "Ascetic preparations of all kinds and degrees of rigor were practiced- prolonged fasts, absolute continence, severe bodily mutilations and painful flagellations, uncomfortable pilgrimages to holy places, public confession, contributions to the church funds- in fact, nearly every form of self-mortification and renunciation practiced by the saints and mystics of all ages."
- Mystical and ecstatic practices were also part of the mystery religions. "Ecstasy might be of a passive character resembling a trance, or of an active orgiastic character of excitation resembling what Plato calls 'divine frenzy.' According to the means of induction, the temperament of the initiate, and his spiritual history, ecstasy might range anywhere from non-moral delirium to that consciousness of oneness with the Invisible and the dissolution of painful individuality which marks the mystics of all ages" (Angus, 1925). "The subjects became 'in God', 'possessed of the deity,' and 'full of God.'"
- "Sacred meals played an important part in the Mysteries as sacraments of union with the deity, but the precise significance of these meals is disputed.

- Common meals of a religious character were in vogue in antiquity" (Angus, 1925).
- "All the mystery-gods were primarily saviour-gods. To initiation was ascribed a sacramental efficacy which atoned for a man's past, gave him comfort in the present, a participation in the divine life, and assured to faith an hereafter of such dazzling splendor that the trials and conflicts of this earthly existence were dwarfed into insignificance" (Angus, 1925).

Four of the more prominent mystery religions were cults to Demeter, Dionysus, Isis and Cybele. The cult of Demeter was situated at Eleusis, which was west of Athens. Demeter was an Olympian goddess of grain. This cult was one of the oldest, and origins date back to the 15th century BCE. The cult came to be known as both the mysteries of Demeter and also the Eleusinian mysteries. "By the Hellenistic-Roman period, participation in the mysteries was understood as a personal religious experience that had the power to bestow happiness on an individual and assistance through this life and after death. Beginning in the 7th century, Eleusis acquired immense prestige as a holy place and a shrine of pilgrimage" (Tripolitis, 2002).

The cult of Dionysus (known to the Romans as Bacchus) was the second most popular mystery cult. The origins of Dionysus are believed to be from around the late 2nd millennium BCE. "His popularity was due not only to the fact that the initiate into his mysteries acquired a new status, as did the initiates in the Demeter rites, but he was also made a member of a group of like-minded individuals who spoke the same language and had a similar hope for the hereafter."

"Bacchus's popularity continued through the 4th century CE, as attested by the literature and iconography of the period. During this time, he was considered the god of wine and of joy. It is this aspect of the god that appealed to many of the affluent of Italy." (Tripolitis, 2002).

"The Egyptian deities were the first of the eastern deities to become important in the Hellenistic world, and during the first two centuries of the common era they were the most popular and widespread of the non-Greek deities" (Ferguson, 2003). The most important of these Egyptian deities was the goddess Isis. She became known to the Greek world as early as the 5th century BCE. She was often portrayed suckling an infant (most often Horus). According to Ferguson many have claimed this to be the precedent for the pictures of Madonna and Child in Christian art. Once initiated into the cult, the man or woman was signified to have "died to the old life and was reborn to a new course of life and salvation under the protection of Isis" (Tripolitis, 2002).

Cybele was a goddess of Anatolian origin. Anatolia is also known as Asia Minor and is in what is now Turkey. Her cult can be traced back to the Neolithic Age in which she was known as Earth Mother. Tripolitis reports that Cybele was adopted by the Greeks early in the 12th century and was worshiped widely by the 7th century BCE. It was a popular cult throughout Greece and then Rome. According to Tripolitis its popularly spread throughout the Western World and Asia Minor by the end of the first century CE.

"The mystery cults enjoyed great success during the Hellenistic-Roman period. This was due to the fact that they were international and universal. With the exception of Mithraism, membership was open to all regardless of sex, nationality, or race. At a time of uncertainty and social fluidity, this feature was especially appealing. They were individualistic, addressing the spiritual needs of the individual, and they also provided the devotees with meaningful fellowship with individuals who possessed the same knowledge of salvation. Last, they provided a personal, closer relationship to the divine, protection from the adversities of this life, and the hope of some sort of blissful world after death" (Tripolitis, 2002).

The Eucharist

I mentioned earlier in this chapter that sacred meals played a part in the mystery religions. Doane (1882) maintains that "the Eucharistia is one of the oldest rites of antiquity". He quotes the Roman Cicero (106 BCE) in making a derogatory reference to it: "How can a man be so stupid as to imagine that which he eats to be a God?"

Doane said the ancient Egyptians "annually celebrated the resurrection of their God and saviour Osiris, at which time they commemorated his death by the Eucharist, eating the sacred cake or wafer, after it had been consecrated by the priest, and become veritable flesh of his flesh. The bread, after sacerdotal rites, became mystically the body of Osiris, and in such a manner, they ate their god. Bread and wine were brought to the temples by the worshipers as offerings." Doane said that in Mithraicism there was a sacrament of bread and wine; Mithraicism will be discussed at some length later in this chapter. He also reported that a sacrament of bread and wine were part of other mystery religions as well including the Eleusinian mysteries, the cult of Bacchus, and the mysteries of Adonis. Doane also reported that "the ancient Druids offered the sacrament of bread and wine."

Baptism

Mircea Eliade (1958) wrote that the symbolism of water as cleansing and regenerating was universal and archetypal. Doane (1882) also wrote that baptism was found in many religions. For Buddhists in Mongolia and Tibet, infants were dipped three times in water and then given a name. "The ceremony of baptism was a practice of the followers of Zoroaster, both for infants and adults." "The rite of baptism was also administered to adults in the Mithraic mysteries during initiation." "The ancient Egyptians performed their rite of baptism, and those who were initiated into the mysteries of Isis were baptized." (Doane, 1882).

Doane also wrote that baptism was well known among the Jews prior to the time of Christ "and was practiced by them when they admitted proselytes to their religion from heathenism." Doane said this was unknown until after the Babylonian exile, suggesting that it was learned from the Babylonians.

Aslan (2013) also wrote about the use of baptism by the Jews. "To be sure, baptisms and water rituals were fairly common throughout the ancient Near East. Bands of 'baptizing groups' roamed Syria and Palestine initiating congregants into their orders by immersing them in water. Gentile converts to Judaism would often take a ceremonial bath to rid themselves of their former identity and enter into the chosen tribe. The Jews revered water for its liminal qualities, believing it had the power to transport a person or object from one state to other: from unclean to clean, from profane to holy."

Roman Empire

In 164 BCE the Jewish people gained control of Jerusalem from the Seleucids. This began a period of self-rule once again, which was known as the "Hasmonean" rule. This lasted until 63 BCE when Palestine was conquered by the Roman general Pompey.

Archaeologists have found that the earliest settlements found in Rome were from around 1000 BCE. Rome began to develop into a city around 650 BCE. It was developed by a peoples known as the Etruscans; they likely originated in a part of Italy now known as Tuscany. The Etruscans, likely influenced by the Greeks, portrayed their gods very anthropomorphically. Also like the Greeks, they constructed temples to their gods.

Roman culture, from its beginnings, was heavily influenced by Greek culture. Like the Greeks, around 500 BCE they discontinued being a kingdom and established a republic. Their religions were very similar. The Roman gods had equivalents in the Greek pantheon:

Greek god	**Roman god**
Zeus	Jupiter
Hera	Juno
Poseidon	Neptune
Demeter	Ceres
Athena	Minerva
Apollo	Apollo
Artemis	Diana

Ares	Mars
Aphrodite	Venus
Hephaestus	Vulcan
Hermes	Mercury
Hestia	Vesta
Dionysus	Bacchus
Hades	Pluto

Although the Romans had a republic, all of its citizens were not of equal status. According to Winks and Mattern-Parkes (2004), the highest economic classes had more voting units than the lower ones. There was a class distinction between *plebeians* and *patricians*. The latter received higher status based upon heredity, and they dominated the consulship. The majority of Roman citizens were plebeians, and at the end of the republic perhaps one in four people in Italy were slaves.

At the end of the republic there was a great military commander named Pompey. "In 66 BCE he took over the war against Mithradates VI, whom he immediately defeated; he then campaigned in Armenia, the Caucasus Mountains, and Syria; he notoriously marched on Jerusalem and desecrated the Temple. He deposed the last Seleucid king and turned the kingdom of Syria into a Roman province. He rewarded those who had supported him with kingdoms and alliances with Rome, and it was to Pompey that the entire network of Near Eastern dynasts now owed their loyalty. No Roman general in history could claim greater military achievements. Pompey advertised his victories in ways that made him seem like a new Alexander who had conquered the entire Eastern world" (Winks, 2004).

Pompey had an alliance with Julius Caesar, also a Roman military leader. This alliance ended when Caesar marched into Italy with his army; civil war broke out in 49 BCE. "The civil war that engulfed the entire Roman world between 49 and 45 BCE- for it was fought in Italy, Greece, Macedonia, Spain, Asia, Egypt, and Africa- was an extension of the personal conflict between these men. Each had kings, cities, armies, and innumerable individuals loyal to him, bound by ties of gratitude, and through these they could bully and intimidate others. Thus they drafted enormous armies and flung at one another the combined manpower of the entire Roman Empire plus a score of peripheral kingdoms, in a war of unprecedented scale" (Winks, 2004).

In 48 BCE Pompey was murdered in Egypt. Caesar was the victor in the civil war, but he also was murdered in 44 BCE. His assassin, Brutus, a "friend" and fellow senator, claimed to have done this to liberate Rome from Caesar's tyrannical rule. Brutus was opposed by one of Caesar's generals, Mark Antony as well as Caesar's adopted 18 year old son (who was his grand nephew), Octavian. Antony, Octavian and a senator by the name of M. Aemilius Lepidus formed an alliance. Antony took over the eastern half of the empire and had a sexual and political alliance with Cleopatra of Egypt (they had three children together). The alliance between Antony and Octavian became strained, and they went to war against each other in 31 BCE. Octavian eventually prevailed. Antony and Cleopatra committed suicide, and Egypt became a Roman province.

Octavian became undisputed leader of the Roman Empire. His rule became known as *Pax Romana*, the "Roman peace". It was through military conquest that there now was peace in

Rome, i.e. no more civil war. Octavian remained the ruler until his death in 14 CE.

In 27 BCE Octavian was voted the title "Augustus" (which means *venerable*) by the Roman senate. The territories of the Roman empire doubled under the reign of Augustus. The Roman senate had a vote declaring Julius Caesar a god; after that Augustus referred to himself as *divi filius*, i.e. "son of god".

Theologian Marcus Borg (2009) wrote "Augustus was Divine, Son of God, God, and God from God. He was Lord, Liberator, Redeemer, and Savior of the World- not just of Italy or the Mediterranean, mind you, but of the entire inhabited earth. Words like 'justice' and 'peace,' 'epiphany' and 'gospel,' 'grace' and 'salvation' were already associated with him. Even 'sin' and 'atonement' were connected to him as well."

Judaism during the Roman Period

During the rule of the Hasmoneans, Jewish sects developed that continued to exist in the Roman period. The historian Josephus wrote about four of them. One of these groups was the Pharisees who developed from an earlier group called the *Hasidim* (from the Hebrew root meaning "pious" or "righteous"). This term should not be confused with the term "Hasidism", a current Jewish religious sect. The predominant concern of the Pharisees was to scrupulously keep the Mosaic law. In addition to the written law of the Torah, they developed an "oral" law to help clear up ambiguities of the written law. These oral laws were passed down by word of mouth from generation to generation until they were finally written down around the year 200 CE; today this is known as the *Mishnah*. The Pharisees believed in a resurrection of the dead, a judgment after death that resulted in reward or punishment, and an afterlife. This group was the forerunner of later rabbinic Judaism.

The Sadducees were another Jewish sect. They largely came from Jewish aristocracy and were the group with power during Jesus' day. They considered themselves as followers of the Biblical priest Zadok. Their emphasis was on sacrificial worship in the Jerusalem temple. The local Jewish council, the Sanhedrin, was primarily composed of Sadducees. They considered only the first five books of the Torah as being authoritative. They did not believe in a doctrine of resurrection. After Solomon's temple in Jerusalem was destroyed by the Romans in 70 CE, the sect dissipated.

The Essenes were another Jewish sect of that time period. Our only source for information about them was the Jewish historian Josephus, until a discovery was made in the late 1940s and early 1950s. At a settlement known as Qumran, the "Dead Sea Scrolls" were discovered. This was a spectacular find. Hundreds of documents were found; most written in Hebrew but some in Aramaic. Not only did this find give us information about the Essenes, but more importantly there were partial copies of every book of the Jewish Bible with the exception of the book of Esther. Many of the canonical books were fairly complete. What makes this find so important is that the writings were nearly a thousand years earlier than any previous copies of the Hebrew scriptures that we had. Generally speaking, the earlier the copy of a writing, the more likely that it is closest to the original writer's intent.

The Essenes' beliefs had a lot in common with Zoroastrianism. They believed that an apocalypse signaling the end of times was imminent. Like the Zoroastrians, they believed there would be a final battle between the forces of good and the forces of evil. They identified themselves as the "sons of light" and believed that in the end they would be victorious over the "sons of darkness". Humans had to choose which side they were on; their choice would lead to either eternal reward or eternal punishment. Some of the discovered scrolls indicated that the coming kingdom would be ruled by two messiahs; one a king, and the other a priest.

A fourth Jewish "philosophy" was known as The Fourth Philosophy. These groups were characterized by their demand for national independence, which they believed was ordained by God. Many of these groups would pursue their goals by any means, including assassinations of Jewish leaders whom they felt were in league with Roman authorities. One group that subscribed to this philosophy were known as the Zealots. Reza Aslan (2013) wrote about the Fourth Philosophy and the Zealots. He said the leader of the movement, Judas the Galilean, was put to death for claiming to be the Jewish messiah, as was his father Hezekiah before him 40 years earlier. Aslan said that the Zealots, like the Essenes, were anticipating a coming apocalypse led by a Jewish messiah.

Aslan links Jesus of Nazareth with the Zealots. He points out that Jesus' primary teaching was the coming of the Kingdom of God. "What Jesus was proposing must have been a physical and present kingdom: a *real* kingdom, with an *actual* king that was about to be established on earth. That is certainly how the Jews would have understood it. Jesus' particular conception of the Kingdom of God may have been distinctive and somewhat unique, but its connotations would not have been unfamiliar to his audience. Jesus was merely reiterating what the zealots had been preaching for years. Simply put, the Kingdom of God was shorthand for the idea of God as the sole sovereign, the one and only king, not just over Israel, but over all the world."

Aslan believed the Kingdom of God was a call to revolution, and not necessarily in non-violent ways. Aslan reminds us that in Matthew Jesus is quoted as saying "Do not think that I have come to bring peace on earth. I have not come to bring peace, but the sword." Aslan said that Jesus was in "agreement with the zealots that God's reign required not just an internal transformation toward justice and righteousness, but a complete reversal of the present political, religious, and economic system."

Another group worth mentioning here were the Samaritans. Like the Sadducees, they accepted only a form of the Torah as scripture. Theologically, there were only minor differences between them and most Jews, with the exception of their rejection of the Jewish Temple in Jerusalem and their insistence that the true temple of God was on Mount Gerizim near Shechem in the territory of Samaria. The Samaritans are associated with the Israelites who remained in Palestine during the Babylonian captivity. One might recall that the Jews who returned to Judea from captivity looked down upon those who had not been exiled.

Jesus of Nazareth

Jesus was born in 4 BCE and lived until 30 CE. He was briefly mentioned by the Jewish historian, Josephus, but otherwise all that we know about him comes from later followers. The earliest writings about him come from letters of the apostle, Paul, who wrote in the sixth decade of the common era. Paul had never met Jesus, and he wrote nothing about Jesus' life. The gospels tell stories about Jesus' s life, but it is highly unlikely that they were written by contemporaries of Jesus. The earliest gospel, known as the Gospel of Mark, was believed to have been written around 70 CE, forty years after the death of Jesus. The gospel known as the Gospel of John was believed to have been written between 90 and 95 CE.

Jesus started his public ministry right after being baptized by John the Baptist. Jesus then begins traveling and preaching to people primarily about the coming Kingdom of God. Jesus calls disciples, teaches to crowds of people (often in parables), heals people of illnesses, performs miracles, and exorcises demons. Although many of these activities sound remarkable to modern day ears, historians tell us that such activities were quite commonplace during that time period, and particularly in Galilee.

Miracle Workers of the Day

"Jesus was not the only miracle worker trolling through Palestine healing the sick and casting out demons. This was a world steeped in magic and Jesus was just one of an untold number of diviners and dream interpreters, magicians and medicine men who wandered Judea and Galilee" (Aslan, 2013).

What apparently was remarkable for that time and place was that Jesus did not charge money for these services. Performing miracles and healing the sick was a lucrative profession for others. I will now describe some other miracle workers of that vicinity and time period that historians are aware of:

Honi the Circle-Drawer

He was known through writings of later Jewish rabbis. Honi died about 100 years before Jesus. Honi was a Galilean teacher who was given his nickname "because of a tradition that he prayed to God for much-needed rain, and drew a circle around himself on the ground, declaring that he would not leave it until God granted his request. Lucky for him, God complied. Later sources indicate that Honi was a revered teacher and a miracle worker, who called himself the son of God. Like Jesus, he was martyred outside of the walls of Jerusalem around the time of Passover" (Ehrman, 2012).

Abba Hilqiah

Abba lived in Galilee around the time of Jesus and was the grandson of Honi. He also was known for miraculous deeds including inducing rain.

Hanan the Hidden

Hanan also was a grandson of Honi who performed miraculous deeds.

Rabbi Hanina ben Dosa

This was a "rabbi in Galilee in the middle of the first century CE, just after the time of Jesus. He was famous as a righteous and powerful worker of miracles, who could intervene with God to make the rain fall, who had the power to heal the sick, and who could confront demons and force them to do his bidding. Like Jesus, he was reputedly called the Son of God by a voice coming from the heavens" (Ehrman, 2012).

Simon Magus

This miracle man is described in the book of *Acts* (chapter 8). "Now a certain man named Simon had previously practiced magic in the city and amazed the people of Samaria, saying that he was someone great. All of them, from the least to the greatest, listened to him eagerly, saying 'This man is the power of God that is called Great.' And they listened eagerly to him because for a long time he had amazed them with his magic" (vs. 9-11). The chapter goes on to say that Simon was baptized and was a follower of the apostle Philip.

Simon Magus also is a major character in the apocryphal *Acts of Peter*. "In the ultimate showdown between the heretical sorcerer (Simon Magus) and the man of God (Peter), Simon the magician uses his powers to leap into the air and fly like a bird over the temples and hills of Rome. Not to be outdone, Peter calls upon God to smite Simon in midair; God complies much to the magician's dismay and demise. Unprepared for a crash landing, he plunges to earth and breaks his leg in three places. Seeing what has happened, the crowds rush to stone him to death as an evildoer" (Ehrman, 2012).

Apollonius of Tyana

The life of this miracle worker and neo-Pythagorean teacher of the first century CE was described in a book by Flavius Philostratus in 220 CE. A fascinating description of what's been written about Apollonius is given by Bart Ehrman (2012). "From the beginning his mother knew that he was no ordinary person. Prior to his birth, a heavenly figure appeared to her, announcing that her son would not be a mere mortal but would himself be divine. This prophecy was confirmed by the miraculous character of his birth, a birth accompanied by supernatural signs. The boy was already recognized as a spiritual authority in his youth; his discussions with recognized experts showed his superior knowledge of all things religious. As an adult he left home to engage in an itinerant preaching ministry. He went from village to town with his message of good news, proclaiming that people should forgo their concerns for the material things of this life, such as how they should dress and what they should eat. They should instead be concerned with their eternal souls.

He gathered around him a number of disciples who were amazed by his teaching and his flawless character. They became convinced that he was no ordinary man but was the Son of God. Their faith received striking confirmation in the miraculous things that he did. He could reportedly predict the future, heal the sick, cast out demons, and raise the dead. Not everyone proved friendly, however. At the end of his life, his enemies trumped up charges against him, and he was placed on trial before Roman authorities for crimes against the state.

Even after he departed this realm, however, he did not forsake his devoted followers. Some claimed that he had ascended bodily into heaven; others said that he had appeared to them, alive, afterward, that they had talked with him and touched him and become convinced that he could not be bound by death. A number of his followers spread the good news about this man, recounting what they had seen him say and so. Eventually some of these accounts came to be written down in books that circulated throughout the empire."

Early Christianity

Jesus was believed to have been crucified in the year 30 CE. Caesar Augustus had died in 14 CE, and so his successor, Tiberius, was emperor of Rome at the time of Jesus' death. Jesus' disciples spread the teachings of Jesus throughout Palestine and the Roman world. There also was a Pharisee, by the name of Saul (later called Paul) who was a persecutor of the early followers of Jesus who had a conversion experience and then became one of the chief advocates for the teachings of Jesus.

During the early proselytizing in the first century CE by Jesus' followers, there was no conception of there being "Christians". Jesus' followers were considered to be Jews who were a splinter group of Judaism. What made this group of Jews different from the majority of Jews was their belief that Jesus was the promised messiah. This belief was scoffed at by the majority of Jews who expected a messiah to come who would break the yoke of Roman oppression and restore Israel's greatness, not someone who was killed and defeated by their enemy.

Jesus' followers did find converts, however. This was an extremely slow process initially, but over the next several decades Jesus communities were started throughout the Mediterranean world. From the middle to the late first century the greater church had become predominantly Gentile rather than Jewish. Converts were not required to be circumcised or to follow strictly the Jewish laws, e.g. kosher foods. It was at this point that Christianity became a non-Jewish religion.

The term "Christian" is first found in the book of Acts. From this and the writings of Tacitus many have concluded that the term came to be applied to the followers of Jesus by outsiders, and that it was not originally a term of self-identification. Christians particularly came to be seen as a distinct group from Judaism during the reign of Nero (54-68) who accused the Christians of setting fires in Rome.

The earliest Christians were known for their love and kindness to people. Aristides (125 CE) wrote: "They walk in all humility and kindness, and falsehood is not found among them, and they love one another. They despise not the widow, and grieve not the orphan. He that hath, distributeth liberally to him that hath not. If they see a stranger, they bring him under their roof, and rejoice over him, as it were their own brother; for they call themselves brethren: not after the flesh, but after the Spirit and in God; but when one of their poor passes away from the world, and any one of them see him, then he provides for his burial according to his ability; and if they hear that any of their number is imprisoned or oppressed for the name of their Messiah, all of them provide for his needs, and if it is possible that he may be delivered, they deliver him. And if there is among them a man that is poor and needy, and they have not an abundance of necessaries, they fast two or three days that they may supply the needy with their necessary food."

Early Christianity was very diverse in its beliefs. There was no sacred scripture to refer to. Over time disputes began to emerge over theology. Ammianus Marcellinus, 4th century historian, describes the Christians in his century as thus: "Wild beasts are not such enemies to mankind as are most Christians in their deadly hatred of one another." What a change from the earlier descriptions!

It once was thought that what is now termed the "proto-orthodox" Christian theology was the original beliefs of the "Christians", and that so called heretical theologies only developed over time later. This was the view of Eusebius, Christian bishop and historian of the fourth century CE. However, particularly with the discovery of previously unknown ancient texts (e.g. those discovered in the Dead Sea Scrolls and Nag Hammadi library), scholars' views about this have changed.

Bart Ehrman (2015) notes that people outside of academia are generally unaware of this. "Even among church people, it is scarcely realized that early Christians engaged in heated and often acrimonious debates over completely fundamental issues, such as whether there was only one God or two or twelve or thirty, whether the Jews were the chosen people of God or the evil children of the Devil, whether women could serve as ministers of the church or were to remain silent and subservient to men, whether a Christian should seek to be martyred for the faith or avoid persecution at all costs, whether the Scriptures included the Gospels allegedly written by Matthew and John or those in the names of Mary Magdalene and Jesus' own twin brother Thomas. Each of these positions- and many others on many other issues- had strong and vocal advocates among the Christian faithful of the second and third centuries."

Walter Bauer (1996) did extensive research on the beliefs of the early Christians. He concluded that so called "heresies" actually preceded proto-orthodox doctrines. Of course they were not considered to be heresies at that time by their believers, and the so-called proto-orthodox beliefs were considered at one time by others as being heresy.

"A united front composed of Marcionites and Jewish Christians, Valentinians and Montanists, is inconceivable. Thus it was the destiny of the heresies, after they had lost their connection with the orthodox Christianity that remained, to stay divided and even to fight among themselves, and thus to be routed one after another by orthodoxy. The form of Christian belief and life which was successful was that supported by the strongest organization- the form which was the most uniform and best suited for mass consumption- in spite of the fact that, in my judgment, for a long time after the close of the post-apostolic age the sum total of consciously orthodox and anti-heretical Christians was numerically inferior to that of the "heretics" (Bauer, 1996).

At the end of the second century Christians made up perhaps 2-3% of the empire. At the *beginning* of the fourth century they made up perhaps 5-7%. Everything changed with the conversion of the Roman emperor Constantine to Christianity. At the *end* of the fourth century almost half of the empire called themselves "Christian".

Paganism was the term Christians used for those following the traditional, polytheistic religious practices of the Roman empire. The Romans were very tolerant of various religious beliefs. There wasn't a sense at that time that one would choose a religion or a god over other religions or gods. Religion generally was accommodating of various beliefs about the divine. However, there was a civic expectation that the traditional, national gods (e.g. Jupiter, Mercury) would be honored. People were expected to participate in nationalistic rituals and festivals to honor these gods; that Jews and Christians did not participate was problematic.

Apotheosis

This term refers to the process whereby emperors were deified, usually after their deaths. Already mentioned in this book was the deification of Julius Caesar by the Roman senate after his death and thereby his adopted son, Augustus, being referred to and referring to himself as the son of god. Augustus himself was deified after his death. This happened with many subsequent Roman emperors, as it had in the past with the pharaohs of Egypt.

With the exception of the Hebrews, people of this period did not think in terms of a dichotomy between divine and mortal. There were levels of divinity. When Augustus was declared a god, it did not mean that he was an equivalent to Jupiter. The Greek and Roman religions had various levels for the gods, and some humans, such as some of the emperors, were considered *super*human. When you think about it, even a monotheistic faith such as Christianity today has some remnants of this. Even though there is but one God, some believe in other lesser supernatural beings (e.g. angels and demons). The book of Genesis mentions beings who are the progeny of humans and angels known as the Nephilim,

Mithraism

This was one of the "mystery religions" I did not previously mention. I waited to talk about it until now because of its popularity and importance as a rival to Christianity. Mithra was an Indo-Iranian deity who originated in the 14th century BCE or earlier. In Persian literature he's referred to as Mithra and in Indian scripture as Mitra. In the Hellenistic-Roman world he was known as Mithras. He is a subordinate deity to the supreme deity: Ahura Mazda in Persia or Varuna in India (Tripolitis, 2002).

The worship of Mithra spread throughout Asia Minor during the Persian Empire's prominence. The religion of Mithra became popular in the Roman empire in the late first century CE. "It reached its climax in the 3rd century, at which time its *mithraea*, the Mithraic sanctuaries, were found from one end of the empire to the other" (Tripolitis, 2002).

Participation in the religion was restricted to men. Initiates had to take solemn oaths to not reveal anything about initiation rites. There were seven levels one could achieve within the cult, corresponding to the Sun, the Moon, and the five known planets (Saturn, Venus, Jupiter, Mercury and Mars). The seven grades were:

1. Corax, the Raven
2. Nymphus, the BrideMiles, the Soldier
3. Miles, the Soldier
4. Leo, the Lion
5. Perses, the Persian
6. Heliodromus, the Courier of the Sun
7. Pater, the Father

Mithraic initiation took place in the mithraeum, a cave which symbolized the cosmos. Frequently the ceilings were decorated with stars. "The Mithraists believed that the soul descended into the cosmos from the sun through the seven planetary spheres." Prayers were addressed to the sun three times daily, Sunday was their sacred day, and December 25th was celebrated as the birthday of the god Mithras. (Tripolitis, 2002).

Mithraism was particularly popular in Rome and amongst the military. "Mithraism's emphasis on justice, truthfulness, loyalty, and courage made it especially appealing to the Roman legions." The religion did not demand exclusivity; participants could worship other gods in addition to Mithras. (Tripolitis, 2002)

During these centuries of the Roman empire astrology continued to be popular, as was the worship of the sun. Aurelian, emperor from 270-275 CE gave credit to the sun for a military victory and "erected a large temple to the god whom he worshiped as the only heavenly, almighty, and divine power. The sun was proclaimed the universal god of the empire, and Aurelian promoted the cult of *Sol invictus*, raised it to the status of an official cult, and attempted to establish a quasi sun-god monotheism. Aurelian's sun-god religion was not the religion of Mithras, but the Mithraic cult took advantage of Mithras's association with the sun" (Tripolitis, 2002).

In 308 under the emperor Diocletian there was a dedication of a large altar to Mithras which "established Mithras as the official god of the Roman state, replacing the general sun-god of Aurelian. During this period, Mithraism was at its peak and it appeared as if it might become the sole state religion, but Constantine's triumph in 312 as sole ruler of the empire shattered its hopes" (Tripolitis, 2002).

Gnosticism

The term "gnosticism" refers to a variety of teachings by individuals and groups that include both Christians and non-Christians. There is no orthodox or normative theology in gnosticism; nor is there a gnostic "church". There is no gnostic canon of scripture. Much of gnostic literature was destroyed by the proto-Orthodox Christian Church. However, in 1945 in Egypt some peasants discovered a jar that contained documentary fragments of gnostic documents. The documents are known as the Nag Hammadi Library, and from this discovery we were able to learn more about gnostic beliefs, which previously we knew about only from the writings of its detractors.

Though there is diversity in gnostic beliefs, there are some common elements. First of all there is the notion of *gnosis*, or "knowledge" or "understanding". The gnostics sought a religious knowledge which had a redeeming or liberating effect. They believed only certain individuals were able to gain this knowledge which had an esoteric character. It was ignorance that kept peoples as slaves, and special knowledge that gave salvation. This divine knowledge was reserved for the elite who had the ability to understand it.

The gnostics also believed that within man was a *divine spark*. The physical world is evil, and goal is to escape their evil material bodies so that their spiritual spark can return to the divine. They had a very dualistic view of the world like the Zoroastrians and the Jewish Essenes, but unlike these previous groups linked the material world with evil. The material is not the work of the supreme being but was created by a subordinate being.

According to Kurt Rudolph (1987), "the gnostic movement was originally a non-Christian phenomenon which was gradually enriched with Christian concepts until it made its appearance as independent Christian Gnosis." Early likely influences included Zoroastrianism, Jewish apocalyptic literature, the Essenes, Jewish wisdom teaching (e.g. Proverbs, Wisdom of Solomon, Ecclesiasticus), Jewish scepticism (e.g. Ecclesiastes), Hellenistic philosophy (especially Plato), and Greek and oriental mystery religions.

I will discuss just a few of the gnostic texts recovered from the Nag Hammadi library. One was The Secret Book of John. This is a description of teachings taught by Jesus to his disciple John. Included in this book is a description of God, of which I will share here just a short excerpt:

"The One is a sovereign that has nothing over it. It is God and Parent, Father of the All, the invisible one that is over the All, that is incorruptible, that is pure light at which no eye can gaze. The One is the Invisible Spirit. We should not think of it as a god or like a god. For it is greater than a god, because it has nothing over it and no lord above it. It does not [exist] within anything inferior [to it, since everything] exists within it, [for it established] itself. It is eternal, since it does not need anything. For it is absolutely complete."

The Gospel of Truth from Nag Hammadi does not have an account of Jesus' life, but rather tells the "good news" of God's revelation through Jesus about the saving knowledge (gnosis). "The book focuses on the truth that brings redemption to an anguished humanity languishing in darkness and ignorance, and especially on the one who brought this revealed truth, Jesus Christ" (Ehrman, 2015).

The Treatise on the Resurrection from Nag Hammadi explains that our physical bodies are transitory, and that upon death our spirit ascends to the heavenly realm. Those who in this life are already denying the flesh have begun the process of resurrection.

The Gospel of Philip discovered at Nag Hammadi says "He who has the knowledge (gnosis) of the truth is free. Ignorance is a slave." Ehrman (2015) in regards to this writing said "Among the clearest emphases is precisely the contrast between those who can understand and those who cannot, between knowledge that is exoteric (available to all) and that which is esoteric (available only to insiders), between the immature outsiders (regular Christians, called "Hebrews") and the mature insiders (Valentinians, called "gentiles"). Those who do not understand- that is, the outsiders with only exoteric knowledge- err in many of their judgments; for example, in taking such notions as the virgin birth or the resurrection of Jesus as literal statements of historical fact, rather than symbolic expressions of deeper truths."

Manicheism

With the triumph of "proto-orthodox" Christianity over other Christian beliefs, gnosticism died out for a time until the rise of Manicheism. The founder of this religion, Mani, was born in Mesopotamia in 216 CE. He saw himself as a prophet and the successor to Buddha, Zoroaster and Jesus. He wrote his teachings down. Some considered

Manichaeism as a Christian heresy, and others as a new religion. Due to vigorous missionary activity, the religion spread to the Roman Empire, into northern Africa, and east all the way to China. The great Christian theologian Augustine converted to Manicheism for a time until converting again to Christianity. It shared with other gnostic sects a dualistic view of good and evil and the importance of gnosis to gain salvation. Remnants of the religion continued until about the 13th or 14th centuries in the east.

Proto-Orthodox Christianity

In 313 CE the emperor, Constantine, converted to Christianity. In 380 CE Emperor Theodosius I made Christianity the official state religion and ended state support for paganism and made paganism illegal. In 325 Constantine financed and convened a Christian council in the city of Nicaea. From this council came the Nicene Creed which delineated what it considered correct belief. As a religion, Christianity was unique in two respects: like Judaism it forbid worship of any other gods, and unlike Judaism (and other religions) it emphasized *correct* beliefs. Generally religions emphasized correct behaviors and practices, not what one *believed*.

Common Religious Themes

T.W. Doane (1882) did extensive research on Christian beliefs and similarities in other religions from earlier times. I will now outline some of these proto-orthodox Christian teachings and Doane's research into similar teachings from other religions.

Virgin Birth

In the gospels of Matthew and Luke Jesus is said to have been born of a virgin named Mary. Virgin birth is not mentioned in the other two gospels, and the apostle Paul never speaks of it either. Miraculous births have happened previously in the Hebrew scriptures. Isaac was born to a post menopausal, 90 year old Sarah. The barren Hannah gave birth to the prophet Samuel. Samson was born to a barren woman. John the Baptist was born to elderly parents and a post menopausal mother. The Roman Catholic Church teaches that Mary, the mother of Jesus, had a remarkable birth herself. Although conceived in the normal way, God reportedly erased the stain of original sin from her; this is known as Mary's immaculate conception.

Doan maintains that many divine figures reportedly had miraculous births including Crishna, Buddha, the Siamese god Codom, Fo-hi of China, Lao-tsze, the Chineese sage Yu, Confucius, the Egyptian god Horus, the Egyptian god Ra, Zoroaster, Romulus the legendary founder of Rome, and many Greek/Roman heroes who were said to be progeny of the unions of mortals and gods. These include Hercules, Bacchus, Mercury, Apollo, Prometheus, and Perseus.

Divine Child

In the Gospel of Matthew the infant Jesus is visited by wise men from the East who bring gifts to celebrate the birth of the one they believe to be "the king of the Jews." In Luke's gospel, the birth of Jesus was announced to shepherds in the field. They were told a messiah was born. They went to Bethlehem to visit the infant Jesus.

Doan maintains that the recognition of divinity in children is a common theme. Doane reports that Crishna was adored by shepherds and Magi and was presented with gifts. He said the infants Buddha, Confucius, Mithras and Socrates were said to be visited by wise men who paid homage.

Humble Birth Place

In Luke we are told that Jesus after being born was laid in a manger as there was no room in inns for the family to stay. Doane reports that rather than a stable, many early proto-Orthodox theologians maintained that Jesus was actually born in a cave (Eusebius, Tertullian, Jerome). Doane maintains that it was a quite common theme for divine births to be in very humble places. Doane said there were stories that the following were born in caves: Crishna, Abraham, Bacchus, Adonis, Apollo, Mithras, Hermes, and Attys. Many were said to have had a bright light shining around them including Crishna, Buddha, Bacchus, Apollo, and Zoroaster.

Royal Descent

In chapter one of the Gospel of Matthew, Jesus' genealogy is given, and he is said to be the descendant of King David. Doane reports that many divine beings, often despite humble beginnings, were said to be of royal descent, including Fo-hi, Confucius, Horus, Hercules, Crishna, Buddha, Bacchus, Perseus, and Aesculapius.

Slaughter of the Innocents

The Gospel of Matthew tells us that King Herod heard that there was a birth of an infant who was to become "king of the Jews". He wanted this infant killed. In order to try to accomplish this, we are told that he had "all children in and around Bethlehem who were two years old or under" killed. This reminds us of the story of Moses. Pharaoh, concerned about the growing Israelite population, reportedly had all the male Israelite infants killed.

Doane also said Buddha and Zoroaster were in danger as infants because the ruling kings were fearful of them and wanted to get rid of them. Doane quotes sources who tell a similar story to that of Jesus in regards to Crishna:

"A heavenly voice whispered to the foster father of Crishna and told him to fly with the child across the river Jumna, which was immediately done. This was owing to the fact that the reigning monarch, King Kansa, sought the life of the infant Saviour, and to accomplish his purpose, he sent messengers to kill all the infants in the neighboring places."

Birthdate of December 25

The significance of the date of December 25 is that it marks the winter solstice, i.e. when we have the shortest day of the year. After this the sun rises higher in the sky. Thus it is often known as the birth date of various sun gods. Doane notes this date as the birthdate of Buddha, Mithras, Osiris, Horus, Hercules, Bacchus, Adonis and "other personifications of the Sun."

Temptation by Evil

The writer of Matthew tells us in chapter 4 that Jesus was tempted by Satan in the wilderness. Doane says that Zoroaster also was purported to be tempted by the devil. Doane also said there is a very similar myth about Buddha to the Matthew story about Jesus. Just as Jesus was tempted by the devil before embarking on a preaching ministry, Buddha was tempted by an evil spirit just before going forth to adopt "a religious life". Both fasted. Both were tempted with great worldly power and riches. Jesus responded with "Away with you, Satan!" Buddha responded with a similar "Get thee away from me." After Satan departed Jesus, angels appeared that waited on Jesus. After the evil one left Buddha, "the skies rained flowers, and delicious odors pervaded the air."

Descent into Hell

In the Apostle's Creed is the remarkable statement that "Jesus descended into hell". There is nothing in the New Testament canon that explicitly says this. However, there is an apocryphal writing, the Gospel of Nicodemus, that does discuss this. Doane maintained that "the reason why Christ Jesus has been made to descend into hell, is because it is a part of the universal mythos, even the three days' duration. The Saviours of mankind had all done so, he must therefore do likewise."

"Chrishna, the Hindoo Saviour, *descended into hell*, for the purpose of raising the dead (the doomed), before he returned to his heavenly seat.

Zoroaster, of the Persians, *descended into hell.*

Osiris, the Egyptian Savior, *descended into hell.*

Horus, the virgin-born Saviour, *descended into hell.*

Adonis, the virgin-born Saviour, *descended into hell.*

Bacchus, the virgin-born Saviour, *descended into hell.*

Hercules, the virgin-born Saviour, *descended into hell.*

Mercury, the Word and Messenger of God, *descended into hell.*

Baldus, the Scandinavian god, after being killed, *descended into hell.*

Quetzalcoatle, the Mexican crucified Saviour, *descended into hell.*

All these gods, and many others that might be mentioned, remained in hell for the space of three days and three nights. They descended into hell, and on the third day rose again" (Doane, 1882).

Church Fathers Explain

The early "church fathers" were aware of the similarities between Christianity and other religions. Doane maintains "The early Christian saints, bishops, and fathers, *confessedly* adopted the liturgies, rites, ceremonies, and terms of heathenism; making it their boast, that the pagan religion, properly explained, really was nothing else than Christianity; that the best and wisest of its professors, in all ages, had been Christians all along; that Christianity was but a name more recently acquired to a religion which had previously existed, and had been known to the Greek philosophers, to Plato, Socrates, and Heraclitus." Doane quotes some early church fathers:

Eusebius: that the Christian religion was "known to the ancients" (Eccl. Hist., lib. 2, ch.v.)

Clement of Alexandria: "Those who lived according to the Logos were really Christians, though they have been thought to be atheists; as Socrates and Heraclitus were among the Greeks, and such as resembled them."

Justin Martyr who was born around 100 CE and converted to Christianity around 130 was a defender of the Christian Faith. In his "apology" to Emperor Adrian he is quoted by Doane as saying:

"By declaring the Logos, the first begotten of God, our master Jesus Christ, to be born of a virgin, without any human mixture, to be crucified and dead, and to have rose again, and ascended into heaven; we say no more in this, than what you say of those whom you style the Sons of Jove. For you need not be told what a parcel of sons, the writers most in vogue among you, assign to Jove; there's Mercury, Jove's interpreter, in imitation of the Logos, in worship among you. There's Aesculapius, the physician, smitten by a thunderbolt, and after that ascending into heaven. There's Bacchus, torn to pieces; and Hercules, burnt to get rid of his pains. There's Pollux and Castor, the sons of Jove by Leda, and Perseus by Danae; and not to mention others, I would fain

know why you always deify the departed emperors and have a fellow at hand to make affidavit that he saw Caesar mount to heaven from the funeral pile?"

"As to the son of God, called Jesus, should we allow him to be nothing more than man, yet the title of the son of God is very justifiable, upon the account of his wisdom, considering that you have your Mercury in worship under the title of the Word and Messenger of God."

"As to the objection of our Jesus's being crucified, I say, that suffering was common to all the forementioned sons of Jove, but only they suffered another kind of death. As to his being born of a virgin, you have your Perseus to balance that. As to his curing the lame, and the paralytic, and such as were cripples from birth, this is little more than what you say of your Aesculapius."

Saint Augustine is quoted by Doane as saying *"for the thing itself which is now called the Christian religion, really was known to the ancients, nor was wanting at any time from the beginning of the human race, until the time when Christ came in the flesh, from whence the true religion, which had previously existed, began to be called Christian; and this in our days is the Christian religion, not as having been wanting in former times, but as having in later times received this name."*

Conclusions

In exploring the history of religion it has become evident to me that certain themes have developed that have been very important in religions. These are eight of what I think are among the most important:

1. Sacrifice and other rituals
2. Sacred Meals
2. Development of laws and rules
3. Worship of the sun
4. Water symbolism
5. Battle between good and evil
6. Social justice and love
7. Saving knowledge

1. Gods were first worshiped with rituals, particularly with sacrifices. There is archaeological evidence of animal and human sacrifice four to five thousand years ago. This was the way that the earliest characters in the Hebrew scriptures worshiped god. We are told the offspring of Adam and Eve, Cain and Abel, made offerings to God; one was of grain, the other an animal sacrifice. Noah, (like Atrahasis in the Mesopotamian flood story that was written 1,000 years before the Noah account) made animal sacrifices to god after the waters subsided from the flood. Abraham was directed by god to make a human sacrifice of his son, Isaac, although he ended up sacrificing a ram instead.

Sacrifices continued to be a major part of the worship of god in Judaism up until the destruction of the second temple in 70 CE. Other forms of worship then became predominant, i.e. prayer, reading of scripture, and following the law. However, the idea of the importance of sacrifice made a return with the theology of the proto-orthodox Christians who saw Jesus, as the only son of god, as making the supreme sacrifice for the sins of mankind. Often sacrifices throughout history were made to atone for sins. The belief was that being the son of god, this sacrifice was so tremendous that it would pay the price for all of the sins of mankind, present and future. So although sacrifices are not part of the practice of Christianity, the idea of it is a most important part of the theology of the proto-orthodox. So from the very earliest beginnings of religion, sacrifice has been and continues to be an extremely important ingredient.

We still can see some remnants of sacrifices in Christianity and other religions. In Roman Catholic and Anglican churches votive candles are often available to light to accompany a prayer.

Similarly, in Buddhism incense is often burnt as a sacrificial offering. Recently I visited a Buddhist temple in Shanghai on New Year's Day. It was packed with people who burned incense, which I was told was a New Year's tradition in the hopes that this would bring good luck in the coming year.

2. Another very early idea in religion was the idea of a sacred meal. A characteristic of early religion was *animism*, which is the belief that everything has a spiritual essence. Several relatively modern "primitive" peoples, and it is believed many prehistoric peoples, believe(d) that the essence of an animal or human being can be absorbed or assimilated by eating it/him/her. That is the basis for cannibalism.

T.W. Doane maintains that the Egyptians celebrated the resurrection of the god Osiris by eating a sacred cake which became mystically the body of Osiris. During Greek and Roman times the mystery religions had sacred meals of bread and wine. The Eucharist became a sacrament of the Christian church which involves the imbibing of grape juice or wine and bread. While Protestants primarily believe this is done in remembrance of Christ (Luke 22:19), Roman Catholics believe they are actually consuming the body of Christ. This process is known as transubstantiation. Where would such an idea come from? The concept is very similar to totenistic beliefs of neolithic times.

3. Early on hominids existed as hunter-gatherers in bands which are groups of families of less than 100 people. Tribes are groups of people linked by common ancestral ties and may be as large as a few thousand people. As larger and larger groups developed, it became necessary to have rules to keep order. The first law codes that we have uncovered come from Mesopotamia and date back to the third millennium BCE. For the Israelites, tradition ascribes to Moses the formation of laws for their worship of god. In later Judaism, keeping of the laws was particularly important for the sect known as Pharisees.

Certainly for societies, rules and laws are important for keeping peace and order. Rules and laws also continue to be important in some religions. They particularly seem to be stressed in more fundamentalist religions, including in Christianity. However, while Jesus said he has not come to abolish the law, he does stress that what's most important is to follow the spirit of the law rather than the letter of the law. He said the reason for the laws is to love god and to love one's neighbor. He rejected legalism.

4. The worship of sun gods goes all the way back at least to the third millennium BCE in Egypt. Early Egyptian sun gods included Ra, Aten, and Amun. Sun gods were also important in the religions of Assyria and Babylonia and gave rise to astrology and then astronomy. Solar deities continued to be important in the Greco-Roman worlds. In fact, the Roman emperor Aurelian (270-275) promoted the cult of *Sol invictus* (which means *unconquered sun*). He established it as an official cult and attempted to establish it as the primary religion of the Roman empire. The mystery cult, Mithraism, also was a solar religion. Tripolitis (2002) maintains that Mithraism came close to becoming the sole state religion of the Roman Empire if not for the conversion of Constantine to Christianity, which he then promoted.

Mircea (1958) reported that it was once thought that sun-worship was common to all of mankind early on in history, although Mircea believed the practice was more limited (Egypt, Asia, Europe, Peru and Mexico).

Christianity has incorporated some elements of these previous solar religions. Hawkes (1962) even maintains "I do not think it would be an exaggeration to say that in the fourth century and for some time afterwards there was for very many people of the western Empire a total confusion between state Christianity and the state sun worship it displaced." For one thing, the date chosen to celebrate the birth of Jesus is December 25, the time of the winter solstice (the time when the sun is resurrected from its lowest point in the sky). Below is the photo of a Christian monstrance, otherwise known as an ostensorium or ostensory. These were used to hold the Eucharistic host in the middle of the rays of the sun. Still to this day many on Easter morning participate in an Easter sunrise service; this is a celebration of the resurrection of the *Son* with the resurrection of the *Sun*.

5. Water has always been important to religions. It is, after all, a necessity for life as we know it. "The tradition of the primeval waters, whence all the worlds were born, can be found in a great many different versions in ancient and 'primitive' creation beliefs" (Eliade, 1958). The Babylonian *Enuma Elish* describes the existence of primeval waters before the heavens and earth were created. The first creation story in the Hebrew book of Genesis in chapter one also describes the primeval waters' existence prior to god's acts of creation.

Many religious cultures have used the immersion into water to symbolize the cleansing and purifying of the old and creation of new life. This was seen in the many "deluge" or "flood" stories of the ancient near east. Humanity returns to the waters from whence it came, and this is followed by a new era, a new humanity.

This pattern is also seen with baptism. "All that one may call the 'prehistory' of Baptism sought the same object- death and resurrection, though at different religious levels from that of Christianity. There can be no question here of 'influences' or of 'borrowings', for such symbols are archetypal and universal" (Eliade, 1958).

The apostle Paul explains the significance of baptism in his letter to the Romans (6:3-4): *"Do you not know that all of us who have been baptized into Christ Jesus were baptized into his death?* [4] *Therefore we have been buried with him by baptism into death, so that, just as Christ was raised from the dead by the glory of the Father, so we too might walk in newness of life."*

As was discussed earlier in this book, baptism was a custom in many religions, including in Judaism, and was symbolic of the washing away of sins and the beginnings of a new life.

6. The idea of a cosmic battle between good and evil originated with Zoroastrianism. Zoroaster taught that there was but one supreme god, named Mazda. He was in battle with an evil counterpart, Ahriman. Zoroaster believed in an afterlife; after a day of judgment, good people would go to heaven and evil people would go to hell. Zoroaster also believed in a final cosmic battle between good and evil. He believed in a coming divine savior who would play a role in humanity's destiny. The teaching was extremely dualistic: good versus evil, saved versus damned. There was no middle ground. Many credit Zoroastrian thought with such concepts as a Day of Judgment, heaven and hell, a coming divine savior, angels and demons.

A genre of literature developed in both Judaism and later Christianity that reflected many of these ideas; it is known as *apocalypticism*. It was a very important concept for the Jewish sect known as the Essenes. Key elements include a very dualistic view of the world (i.e. good versus evil) and the world's ending in an apocalypse in which good destroys evil. Apocalyptic literature in the Bible includes the book of Daniel and especially the book of Revelation. This viewpoint is still very popular with a certain segment of Christians, as evidenced by the popularity of such books as "The Late Great Planet Earth" and the "Left Behind" series of books.

7. A tremendous change happened in religion during what is known as the Axial Age (800 to 200 BCE). During this period of time religions began to change throughout the

world in terms of de-emphasizing rituals and rules and emphasizing love, justice, and individual spiritual growth. These changes were reflected in the Mediterranean world, India, and China. These ideas continue to be emphasized in all of the great religions of the world today. This will be discussed a great deal in the next book (volume 3) of this series, "Evolution of Morality"

8. Another great change occurred with the idea that it was important what *beliefs* one had. For millennia religions focused on ritual, i.e. what one *did* to please the gods, not what one *believed*. It did not matter what beliefs one held. I believe this started to change with the emphasis on contemplation by the Greek philosophers. The Greek philosophers emphasized thinking and reason. They emphasized thinking above ritual. Plato established The Academy, often considered by historians as the first institution of higher learning in the western world. Plato believed that through contemplation one could better understand the divine.

Gnosticism was a philosophy that evolved and stressed the notion of *gnosis*, a special knowledge that led to salvation that only certain individuals were capable of understanding.

Though there is diversity in gnostic beliefs, there are some common elements. First of all there is the notion of *gnosis*, or "knowledge" or "understanding". The gnostics sought a religious knowledge which had a redeeming or liberating effect. They believed only certain individuals were able to gain this knowledge which had an esoteric character. It was ignorance that kept peoples as slaves, and special knowledge that gave salvation. This divine knowledge was reserved for the elite who had the ability to understand it.

Christians had extremely diverse views in the first few centuries after Jesus' death. "The diverse manifestations of its first three hundred years- whether in terms of social structures, religious practices, or ideologies- have never been replicated." "The existence of wildly diverse expressions of Christianity is abundantly attested in our early sources, many of which bemoan the fact as a sorry state of affairs" (Ehrman, 2011).

All of these Christian groups believed that their beliefs were the right beliefs- that their positions were the true, *orthodox* positions, while other groups of Christians who believed differently were *heretic*. Eventually one group won out- the beliefs advocated by the Roman church. Their scriptures were promoted and replicated, and the scriptures of other groups of Christians were denigrated and often destroyed. Only in the last century were some of these lost scriptures discovered, i.e. Nag Hammadi library.

There developed such an insistence on having correct belief that creeds were developed. The first was the Nicene Creed of 325 CE, developed by a council that met in Nicea of that year. Six more ecumenical councils met between 381 and 787 CE to hash out theological differences, primarily discussions about the nature of Jesus (in what way he was human versus divine) and coming to some consensus about trinitarian theology.

The insistence on holding correct beliefs perhaps peaked with the Protestant Reformation. Martin Luther taught a doctrine known as *sola fide*, or justification by faith alone. He taught that good works did not matter; what mattered was believing the Gospel. So in other words, the predominant religious practice for millennia, i.e. ritual, was completely thrown out by Luther, who taught that the only thing that mattered was a correct belief.

My own belief is that many of these methods for worshiping god have become outdated. Various rituals can be helpful in imparting a sense of reverence and reinforcing a sense of community. However, the idea of making sacrifices to a god to appease or placate makes no sense to me. Nor do I necessarily agree with the concept of a need to make payment for sins or mistakes. That is not to say that society does not need rules and laws, and that often there needs to be external consequences for the breaking of those laws. However, particularly for those at higher stages of spiritual development, I don't think the only reason people do good is out of fear of punishment. This is a topic that will be further explored in subsequent volumes of this book series.

I also disagree with a rigid, dichotomous view of good and evil. Particularly due to my training and experience as a psychologist, I know that people, the world, and life cannot be neatly divided into good versus evil, black versus white, or right versus wrong. Life, including morality, is filled with shades of gray. Cognitive psychotherapy, perhaps the most effective, evidence-based psychotherapy, stresses the amelioration of cognitive distortions, such as inflexible, absolutist thinking in order to relieve emotional distress. The Diagnostic and Statistical Manual of Mental Disorders (DSM-V) lists inflexibility about matters of morality, ethics or values as a symptom of Obsessive-Compulsive Personality Disorder. This too will be further explored in subsequent volumes, particularly the next volume "Evolution of Morality".

One religious theme I hope becomes more prevalent in religions is the focus on justice and ever more inclusive love. This is the major theme of the great spiritual leaders since the Axial Age. Jesus taught that the basic message of the law and the teachings of the prophets was to love God and to love one's neighbor (Matthew 22:36-40). This too will be further explored in this book series.

Another religious theme that I agree with is the importance of knowledge. However, unlike the gnostics, I do not believe that there is a secret, esoteric knowledge that provides salvation. Nor do I believe that only holding an orthodox belief system will provide salvation. I believe that knowledge of god is an ongoing process, i.e. that revelations about god, the material universe, and the spiritual realm is an ongoing process. I also believe that we need to learn about god through various disciplines, not just through ancient scriptures or through theology. My hope is that critical thinking and science become of paramount importance to religion. My hope is that the study of god and religion will become *integral*. This too will be explored further in this book series.

I also believe that *evolution* is perhaps the best term to use to describe god's ever unfolding kingdom. This is a term many religious folks have felt antipathy toward. Evolution has been perceived by many as being contrary to scripture, and even more scary as contrary to people's world views. Many people hold a Homocentric world view, i.e. that mankind is the center of god's universe, the one and only "apple of god's eye". Galileo's and Copernicus' scientific discovery that the sun and not the earth was the center of the solar system was so threatening to the people of that time, that Galileo spent his later years under house arrest due to charges of heresy, which was ordered by Pope Urban VIII. Just as a heliocentric view of the solar system was threatening to the people of that time period, so is evolution threatening to many people of this time period, but the evidence is overwhelming. I believe we need to be open-minded to such new revelations and to change our world views accordingly. I believe that evolution is actually the best evidence there is for the existence of god. This certainly will be explored much more in subsequent volumes of this book series.

Group Discussion Questions

Session #1
(Forward and Chapter 1)

What was your earliest conceptions about the beginnings of religion and the worship of god?

When you were learning things in school, did you learn anything in your classes that contradicted your early conceptions about the beginnings of mankind and religion? How did you reconcile these discrepancies?

What are your beliefs about evolution? What impact does evolution have on Judeo-Christian beliefs? Is there conflict for you between evolution and your religion?

Are humans different in kind or degree from animals?

How much does biology affect who we are, as opposed to the environment that we grow up in? In other words, what effects does *nature* have versus *nurture*?

Of the following traits (enduring characteristics), what impact does biology have versus circumstances, upbringing or culture: intelligence, homosexuality, masculinity/femininity, creativity, personality?

What do you believe is the cause of racism?

What is your reaction to the material in the book about the Y-chromosome Adam and mitochondrial Eve?

According to the research presented in this book, how is it hypothesized that the first conceptions of gods originated?

What rituals are important in your life? Do you feel rituals still play an important part in religion?

What are the benefits of myths?

What questions, comments or reactions do you have about information from the book thus far?

Session #2
(Chapters 2 and 3)

What importance do you put on sacrifice in your own religious beliefs?

Do you believe all sins require a price to be paid, and that the greater the sin the greater the requirement for atonement?

What are your past and present beliefs regarding Hades/Hell/Sheol?

What are your reactions to finding out Mesopotamia had much literature that predated by centuries similar Hebrew writings?

What are your beliefs about the god who instructed Abraham to go to Canaan?

What are your thoughts about Sigmund Freud's hypotheses about Moses and Yahweh?

Magic was part of Egyptian culture. What is the difference between magic and miracles? Is magic part of our own culture?

What is your reaction and thoughts to the similarities between the Egyptian god Horus and Jesus Christ?

Session #3
(Chapters 4 and 5)

Do you believe the Hebrews were god's "chosen" people? Explain.

Do you believe god gets angry and is vindictive? Do you believe god orders the annihilation and slaughter of peoples for whom he is displeased?

Do you believe the Canaanites were evil for worshiping gods other than Yahweh?

Is it a surprise to you that archaeological evidence suggests that the Hebrews for the most part seemed to be indigenous Canaanite peoples, and that there was not a mass exodus from Egypt or a major incursion of Canaan by foreign invaders?

Are you surprised that there is evidence for human sacrifices to Yahweh?

What are your thoughts about the suggestion that the god of Israel was an amalgamation of the gods El and Yahweh?

The Levant was ruled by various empires: the Assyrians, the Babylonians, the Persians, the Greeks and the Romans. Why do you think that empire building and the conquest of nations has been a common phenomenon throughout history?

Astrology has a long history. Despite the lack of demonstrated validity, astrology remains quite popular. Why do you think this is?

Comparing and contrasting Judaism and Zoroastrianism, which religion do you think is closest to modern Christianity? Explain.

What was the significance of the "Axial Age"?

Group Discussion Questions

Session #4
(Chapter 6)

What was "Hellenization"? Was it a positive development for the Jews?

What do you think is the difference between philosophy and theology, and which do you most relate to?

What are the similarities between Christianity and the Greek and Roman "Mystery Religions"?

What was the appeal of early Christianity and the Mystery Religions to the people of that time?

What do you think people look for in religion now? Do you think there have been any changes in regards to what people look for in religion?

What does it mean to be a "person of faith"?

Church attendance and participation continues to wane. Why do you think this is?

The author maintains that one common theme of religions has been a "saving knowledge". What knowledge do you believe is important and "saving"?

In regards to salvation, is it a concept that should apply only to individuals or also to larger entities such as cultures or species?

Jesus preached a "gospel" or "good news". What is the good news?

Appendix A
The Pharaoh Akhenaten's Hymn to the Sun

A

You rise glorious at the heavens' edge, O living Aten!
You in whom all life began.
When you shone from the eastern horizon
You filled every land with your beauty.
You are lovely, great and glittering,
You go high above the lands you have made,
Embracing them with your rays,
Holding them fast for your eloved son.
Though you are far away, your rays are on earth;
Though you fill men's eyes, your footprints are unseen.

B

When you sink beyond the western boundary of the heavens
The earth is darkened as though by death;
Then men sleep in their bedchambers,
Their heads wrapped up, unable to see one another;
Their treasures are stolen from beneath their heads
And they know it not.
Every lion comes out from his lair,
All serpents emerge and sting.
Darkness is supreme and the earth silent;
Their maker rests within his horizon.

C

The earth brightens with your rising,
With the shining of your disk by day;
Before your rays the darkness is put to flight.
The people of the Two Lands celebrate the day,
You rouse them and raise them to their feet,
They wash their limbs, they dress themselves,
They lift up their arms in praise of your appearing,
Then through all the land they begin their work.

D
Cattle browse peacefully,
Trees and plants are verdant,
Birds fly from their nests
And lift up their wings in your praise.
All animals frisk upon their feet
All winged things fly and alight once more-
They come to life with your rising

E
Boats sail upstream and boats sail downsteam,
At your coming every highway is opened.
Before your face the fish leap up from the river,
Your rays reach the green ocean.
You it is who place the male seed in woman,
Who create the semen in man;
You quicken the son in his mother's belly
Soothing him so that he shall not cry.
Even in the womb you are his nurse.
You give breath to all your creation,
Opening the mouth of the newborn
And giving him nourishment.

F
When the chicken chirps from within the shell
You give him breath that he may live.
You bring his body to readiness
So that he may break from the egg.
And when he is hatched he runs on his two feet
Announcing his creation.

G
How manifold are your works!
They are mysterious in men's sight.
O sole, incomparable god, all powerful,
You created the earth in solitude
As your heart desired.
Men you created, and cattle great and small,
Whatever is on earth,
All that tread the ground on foot,
All that wing the lofty air.
You created the strange countries, Khor and Kush
As well as the Land of Egypt.
You set every man in his right place
With his food and his possessions
And his days that are numbered.
Men speak in many tongues,
In body and complexion they are various,
For you have distinguished between people and people.

H
In the Netherworld you make the Nile-flood
Leading it out at your pleasure to bring life for the Egyptians.
Though lord of them all, lord of their lands,
You grow weary for them, shine for them,
The Sun Disk by day, great in your majesty.
To far lands also you have brought life,
Setting them a Nile-flood in the heavens
That falls like the waves of the sea
Watering the fields where they dwell.

I
How excellent are your purposes, O lord of eternity!
You have set a Nile in the sky for the strangers,
For the cattle of every country that go on their feet.
But for Egypt the Nile wells from the Netherworld.
Your rays nourish field and garden
It is for you that they live.

J
You make the seasons for the sake of your creation,
The winter to cool them, the summer that they may taste your heat.
You have made far skies so that you may shine in them,
Your disk in its solitude looks on all that you have made,
Appearing in its glory and gleaming both near and far.
Out of your singleness you shape a million forms-
Towns and villages, fields, roads and the river.
All eyes behold you, bright Disk of the day.

K
There is none other who knows you save Akhenaten, your son,
You have given him insight of your purposes
He understands your power.
All the creatures of the world are in your hand
Just as you have made them.
With your rising they live, with your setting they die.
You yourself are the span of life, men live through you
Their eyes filled with beauty till the hour of your setting
all labour is set aside
When you sink in the west.

L
You established the world for your son,
He who was born of your body,
King of Upper Egypt and Lower Egypt,
Living in Truth, Lord of the Two Lands,
Neferkheprure, Wanre
The Son of Re, Living in Truth, Lord of Diadems,
Akhenaten great in his length of days.
And for the King's Great Wife,
She who he loves,
For the Lady of the Two Lands, Nefernefruaten-Nefertiti
May she live and flower for ever and ever.

Bibliography

Chapter 1

Bellah, Robert N. (2011). Religion in Human Evolution: From the Paleolithic to the Axial Age. Cambridge, Massachusetts: The Belknap Press of Harvard University Press.

Bergounioux, O.F.M. and Goetz, Joseph. (1966). Primitive and Prehistoric Religions. New York, New York: Hawthorn Books.

Christian, David (2011) Maps of Time: An Introduction to Big History. Berkley: University of California Press.

Christian, David, Brown, Cynthia and Benjamin, Craig (2014). Big History: Between Nothing and Everything. New York, New York: McGraw-Hill Education.

De Waal Malefijt, Annemarie (1968) Religion And Culture: An Introduction to Anthropology of Religion. Long Grove, IL: Waveland Press.

Donald, Merlin (1991). Origins of the Modern Mind: Three Stages in the Evolution of Culture and Cognition. Cambridge: Harvard University Press.

Durkheim, Emile (1912). The Elementary Forms of Religious Life. New York: The Free Press.

DK Publishing (2009). Prehistoric Life: The Definitive Visual History of Life on Earth.

Eliade, Mircea (1978). A History of Religious Ideas: From the Stone Age to the Eleusinian Mysteries. Chicago, IL: The University of Chicago Press.

Fagen, Brian M. and Durrani, Nadia (2014). People of the Earth: An Introduction to World Prehistory, 14th Ed. Pearson.

Hawkes, Jacquetta (1976). The Atlas of Early Man. New York, New York: St. Martin's Press.

James, E.O. (1957). Prehistoric Religion. New York, Nenw York: Frederick Praeger.

Lee, Richard B. and Daly, Richard (1999). The Cambridge Encyclopedia of Hunters and Gatherers. Cambridge, UK: Cambridge University Press.

Petitt, Paul (2002). Origins of burial. British Archaeology, Issue 66

Roberts, Alice (2011). Evolution: The Human Story. New York, New York: DK Publishing.

Smith, William Robertson (2002). Religion of the Semites. New Brunswick, NJ: Transaction Publishers.

Tyler, Edward Burnett (1874). Primitive Culture. New York, New York: Henry Holt and Company.

Wade, Nicholas (2006). Before the Dawn: Recovering the Lost History of Our Ancestors. New York, New York: Penguin Books.

Winks, Robin and Mattern-Parkes, Susan (2004). The Ancient Mediterranean World: From the Stone Age to A.D. 600. New York, New York: Oxford University Press.

Wright, Robert (2009). The Evolution of God. New York, New York: Little, Brown and Company.

Chapter 2

Bottero, Jean (2001). Religion in Ancient Mesopotamia. Chicago, IL: University of Chicago Press.

Dalley, Stephanie. (1989). Myths from Mesopotamia. New York: Oxford University Press.

Davies, W.W. (1905). The Codes of Hammurabi and Moses. Cincinnati: Jennings and Graham.

Fagen, Brian M. and Durrani, Nadia (2014). People of the Earth: An Introduction to World Prehistory, 14th Ed. Pearson.

George, Andrew (1999) translator. The Epic of Gilgamesh. London: Penguin Books.

Gordon, Cyrus & Rendsburg, Gary (1997). The Bible and the Ancient Near East. New York: W.W. Norton & Company.

Hawkes, Jacquetta (1976). The Atlas of Early Man. New York, New York: St. Martin's Press.

Holland, Glenn S. (2009). Gods in the Desert: Religions of the Ancient Near East. Lanham, Maryland: Rowman & Littlefield Publishers, Inc.

Kramer, Samuel Noah (1956). History Begins at Sumer: Thirty-Nine Firsts in Recorded History. Philadelphia, PA: University of Pennsylvania Press.

Smith, William Robertson (2002). Religion of the Semites. New Brunswick, NJ: Transaction Publishers.

Winks, Robin W. & Mattern-Parkes, Susan P. (2004). The Ancient Mediterranean World: From the Stone Age to A.D. 600. New York: Oxford University Press.

Chapter 3

Fagen, Brian M. and Durrani, Nadia (2014). People of the Earth: An Introduction to World Prehistory, 14th Ed. Pearson.

Freud, Sigmund (1939). Moses and Monotheism. New York: Vintage Books.

Gordon, Cyrus & Rendsburg, Gary (1997). The Bible and the Ancient Near East. New York: W.W. Norton & Company.

Hawkes, Jacquetta (1976). The Atlas of Early Man. New York, New York: St. Martin's Press.

Holland, Glenn S. (2009). Gods in the Desert: Religions of the Ancient Near East. Lanham, Maryland: Rowman & Littlefield Publishers, Inc.

Murdock, D.M. (2009). Christ in Egypt: the Horus-Jesus Connection. Stellar House Publishing.

Pinch, Geraldine (2002). Egyptian Mythology: A Guide to the Gods, Goddesses, and Traditions of Ancient Egypt. New York: Oxford University Press.

Shafer, Byron (1991). Religion in Ancient Egypt: Gods, Myths, and Personal Practice. Ithica, NY: Cornell University Press.

Shaw, Ian (2000). The Oxford History of Ancient Egypt. New York: Oxford University Press.

Winks, Robin W. & Mattern-Parkes, Susan P. (2004). The Ancient Mediterranean World: From the Stone Age to A.D. 600. New York: Oxford University Press.

Chapter 4

Coogan, M. (1998). The Oxford History of the Biblical World. New York, NY: Oxford University Press.

Coogan, M. and Smith, M. (2012). Stories From Ancient Canaan, 2nd Edition. Louisville, KY: Westminster John Knox Press.

Davies, N. (1981). Human Sacrifice In History and Today. New York, NY: William Morrow and Company, Inc.

Day, John (2000). Yahweh and the Gods and Goddesses of Canaan. New York, NY: Sheffield Academic Press Ltd.

Dever, William (2003). Who Were the Early Israelites and Where Did They Come From? Grand Rapids, MI: Eerdmans Publishing

Eliade, Mircea (1978). A History of Religious Ideas: From the Stone Age to the Eleusinian Mysteries. Chicago, IL: The University of Chicago Press.

Finkelstein, I. and Silberman, N. (2001). The Bible Unearthed. New York, NY: Touchstone.

Gordon, C. and Rendsburg, G. (1997). The Bible and the Ancient Near East. New York, NY: W.W. Norton and Company.

Holland, G. (2009). Gods in the Desert: Religions of the Ancient Near East. Lanham, Maryland: Rowman & Littlefield Publishers, Inc.

Levenson, J. (1993). The Death and Resurrection of the Beloved Son. New Haven, CT: Yale University Press.

Olyan, Saul (1988). Asherah and the Cult of Yahweh in Israel. Atlanta: Society of Biblical Literature.

Smith, M. (2002). The Early History of God: Yahweh and the Other Deities in Ancient Israel, 2nd ed. Grand Rapids: Wm. Eerdmans Publishing Co.

Smith, W.R. (2012). Religion of the Semites. New Brunswick, New Jersey: Transaction Publishers.

Tierney, P. (1989). The Highest Altar: The Story of Human Sacrifice. New York, NY: Penguin.

Tubb, Jonathan. (1998). Canaanites. University of Oklahoma Press.

Van Der Toorn, K., Becking, B & Van Der Horst, P. (1999). Dictionary of Deities and Demons in the Bible, 2nd ed. Grand Rapids: Wm. Eerdmans Publishing.

Walton, John (2009). The Lost World of Genesis One. Downers Grove, IL: InterVarsity Press.

Winks, R. and Mattern-Parkes, S. (2004). The Ancient Mediterranean World: From the Stone Age to A.D. 600. New York: Oxford University Press.

Wright, Robert. (2009). The Evolution of God. New York, NY: Little, Brown and Company.

Chapter 5

Armstrong, Karen (2006). The Great Transformation: The Beginning of Our Religious Traditions. New York: Anchor Books.

Bellah, Robert and Joas, Hans (2012). The Axial Age and Its Consequences. Cambridge, Massachusetts: Belknap Press of Harvard University.

Bobrick, Benson (2005). The Fated Sky: Astrology in History. New York, NY: Simon and Schuster.

Bottero, Jean (2001). Religion in Ancient Mesopotamia. Chicago, IL: University of Chicago Press.

Boyce, Mary (1979). Zoroastrians: Their Religious Beliefs and Practices. New York, NY: Routledge.

Campion, Nicholas (2008). A History of Western Astrology: Vol 1 The Ancient World. New York, NY: Bloomsbury.

Coogan, M. (1998). The Oxford History of the Biblical World. New York, NY: Oxford University Press.

Day, John (2000). Yahweh and the Gods and Goddesses of Canaan. New York, NY: Sheffield Academic Press Ltd.

Eliade, Mircea (1978). A History of Religious Ideas: From the Stone Age to the Eleusinian Mysteries. Chicago, IL: The University of Chicago Press.

Finkelstein, I. and Silberman, N. (2001). The Bible Unearthed. New York, NY: Touchstone.

Gordon, C. and Rendsburg, G. (1997). The Bible and the Ancient Near East. New York, NY: W.W. Norton and Company.

Hawkes, Jacquetta (1963). Man and the Sun. London: Cresset Press.

Hick, John (1991). An Interpretation of Religion: Human Responses to the Transcendent. New Haven: Yale University Press.

Holland, G. (2009). Gods in the Desert: Religions of the Ancient Near East. Lanham, Maryland: Rowman & Littlefield Publishers, Inc.

Jaspers, Karl (1953). The Origin and Goal of History. London: Routledge & Kegan Paul Ltd.

Rochberg, Francesca (2004). The Heavenly Writing: Divination, Horoscopy, and Astronomy in Mesopotamian Culture. Cambridge, UK: Cambridge University Press.

Roux, Georges (1992). Ancient Iraq. London, England: Penguin.

Schneider, Tammi (2011). An Introduction to Ancient Mesopotamian Religion. Grand Rapids, MI: Eerdmans.

Snell, Daniel (2011). Religions of the Ancient Near East. New York, NY: Cambridge University Press

Van De Mieroop, Marc (2004). A History of the Ancient Near East. Malden, MA: Blackwell Publishing Ltd.

Van Der Toorn, K., Becking, B & Van Der Horst, P. (1999). Dictionary of Deities and Demons in the Bible, 2nd ed. Grand Rapids: Wm. Eerdmans Publishing.

Waters, Matt (2014). Ancient Persia: A Concise History of the Achaemenid Empire, 550-330 BCE. New York, NY: Cambridge University Press.

Whitfield, Peter (2001). Astrology: a History. New York, NY: Harry N. Abrams, Inc.

Wiesehofer, Josef (2001). Ancient Persia. New York, NY: I.B. Tauris & Co Ltd.

Chapter 6

Angus, S. (1925). The Mystery-Religions: A Study in the Religious Background of Early Christianity. New York: Dover Publications.

Aslan, Reza (2013). Zealot: The Life and Times of Jesus of Nazareth. New York: Random House.

Bauer, Walter (1996). Orthodoxy & Heresy in Earliest Christianity. Mifflintown, PA: Sigler Press.

Borg, Marcus (2011). Speaking Christian: Why Christian Words Have Lost Their Meaning and Power. New York: Harper One.

Coogan, M. (1998). The Oxford History of the Biblical World. New York, NY: Oxford University Press.

Doane, T.W. (1882). Bible Myths and Their Parallels in Other Religions. New York, NY: The Truth Seeker Co.

Durant, Will (1944). The Story of Civilization. New York: Simon and Shuster.

Ehrman, Bart (2011). The Orthodox Corruption of Scripture. New York: Oxford University Press.

Ehrman, Bart (2012). The New Testament: A Historical Introduction to the Early Christian Writings, 5th ed. New York: Oxford University Press.

Ehrman, Bart (2014). How Jesus Became God: The Exaltation of a Jewish Preacher from Galilee. New York: Harper One.

Ehrman, Bart (2015). After the New Testament: A Reader in Early Christianity 11-300 CE, 2nd ed. New York: Oxford University Press.

Eliade, Mircea (1958). Patterns in Comparative Religion. Lincoln, NE: University of Nebraska Press.

Ferguson, Everett (2003). Backgrounds of Early Christianity, Third Edition. Grand Rapids, MI: Wm. Eerdmans Publishing

Hawkes, Jacquetta (1963). Man and the Sun. London: Cresset Press.

Hengel, Martin (1974). Judaism and Hellenism. Philadelphia, PA: Fortress Press.

Jeffers, James (1999). The Greco-Roman World of the New Testament Era. Downers Grove, IL: InterVarsity Press.

Meyer, Marvin (1987). The Ancient Mysteries: A Sourcebook of Sacred Texts. Philadelphia: University of Pennsylvania Press.

Peppard, Michael (2011). The Son of God in the Roman World: Divine Sonship in its Social and Political Context. New York: Oxford University Press.

Philostratus, Flavius (220). The Life of Apollonius of Tyana. Sacramento, CA: reprinted by Ancient Wisdom Publications.

Rudolph, Kurt (1984). Gnosis: The Nature & History of Gnosticism. New York, NY: HarperCollins.

Stark, Rodney (2007). Discovering God: The Origins of the Great Religions and the Evolution of Belief. New York: Harper One.

Tripolitis, Antonia (2002). Religions of the Hellenistic-Roman Age. Grand Rapids, MI: Wm Eerdmans Publishing.

Tuggy, Dale, "Trinity", *The Stanford Encyclopedia of Philosophy* (Winter 2016 Edition), Edward N. Zalta (ed.), forthcoming URL = <http://plato.stanford.edu/archives/win2016/entries/trinity/>

Whitfield, Peter (2001). Astrology: a History. New York, NY: Harry N. Abrams, Inc.

Winks, Robin and Mattern-Parkes, Susan (2004). The Ancient Mediterranean World: From the Stone Age to A.D. 600. New York, New York: Oxford University Press.

Index

Aaron, 136, 138, 145, 157-158, 179
Abba, 265
Abel, 177-178, 287
Abimelek, 107
Aborigines, 217
Abraham, 6-9, 12, 70, 77, 106-109, 113, 135-136, 140, 183, 186, 188, 194, 196, 198, 232, 280, 287, 303
Abu, 132-133
Achaemenes, 223
Achaemenid, 223, 237, 323
Adad, 88, 206
Adam, 1, 42-43, 78
Adonai, 196
Adonis, 255, 280-281, 283
Adrammelech, 210
Adrian, 284
Aegyptiaca, 116
Aemilius, 259
Aesculapius, 280, 284-285
Aethiopicus, 30
Afarensis, 30
Africanus, 30
Ahaz, 185-186, 209-210
Ahmose, 124, 126, 138
Ahriman, 13, 227, 294
Ahura, 226-227, 273
Ain, 54, 59
Akhenaten, 10, 127-129, 138-139, 143, 151, 217, 227
Akkad, 70, 81
Akkadian, 70, 76, 79-81, 83-84, 86-88, 90
Akki, 82
Albinus, 246-247
Alexander, 151, 237-238, 258
Alexandria, 238, 246, 284
Altamira, 49
Amalek, 184
Amalekites, 160, 166
Amarna, 128-129, 132
Amen, 127
Amenemhat, 122
Amenhotep, 9, 126-129, 133, 138
Amenmessu, 134
Amman, 182
Ammianus, 270

Ammon, 172
Ammonites, 184-185
Amorite, 70, 83-84, 135, 160, 162, 166, 168
Amos, 215, 232
Amun, 124-126, 128-129, 132, 139
Anakites, 160
Anamensis, 29
Anat, 133, 141, 152, 175, 189, 193
Anatolia, 55-56, 90, 213, 254
Anaximander, 230
Andrew, 317
angels, 7, 229, 272, 282, 294
Angus, 250-253, 324,
Animism, 6, 58, 60-61, 289
Ankara, 55-56
Ankhesenamun, 129
Ankhesenpaaten, 129
Antecessor, 31
antediluvian, 78
anthropologists, 2, 18-19, 26, 39, 56, 58, 62, 315
Antigonid, 237
Antonia, 326
Antony, 259
Anu, 76, 87, 91, 94, 220
Anunnaki, 85
Anup, 154
Aphrodite, 240-241, 258
Apis, 157-158
Apocryphal, 229
Apollinarian, 251
Apollo, 240, 257, 279-280
Apollonius, 240, 267, 326
Apotheosis, 272
Aqaba, 140, 158, 193, 195
Aqedah, 188
Arabah, 195
Arabs, 79, 211
Arad, 161
Aram, 108, 209
Aramaeans, 79, 172, 206
Aramaic, 81, 84, 172, 214, 261
Ararat, 94
Archimedes, 230
Areians, 223
Ares, 240-241, 258

argon, 23-24
Aristides, 269
Aristotle, 237, 241, 246, 249
ark, 94, 165
Armenia, 79, 258
Armstrong, Karen, 234, 321
Arno, 99
Artemis, 240, 257
Aryan, 223
Asenath, 112
Ashdod, 171
Asher, 169, 192, 204
Asherah, 175, 186, 189, 192, 199, 211, 320
Ashkelon, 171
Ashtarte, 181
Ashur, 207
Ashurbanipal, 211-212
Ashurnasirpal, 206-207
Asshur, 84, 88
Assur, 206-209, 212-213
Assyria, 115, 206-213, 225, 290
Assyrian, 12-13, 73, 79, 90, 146, 206-210, 212-214, 304
Astarte, 133, 141, 152, 189, 193
AstarteChemosh, 184
Astartes, 203
astrologers, 222, 225
Astrology, 13, 216-218, 220, 222, 225, 240-242, 274, 290, 305, 321-323, 326
Astronomy, 212, 218, 240-241, 290, 323
ataraxia, 245
Aten, 9-10, 127-129, 132, 138-139, 141-143, 151, 217, 290
Athena, 240, 257
Athens, 253
Athirat, 192
Atkinson, 63
Atlas, 316-318
Atrahasis, 70, 99, 287
Attys, 280
Atum, 142-144, 149-151
Atun, 248
Augustine, 2, 248, 278, 285
Augustus, 260, 268, 272
Aurignacian, 44, 48-50,
aurochs, 51, 157

australopithecines, 33
Australopithecus, 29-30, 35
Avaris, 123, 132, 171
Axial Age, 12, 15, 229-231, 233-234, 294, 298, 305, 315, 321
Ay, 131
Aztecs, 217

Ba, 123, 143, 147
Baal, 133, 152, 175, 181, 185-186, 189-193, 198-200, 203, 219
Babel, 103, 174
Babylon, 13, 70, 84, 87-88, 94, 100, 102, 106, 207, 209-210, 213-216, 224-225
Babylonia, 84, 211-214, 216, 223, 225, 241, 290
Babylonians, 12-13, 79, 84, 90, 94-95, 99, 139, 146, 167, 187, 199, 207, 212-219, 221-224, 241, 248, 256, 263, 293, 304
Bacchus, 253-255, 258, 279-281, 283-284
Bahrelghazali, 30
Bahri, 122
Balaam, 162-163
Balak, 162-163
Baldus, 283
Baptism, 14, 251-252, 256, 293-294
Bashan, 162
Bauer, 271, 324
Bazile, 39
Bears, 10, 46, 61, 180, 210, 248
Beijing, 63
Bel, 94
Belknap, 315, 321
Bellah, 315, 321
Benson, 321
Bergounioux, 315
Bering, 36, 44
Bethel, 107, 109, 158, 176, 192
Bethlehem, 279, 281
Bible, 9, 26-27, 75, 78, 92-93, 102, 113, 134-136, 138, 145, 179, 196-197, 200, 248, 261, 294, 317-318, 320-324
Bilgamesh, 90
Borg, Marcus, 260, 324

Bottero, 317, 321
Boyce, 226, 228, 321
Brahma, 248
Brahman, 234
Brahmanism, 226
Britain, 48, 217
Bronze, 32, 70, 74, 169-171
Brutus, 259
Buddha, 12, 229-230, 277, 279-282
Buddhism, 230, 288
Buddhist, 256, 288
Bull, 54-55, 91, 157-158, 178
Byblos, 173, 182

Caesar, 259-260, 268, 272, 285
Cain, 177-178, 287
Cairo, 130
Calah, 208
calf, 157-158, 183
Calvanist, 2
Cambyses, 237
Campion, 220, 225, 322
Canaan, 6-11, 107-109, 112-113, 135, 157, 160, 165-167, 169, 171-173, 175, 181, 184, 189, 191, 198, 303-304, 319, 322
Canaanite, 10-11, 79, 81, 83, 107-108, 146, 160-161, 166, 168-170, 172-173, 175, 181, 183, 190, 192, 199, 204, 304, 320
Cannibalism, 63-64, 289
canon, 141, 167, 228-229, 275, 282
canonical, 229, 261
Carthage, 180-186
Catal, 53-55, 157
Catholic, 279, 287, 289
Caucasus, 258
cave, 3, 33, 45-49, 51, 63-64, 113, 243-244, 274, 280
Ceres, 257
Cezaire, 46
Chalcolithic, 74
Chaldeans, 106, 211, 213
Chaldees, 77
Chapelle, 64
Charente, 45
Chauvet, 49

Cheops, 118
Chicago, 46, 315, 317, 320-322
Chiefdoms, 73-74, 114, 160
Chima, 36, 229-230, 278-279, 295
Chou, 63-64
Chrishna, 282
Christ, 3, 225, 229-230, 256, 277, 282, 284-285, 289, 293, 303, 318
chromosome, 38, 40-44, 301
Chronicles, 225
Chthonic, 187
Chuang, 229
Cicero, 255
circumcision, 7, 10108, 139, 141, 188-189, 232
citystates, 75, 85
Clement, 284
Cleopatra, 259
Colossi, 126-127
Confucius, 12, 229-230, 279-280
Constantine, 271, 275, 278, 290
constellations, 219, 222
Coogan, 172, 215, 319, 322, 324
Copernicus, 298
Crishna, 279-281
Croatia, 45
Croesus, 223
Cromagnon, 47
crone, 54
Cronus, 239-240
cuneiform, 70, 80, 90, 99
Cybele, 253-254
Cynics, 246
Cyrus', 223-225, 237, 317-318

daevas, 227
Damascus, 172, 209
Damgalnuna, 87
Damkina, 87
Danae, 284
Daniel, 200, 228, 230, 294, 323
Darius, 237
Darwin, 26
David, 66, 166, 175, 181, 184, 204, 280, 315
Davies, 95, 183, 186, 317, 319
deluge, 122-123, 99, 104, 293

Demeter, 239, 253, 257
demons, 89, 154, 264, 266-267, 272, 294, 321, 323
dendrochronology, 23
Denisovans, 37
deoxyribonucleic, 38
Deuteronomist, 11, 71, 197
Deuteronomy, 11, 176, 198-199, 211, 215
Dever, 167-169, 204, 319
Diana, 257
Diaspora, 224
Dijk, 127-128
Dilmun, 101, 104
dinosaurs, 19
Diocletian, 274
Dionysus, 240, 253, 258
divination, 89, 323
diviners, 89, 176, 264
Djoser, 117-118
DNA, 18, 20, 34, 36-44
Doane, 255-256, 278, 280-285, 289, 324
Documentary Hypothesis, 11, 197, 275
Dorians, 230
Dover, 224
Druids, 256
Dumuzi, 87
Durant, Will, 248, 324
Durkheim, Emile, 57, 315
Durrani, 316-318

Easter, 291
Eblaite, 111
Ecclesiastes, 92, 106, 225, 228, 245, 276
Ecclesiasticus, 276
eclipse, 220
Ecliptic, 220-222
Eden, 1, 42-43, 101, 105
Edom, 168, 172, 193-195, 198-199,
Edomites, 195
Egypt, 7-10, 51, 72, 80, 82, 107, 111-117, 119-129, 131-141, 173-175, 147, 149-153, 155, 157-158, 165, 167, 199, 171-173, 182-183, 188, 194, 197, 199, 203, 209, 211-214, 217, 226, 237-238, 240, 248, 259, 272, 275, 290, 304, 318-319

Ehrman, Bart, 248, 265-267, 270, 277, 296, 324-325
Eissfeldt, 187
Ekron, 171
El, 11, 175, 189-194, 197-200, 304
Elam, 80, 214
Elamites, 80, 83, 211, 223
Eleusinian, 281, 253, 255, 315, 320, 322
Eliade, 256, 293, 315, 320, 322, 325
Elijah, 185, 230
Elish, 70, 99-100, 293
Ellil, 87
Elohim, 11, 197
Elohist, 11, 71, 197
Enki, 74, 87-88, 101, 104, 215
Enkidu, 91-92
Enlil, 87-88, 91, 93, 99, 207, 220
Ennead, 144, 149-150, 153
Enoch, 78, 229
Enosh, 78
Enuma, 70, 99-100, 293
Epicurean, 245
Erech, 75
Ereshkigal, 88
ergaster, 34-35
Eridu, 74
Esarhaddon, 210
Esau, 108
Esh, 200
Essenes, 13-14, 261-262, 275-276, 294
Esther, 225, 261
Ethiopia, 36, 43, 148
ethnographies, 18, 20, 56-57
Etruscans, 257
Eucharist, 255, 289
Eudoxus, 240
eukarya, 27
Euphrates, 72, 82-83, 101, 105, 165, 210
Eusebius, 270, 280, 284
Eve, 1, 42-43, 101, 105, 182, 177, 287, 301
Everett, 243, 325
Exodus, 10-11, 77, 105, 134-136, 138-140, 157-158, 166-169, 179, 183, 187, 193-194, 196, 198, 215, 304
Ezekiel, 168, 182, 187, 215, 230
Ezra, 224-225

Fagen, 316-318
Ferguson, 243, 254, 325
Fetishism, 60
Finkelstein, 169, 192, 200, 204-205, 320, 322
Flavius, 267, 326
Flores, 35
floresiensis, 35
Freud, Sigmund, 9-10, 138-141, 303, 318

Gabriel, 200
Gad, 163
Galilee, 160, 264-265, 325
Galileo, 298
Geb,144, 149-152
Gehenna, 187
Genesis, 1-2, 6, 8, 11, 26-27, 75, 77, 93, 100-101, 103-108, 122, 148, 160, 174, 177-178, 183, 190, 215, 272, 293, 321
genetics, 40, 43
genocide, 166
genome, 38, 40
genus, 27-28, 30-32, 35
geology, 19, 26
Gerizim, 263
Ghazal, 54, 59
Gibeonites, 166, 184
Gilgamesh, 70, 75, 90-93, 99, 105-106, 317
Girgashites, 166
Giza, 118-120
Gnosticism, 226, 251, 275-278, 295, 298, 326
Goetz, 315
Goshen, 113, 137, 139, 157, 159
Gozan, 209
Gravettian, 44, 49-50

Habakkuk, 215, 230
Habilis, 30, 35
Habor, 209
Hades, 86, 176, 228270, 258, 303
Haggai, 255
Halafians, 73
Ham, 94
Hamath, 209

Hammadi,270, 275-277, 296
Hammon, 181
Hammurabi, 12, 70, 84, 94-95, 99, 317
Hanan, 265
Hanukkah, 238
Haran, 6, 107
Harran, 216
Hasidim, 260
Hasidism, 260
Hasmonean, 257, 290
Hassunans, 73
Hathor, 122
Hatshepsutt, 127
Hatti, 171
Hawkes, 216, 290, 316-318, 322, 325
Hebron, 108
Hegel, 229
Heidelbergensis, 31, 34-35, 45
Heliodromus, 273
Heliopolis, 150
Hell, 13, 187
Hellenism, 325
Hellenistic, 268, 249, 253-254, 273, 276, 326
Hellenization, 238, 306
Henotheism, 10, 173
Hephaestus, 240, 258
heptad, 226-227
Heraclitus, 230, 284
Herakleopolis, 121
Hercules, 279-281, 283-284
Hermes, 240-241, 258, 280
Herod, 281
Herodotus, 139, 178
Hestia, 270, 258
Hezekish, 210-211, 262
hieroglyphics,' 80-81
Hilkiah, 212
Hilqiah, 265
Hindoo,282
Hinduism,248
Hinnom, 185-187
Hipparchus, 270
Hiram, 181
Hittite, 84, 133, 135, 176, 160, 165-166, 168, 171,
Hivites, 135, 166

Index

Hobab, 140
Holland, Glenn, 89, 118, 144, 177, 317-318, 320, 322
Homer, 230
Homocentric, 298
homosexuality, 301
Honi, 265
Horeb, 157
Horemheb, 131-132
Horst, 190, 321, 323
Horus, 117, 119-121, 128-129, 144-145, 147, 150, 152-154, 217, 254, 279-281, 283, 303, 318
Hosea, 140, 215
Hoshea, 209
Humbaba, 91
huntergatherer, 57-58, 66
Hurrian, 201
Huyuk, 53-55, 157
Hyksos, 123-124, 139, 171
Hyrcanians, 223

Inanna, 75-76, 82, 87, 216
Incans, 217
India, 36, 61, 229-230, 237, 273, 295
Indonesia, 35
Indra, 227
Iran, 36, 48, 79-80, 212-213, 223, 230
Iraq, 72, 211, 323
Isaac, 7-9, 12, 107-108, 135-136, 140, 183, 186, 188, 194, 196, 198, 279, 287
Isaiah, 12-13, 176, 187, 200, 215, 219, 224, 230, 232-233
Ishkur, 87-88
Ishmael, 200
Ishtar, 82, 87, 91, 94, 105, 216, 241
Ishtumegu, 223
Isis, 144, 150-153, 251, 253-254, 256
Islam, 226
Italy, 48-49, 64, 254, 257-260
Jacob, 7-9, 12, 108-109, 112-113, 122, 135-136, 140, 148, 190, 194, 196, 198, 232

Jacobsen, 92
Jahwe, 197
Jaspers, Karl, 229-231, 233-234, 322

Java, 94
Jebusites, 135, 160, 166
Jehoahaz, 212
Jehoiachin, 212-214
Jehoiakim, 212-213
Jehovah (JEHOVAH), 136, 195-196
Jennings, 317
Jephthah, 184-185
Jerahmeelites, 166
Jeremiah, 13, 186-187, 200, 215, 219, 230, 232-233
Jericho, 83-84, 59, 63, 162, 165, 168, 170, 184
Jeroboam, 205
Jerome, 280
Jerusalem, 102, 106, 158, 166, 173, 176, 186, 192, 204-205, 209-211, 213-214, 219, 224, 239, 268, 257-258, 261, 263, 265
Jesus, 13, 15, 229, 238, 247, 261-266, 268-270, 276-277, 279-282, 284-285, 287, 290-291, 293, 296, 298, 303, 306, 318, 324-325
Jethro, 9, 135, 140, 193
Joas, 321
Job, 101-102, 105, 204-205, 225
Joel, 225
Johannine, 246
Jonah, 225
Jonathan, 200, 320
Jordan, 10, 34, 54, 108, 160, 162-163, 165, 170, 173, 193
Josephus, 116, 260-261, 263,
Joshua, 10, 163, 165-166, 184, 199-200, 203, 215
Josiah, 12-13, 186-187, 211-212, 218
Judah, 12-13, 158, 172, 176, 213, 185-186, 197, 200, 204-205, 209-214, 218-219, 224
Judaism, 2-3, 12-13, 174-175, 211, 226, 228, 243, 246, 256, 260-261, 268-269, 278, 287, 289, 294, 305, 325
Judas,
Jude, 262
Judea, 237-238, 263-264
Judean, 13, 183, 214
Juno, 257

Jupiter, 218, 241, 257, 272-273

Kadesh, 160
Kassites, 70, 84
Kenite, 140, 195
Kenizzites, 166
Khafra, 118-119
Khufu, 118
Kidron, 186
Kish, 76, 78, 82
Kishon, 185
Kramer, 101, 318
Krapina, 45
Kronos, 241
KRST, 154

Laban, 7, 108
Lamentations, 102, 106, 215
,Lanham, 317-318
Lascaux, 33, 49
Latin, 80, 241, 248
Lebanon, 34, 72, 165, 170, 172-173, 181
Lepidus, 259
Levant, 10, 34, 48, 52-53, 72, 86, 90, 134, 141, 166, 168, 170, 304
Levenson, 187, 189, 320
Leviathan, 175
Levite, 135, 182, 188
Leviticus, 11, 178-179, 215
ligers, 37
Logos, 233, 239, 246, 284
Lot, 107-108
Lothan, 175
Lucy, 30
Luke, 15, 279-280, 289
Luther, 296-297
Lydia, 211, 223

Maat, 149, 152-153
Maccabees, 228
Macedonia, 259
Magus, 266
Mahalalel, 78
Malachi, 225
Malaysia, 61
Manasseh, 163, 185-186
Manetho, 116

Mani, 277
Manicheism, 277-278
Marcionites, 247, 271
Marduk, 87-88, 100, 175, 207, 215-217, 241,
Mars, 218, 241, 258, 273
Martyr, 284
Marx, 57
Matthew, 13, 15, 225, 263, 270, 279-282, 298
Mazda, 13, 226-227, 273, 294
Medes, 209, 212, 223
Media, 212, 214
meiosis, 40-42
Melanesians, 37
Memnon, 126-127
Memphis, 116, 122, 129, 158
Menes, 116
Menkaura, 119
Mentuhotep, 121
Mercury, 218, 241, 258, 272-273, 279, 283-285
Merlin, Donald, 65, 315
Merneptah, 133, 138, 167, 169, 171
Mesolithic, 32-33
Methuselah, 78
Mexico, 290
Micah, 215, 232
Midian, 8-9, 135, 140, 158, 162-163, 168, 193-195, 199
Midianite, 8-9, 135, 140-141, 162-163, 193, 195
Mieroop, 208, 213, 223, 237, 323
Mircea, 256, 290, 315, 320, 322, 325
Mishnah, 261
Mitanni, 171
Mithra, 226, 251, 273
Mithraism, 254, 273-274, 290
Mithras, 273-274, 280-281
Mitosis, 40
mlk, 183, 187
Moab, 159, 162-163, 168, 172, 183, 185,
Moabite, 163, 184
Mohamed, 4
Molech, 186-187
monolatry, 174

Monotheism, 9, 58, 62, 128-129, 173-174, 226, 274, 318
monstrance, 291
Montanists, 271
moon, 76, 87, 100, 200, 215-216, 219-222, 248
Mormon, 4
Mosca, 187
Moses, 4, 8-11, 82-83, 94, 103, 105, 134-136, 138-141, 145, 157-158, 160, 162-163, 165, 179, 182-183, 193-194, 196-197, 232, 281, 289, 303, 317-318
Mot, 175, 189, 191
mummification, 123, 146-148
Murdock, 153, 171
Mycenaean, 133, 171

Nabonidus, 215-216
Nabopolassar, 213
Nabu, 218, 241
Nadia, 316-318
Nag, 270, 275-277, 296
Nahor, 8
Nahum, 215
Nammu, 70, 83
Nanna, 76, 83, 117, 216
Napoleon, 80
Naqada, 116
Narmer, 116
Nathaniel, 200
Natufian, 52-53, 170
Nazareth, 262-263, 324
Nazirite, 188-189
Neanderthal, 31, 33-37, 45-47, 64
Nebhepetra, 121
Nebo, 184
Nebuchadnezzar, 213-216, 224
Neco, 212
necromancy, 176
Negeb, 7, 107, 161, 165
Nehemiah, 224-225
Neo, 216, 223, 247-248
NeoAssyrian, 207
NeoBabylonian, 213
Neolithic, 5-6, 32, 34, 52, 54, 61-63, 157, 170, 254, 289
Neoplatonism, 246-247, 249

Nephilim, 160, 272
Nephthys, 144, 150, 152-153
Neptune, 257
Nergal, 87-88, 218, 271
Nero, 269
Netjerkhau, 120
Netjeryhedjet, 121
Nicaea, 278
Nicense, 278, 296
Nicholas, 42, 316, 322
Nicodemus, 282
Nile, 45, 72, 114, 119, 123-124, 142, 171
Nimrud, 208, 213
Nin, 101
Nineveh, 99, 208, 210, 213
Ningal, 88
Ninhursag, 101, 104
Ninib, 218, 241
Ninlil, 87
Ninmah, 88
Ninsun, 90
Ninurta, 87-88, 218
Nippur, 103
nirari, 206
Nirvana, 234
Noah, 93-94, 99, 101, 178, 287, 318
nome, 114, 141
Nous, 247
Nubia, 117, 132-133, 237
Numa, 230
Numenius, 246
Nut, 144, 149-152
Nymphus, 273

Obadiah, 225
Obama, 15
ochre, 51, 59
Octavian, 259-260
Og, 162
Olympians, 239
Olympus, 239
Origen, 2
Osiris, 120, 123, 129, 144, 146-147, 149-154, 158, 255, 281, 283, 289

Paganism, 248, 271, 278

Paleoanthropology, 19
Paleoarcheology, 19
Paleolithic, 5, 32-33, 44-47, 51, 64, 315
Palestine, 123, 133, 156-157, 159, 161, 163, 165, 167, 169-173, 175-177, 179, 181, 183-185, 187, 189, 191, 193, 195, 197, 199, 201, 203-214, 230, 256-257, 263-264, 268
Pantheism, 58, 199
Paramessu, 132
Paran, 160, 194-195, 198
Paranthropus, 30, 35
Parkes, 258, 316, 318-319, 321, 326
Parmenides, 230
Passover, 138, 177, 188, 211, 265
Paul, 4, 247, 264, 268, 279, 293, 316, 322
Peking, 63
Pentateuch, 71, 159, 224
Pepy, 120, 132
Perizzites, 135, 166
Perseus, 279-280, 284-285
Persia, 214, 223, 225, 230, 237, 240, 273, 323
Peter, 266, 323
Pharisee, 14, 260-261, 268, 289
Philip, 237, 266, 277
Philistines, 107, 133138, 157, 168, 171-172, 211
Philo, 182, 238-239, 246
Philostratus, 267
Phoenicia, 181, 183, 211, 214
Phoenician, 79, 172, 181-182, 190, 193, 207
Pierolapithecus, 29
Pinch, Geraldine, 151-152, 158, 319
Paramesse, 132-133
plague, 9, 123, 107, 136-137, 163,
Plato, 3, 14, 230, 241-243, 246-247, 252, 276, 284, 295
Platonism, 246-247, 249
plebeians, 258
Pleistocene, 28, 33
Pliocene, 28
Plotinus, 247
Pluto, 258
polytheism, 58-59, 61, 138, 200

Pompey, 257-259
Poseidon, 239, 257
Potiphar, 112
primatologists, 20
Proconsul, 29
Prometheus, 279
Proverbs, 102, 105, 225, 276
Psalms, 174, 198, 225
Ptah, 142, 158
Ptolemaic, 116, 237-238
Ptolemies, 237
Ptolemy, 240
Pythagoras, 230, 244, 246
Pythagorean, 245, 267

Qoheleth, 106
Quaran, 4
Qumran, 261

Ra, 118-120, 127-129, 142-143, 145, 149-151, 153, 217, 279, 290
RaAtum, 151
race, 39, 93, 255, 285
Rachel, 7, 108
racism, 301
Rameses, 131-134, 138, 157
Ramesside, 131
Ramses, 133, 138, 167-168
Raphael, 200
Re, 124-125, 150
Rebekah, 107-108
Reformation, 296
Rehoboam, 158, 205
Rendsburg, Gary, 78,
Resurrection, 228, 255, 261, 277, 289, 291, 293
Reuben, 163
Reul, 140
Reza, 262,
Rhea, 239-240
Rheims, 196
ritual, 6-7, 12, 15, 33, 46, 58, 61-66, 85, 89, 103, 119, 143, 173-174, 176-177, 182-184, 187, 189, 231, 234, 239, 256, 272, 286-287, 295-297, 302
Robertson, 62, 65, 79, 316, 318
Robustus, 30

Romulus, 279
Rosetta, 80
Rudolfensis, 30
Ruth, 215

Sadducees, 14, 261, 263
Sahara, 44
Sahelanthropus, 29
Sakyamuni, 230
Samaria, 192, 209, 263, 266
Samaritans, 263
Samarrans, 73
Samson, 188, 279
Samuel, 101, 147, 176, 181, 184, 188, 200, 204, 215, 279,
Sanhedrin, 261
Saptah, 134
Sarah, 107-108, 279
Sargon, 70, 76, 81-83, 103, 105, 209-210
Sargonids, 210
Satan, 174, 229, 282
Saturn, 218, 241, 273
Saul, 147, 176, 184, 192, 200, 204, 268
Schneider, 208
Scythians, 223
Seir, 194-195
Seleucid, 237-238, 257-258
Semites, 79, 139, 172
Sennacherib, 210
Senusret, 113, 122
Sepharvaim, 209
Set, 83, 150, 152, 154
Seth, 78, 144, 150, 152-154
Sethnakht, 134
Seti, 113, 132
Setnakhte, 138
Sety, 132, 134
Shaddai, 194, 198
Shalmaneser, 207, 209
shamanism, 62
Shamash, 88, 91, 94, 211, 216
Shanghai, 288
Sharezer, 210
Shechem, 107, 109, 173, 263
Shenazzar, 215
Sheol, 86, 104, 146, 175, 303

Shu, 144, 149-151, 248
Sidon, 173, 181, 193
Siduri, 92, 106
Sihon, 162
Silberman, 169, 192, 200, 204-205
Simbel, 132-133
Sin, 87, 180, 215-216
Sinai, 157-160, 167, 182, 194-195, 198
Sneferu, 118
Sobekneferu, 122
Socrates, 242-243, 280, 284
Sol, 274, 290
Solomon, 104, 181, 204-205, 213-214, 225, 228, 261, 276
solstice, 153, 281, 291
sorcery, 145
Spain, 31, 45, 49, 259
Spencer, 37
sphinx, 118, 120
stele, 167, 169, 171, 184
Stoicism, 241, 245-246, 249
Stonehenge, 63, 217
Succoth, 157
Sumer, 51, 70, 87, 103, 318
Sumeria, 70, 114
Sumerian, 6, 70, 74-84, 86, 88, 90, 94, 99, 101-106, 139, 172, 216, 223
Susa, 80

tabernacle, 104, 177, 179
Tacitus, 269
Tefnut, 144, 149-151, 248
Teman, 194-195
Terah, 6, 107
Tertullian, 251, 280
tetragrammaton, 195
Theban, 121, 124, 151
Thebes, 121-123, 126-129
Theodosius, 278
thermoluminescence, 24
Thucydides, 230
Thutmose, 126-127, 138
ti, 101, 229
Tiamat, 100, 175
Tiberius, 268
Tien, 63-64
Tierney, 184, 186, 220

Tiglathileser, 208-209
Tiglathpileser, 209
Tigris, 72, 101, 206, 210
Torah, 4, 11, 77, 94-95, 103, 178, 197, 224, 260-261, 263
totem/Totenism, 61-62, 66
Transjordan, 159-160, 163, 168
Trinitarian, 247-249, 296
Trinity, 149, 216, 246-248
Tripolitis, 242, 245-247, 249-250, 253-255, 273-275, 290
Tritolsaiah, 232
Tubb, 192
Tugenensis, 29
Tunis, 180
Turkey, 36, 53-56, 77, 106-107, 254
Tutankhamun, 129-131
Tutankhaten, 129
Tyana, 267
Tyler, 58-60, 63, 316
Tyre, 173, 181

Ubaid, 70, 74, 76, 79
Ugarit, 172-173, 189
Ugaritic, 83, 172, 176, 189-190, 192-193
Upanishads, 229
Ur, 70, 76-78, 82-83, 87-83, 90, 95, 103, 106, 216
Urfa, 77, 106
Uruk, 70, 75-76, 78, 90-91
Utnapishtim, 92-93, 99
Utu, 88, 216

Valentinians, 271, 277
Van Der Toorn, 190-191, 193, 195, 197, 216
Varuna, 226, 273
Venus, 50, 216, 241, 248, 258, 273
Virgin, 97, 153, 277, 279, 283-285
Vishnu, 248
Vulcan, 258

Wade, 42-44
Wadis, 185
Weber, 57, 63
Wellhausen, 197

Wells, 37
Whitfield, 218-219, 241
Winks, , 258-259
Wolff, 181
Woolley, 77

Xenopohanes,, 230

Yahweh/YHWH, 8-13, 71, 82, 104, 135, 140-141, 147, 162, 174-179, 182-187, 195-200, 203, 205, 210-212, 224, 303-304

Zababa, 76, 82
Zadok, 261
Zagros, 114, 207, 213
Zaphenath, 112
Zarathustra, 230
Zealot, 14, 262-263
Zechariah, 200, 225
Zedekiah, 214
Zeno, 245
Zephaniah, 215
Zerubbabel, 215
Zeus, 239-241, 257
ziggurat, 70, 74-76, 83, 85, 88-89, 91, 103
Zipporah, 136, 193
Ziusudra, 99
zodiac, 222
Zoroaster/Zoroastrian, 13, 226-228, 256, 262, 275-277, 279-283, 294, 305
zygote, 41

www.ingramcontent.com/pod-product-compliance
Lightning Source LLC
Chambersburg PA
CBHW070529010526
44118CB00012B/1081